JEWISH IN AMERICA

JEWISH IN AMERICA
Living George Washington's Promise

Richard L. Rubin

A RICHARD MAREK BOOK

PARK INTERNATIONAL PUBLISHING
PURCHASE, NEW YORK

Published in the United States by:

Park International Publishing
36 The Crossing
Purchase, NY 10577

Manufactured in the United States of America

Cover design by Marja Walker

For my children and grandchildren

Table of Contents

Washington's Promise

Writing to the Touro Synagogue in Rhode Island in 1790, George Washington, co-founder and first president of the United States of America, made the following promise of unqualified citizenship to the Jews of America:

> All possess alike liberty of conscience and immunities of citizenship . . . For happily the Government of the United States, which gives to bigotry no sanction, to persecution no assistance, requires only that they who live under its protection, should demean themselves as good citizens. . . . May the Children of the Stock of Abraham, who dwell in this land, continue to merit and enjoy the good will of the other Inhabitants, while every one shall sit under his own vine and fig tree, and there shall be none to make him afraid.

Introduction

In the fall of 1947, when I was eighteen years old, I fell in love with Hélène Emily Rice, daughter of Willard Martin Rice IV and Henriette Ravier Jones. Like me, Hélène ("Len") was a freshman at Brown University. But while I was a talkative, outgoing city boy from New York, she was a quiet, very shy country girl from rural Delaware. Most telling of all, I was Jewish—but she was not.

Then, as now, I wasn't a religious Jew—and I had a strong desire to stay that way. Nevertheless, I was close to my Jewish family and felt a kinship with the Jews as a people. Hence, I had no thoughts of "marrying out." After all, during a period of intense anti-Semitism, I had lived comfortably as a Jew in New York City, sheltered by my family and my Jewish classmates, whom I thought of not as "Jews" but as "friends." Similarly, Len had grown up in an insular, mostly Protestant cultural environment. As a result, neither of us was familiar with the culture of the other.

As our love deepened and we talked of marriage, we knew we would eventually have to deal with family problems stemming from our cultural and religious differences. My parents were initially unhappy at the thought of intermarriage, and Len's Grandmother Rice, an officer of the Daughters of the American Revolution, was appalled. Neither side of the family believed such a marriage could last. Yet, as of this writing, Len and I have been married for sixty-six years. Our experience together has been a main motivator for me to study the issues of cultural distinctiveness and, more specifically, of what it means

1

to be an American Jew. Had I married a Jewish woman, this book would never have been written.

In college, personal, familial, and social issues required grappling with questions to which I had previously paid little attention. Mixing into the Gentile world, I gradually learned to distinguish between different religious cultures. After college, I learned even more about the distinctiveness of Jewish culture and its values, both from my experience and from what I read.

Growing up in the 1930s and '40s, I came of age at a time when social scientists were reporting that over 50 percent of the non-Jewish public held negative views of the Jewish people, with many Gentiles believing in a worldwide Jewish "conspiracy." As a result, most less-religious Jews, myself included, saw themselves as resisters against anti-Semitism, rather than as bearers of the positive elements of Jewish life and culture.

Over the decades that followed, I came to recognize a distinctive Jewish-American subculture that had resulted from the melding of traditional Jewish values with quintessentially American (and Protestant) ones; it was a subculture into which most American Jews chose to enter. Indeed, they adopted certain ideas—pluralism, the value of diversity, and democratic equality—that were largely alien to their European forebears. The fusing of two distinct cultures had produced a kind of hybrid Jew, one cognizant of his or her ancestors' experiences in Europe, but imbued with the ideas and values of a new and heterogeneous homeland in America.

From studying the social sciences and teaching about immigrant transformation in America at Columbia University and Swarthmore College, I've come to what I believe are important conclusions about the unique and positive nature of present-day American Jewish culture—conclusions not only dependent on colorful anecdotal experience, but anchored in new social science research that makes clear that the "Americanized" Jew is distinctive in many ways, both from other American groups and from Jews in other nations.

Jewish assimilation in Europe and Jewish Americanization are distinguishable from each other because the terms of Americanization for immigrants are less stringent, less demanding, for citizenship. While assimilation speaks to the absorption of newcomers into the body and culture of the new host nation, Americanization—the terms of American citizenship—permits a dual or hybrid identity that does not require a full change from the "old" culture. Underpinning Americanization is the original ideal of pluralist democracy that George Washington proclaimed at the country's beginning, an ideal quite different from European ones. We are not a nation with a common culture and history to protect, he wrote in his welcoming letter to a small Jewish congregation in 1790, but rather a nation of diverse peoples under a common democratic government that requires allegiance—and it is the job of the new government to protect the *differentness* of its peoples. Thus, Washington made an unqualified promise of protected pluralist citizenship for Jews—the first such promise ever made to them—in a country where "every one shall sit under his own vine and fig tree and there shall be none to make him afraid."[1] It was a promise of minority protection that has been kept.

The American formulation of citizenship in a new nation of people from different national origins was, as the scholar Lawrence Fuchs points out, "a kind of *voluntary* pluralism in which immigrant settlers from Europe and their progeny were free to maintain affection for and loyalty to their ancestral religions and cultures, while at the same time claiming an American identity by embracing the founding myths and participating in the political life of the Republic."[2] Political principles and participation in the rites of republican life were thus the central basis of citizenship, not the commonality of religion, culture, or history. The duality of identity, the essence of American pluralism, which combined an old identity with new American citizenship, has allowed the successful absorption of huge numbers of people of different national origins, religions, and, of late, races.

My purpose in writing this book is to further identify and specify the nature of this new hybrid American-Jewish culture, in order to help perpetuate that culture and the identity of Jewish "peoplehood." For the great majority of American Jews, who claim that religious belief is not the principal source of their identity as Jews, a rebirth of religiosity as a key to Jewish continuity is unlikely to happen. This is because American Jews, as evidence will show, have become by far the most secular and minimally religious group in America, a trend unlikely to be reversed. This book is meant to identify, inform, and define the unique culture of these American Jews of "fusion," who are more than a religious group, but a "people" with a specific culture that has been transformed by their Jewish experience of the past, and by their unique experience in America.

Questions about the importance and essence of nonreligious Jewish "culture" were raised, but not answered, by Sigmund Freud over a century ago. At various times called an apostate or a renegade Jew because of his atheism and his questioning of the Jewish origins of the historic Moses, he nevertheless shared with certain other assimilative Jews, atheists or not, a bond of connection to the Jewish people, and to their values and psychology. Writing to the woman who would be his future wife, Martha, he stated that "even if the form wherein the old Jews were happy no longer affords us any shelter, something of the core, of the essence of this meaningful and life-affirming Judaism will not be absent from our home."[3]

This search for that inner identity of nonreligious Jews, though then resistant to definition, is captured in the preface Freud wrote for the Hebrew translation of his *Totem and Taboo* in 1930. Though a rationalist and scientist of the Enlightenment, he nevertheless said that he had never repudiated his people, unlike many of the upward-striving German and Austrian Jews of that period. Yosef Yerushalmi, in his analysis of Freud's response to assimilative pressures, quotes Freud's preface:

> If the question were put to him [Freud is here referring to himself]: "Since you have abandoned all these common characteristics of your compatriots, what is left to you that is Jewish?" he would reply: "A very great deal, and probably its very essence." He could not now express that essence in words, but some day, no doubt, it will become accessible to the scientific mind.[4]

A large segment of highly educated Americans, assimilative but nonetheless identifying themselves as cultural Jews, are still largely uninformed about their own culture and history, a culture built upon both religious origins and historical experiences before and after their immigration to America. In an attempt to remedy this deficiency, I will address certain questions and themes in the following chapters to give more shape to the meaning of Jewish culture. This book, then, is not simply about American Jewish history and present-day Jewish beliefs and behavior, but also about cultural development. It focuses on the growing fusion of American and Jewish ideals within the context of broad transformative changes in American life to which the majority of Jews have always responded. How did prior Jewish history actually help shape the Protestant Reformation in America? How, in turn, did the specific American version of the Protestant-pluralist culture subsequently reshape the culture of successive generations of American Jews? What were the origins of American social and political life that made America the first Christian-dominant country to grant citizenship to Jews from its very founding? How were Jews initially integrated into society, and how was that relationship later changed by a virulent anti-Semitic reaction almost a century later? Why, then, after such a strong period of intense anti-Semitism, did popular anti-Semitism decline so rapidly after the Second World War? And what factors led to the Jewish Golden Age of renewed opportunity, declining discrimination, and disproportionately high levels of accomplishment in just the last sixty years?

Do these remarkable changes for individual Jews require Jews as a group to pay a price in terms of their distinctiveness and continuity? New large-scale research has now given clear answers to whether, and to what extent, Jewish distinctiveness of culture still exists in a contemporary era of openness—that is, how Jewish thoughts, values, and perspectives may still differentiate them not only from other groups of Americans but from Jews of other nations as well.

In the second half of the book, I pose additional questions. Is America different from other Western European countries that attempted to integrate and protect their assimilative Jewish populations, like

Germany and France, and ultimately failed to do so, leading to disaster and destruction? What is unique, if anything, about American pluralism that can continue to spur optimism in Jews and other minorities about their place in America? What is likely to come from successful American assimilation, with its rapidly growing rate of intermarriage among Jews? What will happen to the Jews of the future as increasing secularity and significant intermarriage shape group consciousness? How do older and younger Jews differ in their relationship to Israel, given the substantial gaps between generations?

At the end of the book, I will provide answers to old questions and probe new questions that arise from those very answers. Why, I will ask, is there such a disproportionately high level of Jewish participation and accomplishment in the professions of medicine, science, academics, and law (as well as in the related fields of art, music, and literature)? Is that disproportion related to those undescribed essences of Jewish culture—the life-affirming elements of Judaism that Freud spoke of—and their fusion with important elements of pluralism in American culture, which together may be responsible for most of these new hybrid American Jews? Without invoking theories of superior genetic endowment, or the idea of Jewish "chosenness by God," I will advance the idea that culture counts, and that a distinctive and well-defined Jewish-American culture that could continue to be transmitted generationally should be an important foundation of future Jewish education on which to build confidence and Jewish continuity.

The final chapter addresses a crucial contemporary question: What is the future of Jewish life in a world of terrorism, with the renewal of anti-Jewish hostility both in Europe and the Middle East, and the American role in determining that future? Whereas during the rise of Western Christendom Jew-hatred produced terror for Jews through banishment, the Inquisition, and the threat of death, the Muslim world of the time largely treated Jews more humanely as a special minority, a protected group, albeit one more heavily taxed than Muslims. But since the establishment of the Jewish state of Israel in 1948, Muslim anti-Semitism, often violent, has ended almost 1,400 years of peaceful coexistence of Jews and Muslims in the Middle East.

This chapter deals specifically with growing anti-Jewish activities in Europe, particularly in France, which is home to the last substantial post-Holocaust Jewish population left in continental Europe. There, assassinations and kidnappings by young fundamentalist Muslims threaten French Jewish security, and have already provoked in France the highest percentage of emigrating Jews among Western European nations, at almost 20 percent (and rising) of its post–World War II population. The continuing emigration of even more of France's Jewish population—at 475,000 the third largest in the world after Israel and America—becomes the focus of the Jewish future and the role of America in securing that future.

Author's Note

Before each chapter of history or social analysis of American Jewish life, I have added a brief prologue describing some personal experiences that inspired and have unique relevance to that chapter. These background observations serve as connective links between each chapter, so that by the end of the book the prologues may better connect the reader to the writer.

Prologue to Chapter One

When I started this book I knew little about the long history of Jews in Europe and later in America, little about rabbi intellectuals such as Maimonides and Hillel, and practically nothing about the roots of Protestantism. I had thought that the founding of the United States was simply an extension of the European Enlightenment, but what I found instead was that the pre-Enlightenment Protestant Reformation was key to America's creation and a light in the darkness of Christendom for Jews.

In the colonies of Protestant America there were no enforced Jewish ghettos, as there were in Europe, even before Independence. There had been little fusion of cultures in the Europe of the 1650s when the first community of Jews arrived in America. And although there had been a significant amount of cultural fusion in the Muslim-dominated parts of Spain centuries earlier, when the Christian armies forced out the Muslims from those parts of Spain, they brought with them the Spanish Inquisition. In the summer of 1492, all Jews were forced to leave Spain under penalty of death if they remained.

What changed in Western Christendom after the Jewish expulsion from Spain was the advent of the Protestant Reformation in Europe in the following century, and, later, the development of a particular variant of Protestantism in America. The Protestantism of the colonies was uniquely shaped by the American experience—no European country where Protestantism contested Catholicism's hold on Christianity had close to the same amount of territory as North America; and none had the multiplicity of settlements by *differing* Protestant churches and sects, which in America numbered in the hundreds. Protestantism's multiple voices and America's natural resources together produced a religion open to diversity, a landmass of great opportunity, and superb political leaders to make a new government work.

Each immigrant who came to the United States brought a distinct cultural inheritance from his birth nation that fused with the equally distinct culture of America. Immigrant Jews entered in the same way, but with a big difference. They came to an America populated predominantly by Christians, and as Jews they belonged to a religious group long demonized by much Christian theology. One would expect European settlers in America to have evinced a level of Christian anti-Semitism similar to that in their native countries. But that didn't happen.

The first community of Jews in America served as a test among Protestant settlers of how far their tolerance of differentness would extend. Would it extend to more than other denominations of Protestants? To Catholics? To Jews? To the nonreligious? The answers ultimately given to these questions at the founding of the United States were crucial to the birth and flourishing of democracy. For Jews in particular, America offered untrammeled political freedom such as they had never enjoyed anywhere else in the Christian world. Protestants had formed an electorally governed country, but with no special privileges for their own religion. Jews, required in parts of Europe to convert to Christianity in order to receive certain privileges of citizenship (such as university admission), were in America free of religious disabilities. This new political freedom for Jews and their elimination as a special political class led, paradoxically, to the potential loss of their historic identity resulting from full assimilation, a problem that still confronts Jews today.

For the early Jewish settlers of the seventeenth and eighteenth centuries, as well as for the much more numerous Jewish immigrants of the nineteenth and twentieth centuries, there were big challenges to the values and traditions they brought with them. My immigrant grandparents and great-grandparents, who came to America from Europe in the latter half of the nineteenth century, were part of that experience. As Orthodox Jews who considered themselves members of a "people apart," they thought traditionally of *group* interests—is it good for the Jews?—rather than their own. But they faced a new country where pluralism, egalitarianism, and individualism were the prevailing and contrasting values.

My parents, on the other hand, fell far from the Orthodox tree, linking themselves first to Conservative and then to Reform Judaism. In practice, however, they were altogether nonreligious Jews: God and the Bible were rarely, if ever, subjects of discussion in our family. My parents were comfortable with the uncertainty of life without a belief in God, and secular in all ways. Yet they still, unquestionably, considered themselves part of the Jewish people, as do I.

My parents' forebears were part of the massive European immigration to America that occurred in the last decades of the nineteenth century, and part of the subsequent fusion of Jewish culture with a powerful Protestant American culture of diversity and pluralism. My mother's family began its life in America in Houston, Texas; my father's family in New York City, over two thousand miles away. The great distance between them would have spanned three or four countries in Europe, but here it was within just one giant country.

What will happen to my grandchildren? Will they too be linked to the Jewish people, and to that particular Jewish humanism that exists today, even if not to God and the Jewish religion? I don't know whether the distinctive qualities of Jewish life that I find so valuable, and that I describe in this book, will preserve them as part of an extraordinary, continuous history of Jewish peoplehood. But I have hope, and this book is written for them.

Chapter One

The Fusion of Cultures

Jews have been often called, by themselves as well as others, a "People of the Book." I prefer "a people of books"—of learning, study, and education. While the motivation for the study of religious writings has all but disappeared for most American Jews, their motivation for educating themselves has only intensified. Today, American Jews have on average two and a half more years of formal college education than non-Jewish Americans, and three times the number of postgraduate advanced degrees.[1] The deep commitment to study and the intellectual life is not, of course, unique to Jews—it is just more prevalent and intense among them than among non-Jews. And it yields a disproportionately large representation of Jews in the fields of science, medicine, academics, and law, where they are currently up to ten times more numerous in proportion to their percentage of the general population (2 percent) than is the rest of that population. This has resulted from the fusion of historic Jewish traits and values with an American (primarily Protestant) culture of intense individualism, freedom of conscience, and ambition for worldly "success."

Most Jews who immigrated to America in the last decades of the 1800s and the beginning decades of the 1900s were from Eastern Europe, a region scarcely touched by the modernizing industrial and cultural influences of Western Europe. The massive influx of more than two and a half million poor Jews increased the American Jewish

population tenfold in little more than a generation, markedly alter-
ing the American Jewish world, which was until then dominated by a
small group of relatively affluent and assimilated German and Central
European Jews. Immigrants from Europe's socially restricted and economically deprived Eastern territories sought not only economic and
political freedom, but also an escape from the strictures of traditional
Jewish life. The scholar Stephen Greenblatt has described what was
driving them:

> When they boarded the ship taking them to America, they were
> not following a spiritual leader, and they were not seeking any
> intensification or purification of their faith. They were part of a
> large transnational religious community that was pulling away
> both from the severe piety of the most dourly orthodox of their
> contemporaries, the *mitnagdim*, and from the mystical enthu-
> siasm of the *Hasidim*. Embattled, impoverished, and bloodied,
> a whole generation, deeply steeped in tradition, was preparing
> to embrace new forms of existence and poised to listen to the
> voices other than those of their rabbis.[2]

Jews would be just one of more than two hundred different religious churches and sects, and just one of many unrestricted religious-
minority groups. My focus here is particularly on the largest, most
eagerly assimilative segment of Jewish immigrants, acknowledging
that all Orthodox Jews together, from the Hasidim to the Modern Orthodox, now number only about 12 percent of American Jews.[3] Most
of the rest have accepted the challenge of integrating their culture with
that of Gentile Americans, whatever the risk of total assimilation. The
effort to maintain for oneself a balance between Jewish values and traditions and those of non-Jewish Americans became the characteristic
Jewish experience of assimilative life.

There is, of course, a wide variety among these assimilative Jews—
Conservative, Reform, Reconstruction, and others[4]—in the nature
and extent of their religious practice and belief; but they are as one in
their unwillingness to be governed strictly by *halachah*, the religious

law of Orthodoxy. But although they are mostly secular and Americanized, doubtful even of the "chosenness" of the Jewish people, these assimilatives still identify themselves as Jews. They perceive a certain common Jewish destiny, and a certain social and political *like-mindedness* of Jews that distinguishes them from other groups of Americans. In short, assimilative Jews want to be both "like" and "unlike"—mostly absorbed into American ways, but not completely.

Where the fusion of Jewish and American culture will lead in the future is unclear, but frequent laments about the coming disappearance of American Jewry as a distinct group (excluding Orthodox Jews) do not give sufficient credit to the regenerative elements found in all variants of Jewish life throughout thousands of years of history. Although, in the past, there have been substantial losses in the number of Jews worldwide owing to total assimilation in Europe, there is in modern America a vibrant and thriving, but not totally assimilated, Jewish community that is unlikely to disappear.

The nature and extent of American assimilation differs widely from the classical model of the more homogeneous nations of Europe. The pluralist culture of an immigrant nation has made Americanization rather than assimilation a special process of group integration. While the number of self-identifying Jews may increase or decrease in the future, Jewish life in America will differ from the past in many ways. Without doubt, there will be greater further sectarianism. Despite growing anti-Zionism and anti-Semitism outside the United States, the decline of anti-Semitism inside the United States over the last half century can only lead to greater diversity—a diversity long inhibited by the closing of Jewish ranks in reaction to earlier social anti-Semitism in America.[5] I seek to find the combined influence of the Jewish past and the American past that, together, shape the present-day values and behavior of "Americanized" Jews.

In a related response to the more open and positive social and economic environment facing American Jews in the last four or five decades, the rapid increase in marriage between born Jews and Gentiles—from about 7 percent of Jews in 1950, when I married, to approximately 50 percent half a century later—is certain to provide a further challenge to the unity of an intellectually sensitive and fractious group whose attempts at unity have largely been motivated in reaction to the hostility of the non-Jewish world.[6] In the next four decades, when almost half the children of presently self-identifying American Jews will be the product of one parent born a Gentile, can there be any doubt that, for many reasons, relationships will be different? Already, the relations are strained between intermarried families who think of themselves as Jewish and those more traditional Jews who view children of only patrilineal descent as non-Jewish. The disagreements among Jews on this issue alone are bound to inflame differences of opinion on the question of "Who is a Jew?"

What is unusual in American life is not that various cultural traditions brought by immigrants are retained in some form or other—that is, that the melting pot never fully melts the immigrants.[7] What is unusual, however, is that after many of the external traditions have dropped away—such as keeping kosher homes and maintaining regular Sabbath attendance—a group of mostly assimilative American Jews, almost half of whom are unaffiliated with any temple or synagogue, have maintained or acquired a distinctive set of religious, social, and political values (as recent social science can now identify).[8]

Recent research attests that even after four or five generations of assimilative life in America, the majority of Jews maintain a unique, and in some respects surprising, set of attitudes and values. While other groups of Americans share many of these attitudes and values, there remains a clear and significant "differentness" of Jews on matters ranging from political attitudes and voting behavior to specific social and moral values, such as those concerning abortion and sexuality, and even to one's conception of (or disbelief in) God. What these values, attitudes, and beliefs are, how they got that way, and whether and how they may be passed on is the story of millions of American Jews who are minimally religious but culturally bound to Jewish life.

The "muse of fusion" between different cultures or civilizations, as Cynthia Ozick has noted, has brought major changes historically in the character, qualities of intellect, and life approaches among Jews. For example, Ozick points to the emphasis on study and analytical thinking so common among Jews. She argues that it is not characteristic of ancient Jews, but comes from later rabbinical Judaism's encounter with Greek culture:

> The source of study-consciousness, the source of intellect as the paramount tool of right conduct, is the Socratic, not the biblical, font. It was the gradual superimposition of the Socratic primacy of intellect upon the Jewish primacy of holiness that produced the familiar, and now completely characteristic, Jewish personality we know. Because the Jewish mind has wholly assimilated the Platonic emphasis on the nobility of pedagogy, on study as the route to mastery and illumination, there is no Jew alive today who is not also resonantly Greek; and the more ideally Jewish he is in his devotion to Torah, the more profoundly Greek he is.[9]

Encounters with the Muslim Golden Age and the European Enlightenment have also left marked imprints on Jewish thinking and approaches to life, particularly in opening Jewish studiousness to the new secular fields of science and mathematics. In the same way, the Jewish encounter with America has made American Jews not only distinct from American Gentiles, but from other geographic and sociologic concentrations of Jews as well.

The unique founding of America, with the deep imprint of the Protestant Reformation on the diverse religious denominations and sects of its population, provided a special governmental and political environment for its Jews. The decision by the Founders not to blend Protestant Christianity, Deism, or any other religion with the new nation's government gave to Jewish Americans, from the very start, a status as full citizens that no Jews enjoyed in any other nation at that time—despite the fact that several states with established religions took decades to conform their constitutions to the secular federal one.

Much has been written about recent Jewish success in penetrating into high levels of professional, intellectual, and business circles; and much, too, has been made of the impact of Jews on literature, science, music, and comedy. Far less, however, has been noted of the influence of American Protestant values and concepts on American Jewish religious, political, and personal attitudes—values and concepts such as individualism, material success, pluralism, diversity, and the separation of religion from government, none of which were part of traditional Jewish culture. Indeed, what makes most contemporary American Jews distinct not only from non-Jewish Americans but from Jews of other nations is this synthesis of American and Jewish culture, one that goes beyond religious belief alone. As Stephen Whitfield observed in *In Search of Jewish Culture,* "Difference is how to begin to understand culture—and indeed to grasp the making of the self, which is formed in relation to the Other."[10] It was, in fact, my sense of such a "difference" in Jewish-American family life, culture, and psychology that spawned, when I was just eighteen years old, my serious interest in the interaction of Jewish and American cultures.

The threat to Jewish group cohesion and continuity in America has become even greater as hostility toward Jewish involvement in social, economic, and personal relationships has continued to decline. While anti-Semitism in Europe has been resurgent—it has deep religious roots going back many centuries—present-day anti-Semitism seems largely confined to the Middle East and related to hatred of Israel. But America has remained, so far, relatively resistant to the virus. Although academia has seen some anti-Israel agitation, and there are continued sporadic anti-Semitic acts, all the major indicators of sociological integration in the last fifty years have pointed to a dramatic decline in anti-Semitism in business, law, academia, and social organizations.

American Jews need only look back to the 1940s, 1950s, and early 1960s to see how many restrictions on Jewish participation and advancement in American life have been removed. Those decades had followed many earlier ones of severe anti-Jewish restrictiveness, including low Jewish admission quotas to top colleges and universities, restrictions on where Jews could buy homes, resort/hotel discrimination, and, most important, severe limitations on employment opportunities.[11] I myself was directly affected by these restrictions:

my parents had to rent our house in Riverdale, New York, because a restrictive covenant in its deed forbade its purchase by "Jews, Negroes, and Orientals." I was dissuaded from my initial choice of college (Princeton) by my high school principal because of its low quota for Jews; and before graduating from Brown University in 1951, I was advised by the dean not to bother applying for a job in major industries such as steel, automobiles, and chemicals, because, he said, they did not hire Jews. While there were no laws mandating such restrictions, neither were they forbidden by law, and they were quite common. Much has changed for the better in both law and custom over the last half-century, and most, if not all, anti-Jewish restrictions have disappeared.

I realize there's a risk in generalizing about people of any race, creed, or ethnicity; assimilative Jews are themselves particularly suspicious of such generalizations, having long been the victims of negative stereotypes. And after all, even within any particular group, there are many who do not share its predominant beliefs, values, or traits, while there are often outsiders who do. Indeed, there are many Gentiles who share some of the defining characteristics of assimilative Jews.

All that said, it is permissible to generalize about certain groups so long as we are careful not to indulge in facile negative stereotyping. I could hardly discuss the Puritan settlers in New England, for example, without distinguishing them from Christian settlers elsewhere in the colonies.

The shameful memories of past anti-Jewish discrimination and stereotyping tend to induce enlightened and sympathetic Gentiles (and many assimilative Jews as well) to play down the differences between Jews and Gentiles. Fuzzy universalism aside, however, different peoples are just that: different. There are important differences between Jews and Gentiles—psychological, attitudinal, intellectual, etc.—of which even many Jews are only vaguely aware. Respect for differences, rather than blindness to them, is the beginning of tolerance, and a prerequisite for a successful democracy. It is not by chance that a substantial majority of the white lawyers for, and financial contributors to, the civil rights movement of the 1960s were Jewish; a disproportionate number of white student freedom riders were Jewish as well. An acute sense of injustice and a strong empathy with oppressed peoples, born of their own legacy of persecution, produced a tenfold overrepresentation of Jews among white civil rights activists.[12] New research finds significant differences between Jews and Gentiles (especially Christians) on other key issues in America, from race to abortion to beliefs (or lack of such) about God, heaven, and hell that indicate a kind of Jewish community of thought. These differences point to certain attitudes, ideas, and sensibilities that, while not exclusive to Jews, are disproportionately found among them. Religion, historical experience, and a particular interpretation by Jews of American values have combined to develop a commonality of outlook and culture that is not just distinctive but *very* distinctive, not necessarily in kind, but in emphasis and degree.

The late American artist Robert Motherwell once related to me an incident that demonstrated the increasing American openness to Jews over the last half century, and its psychological effects on them. Motherwell, a patrician WASP by upbringing, was at a raucous New York party given by fellow painter Mark Rothko, a Jew, when he glanced over to a dark corner and saw David Sylvester—an eminent, highly assimilative English (and Jewish) art critic and historian—standing alone. As Motherwell walked over to him, he noticed tears rolling down Sylvester's cheeks. "What's wrong, David?" Motherwell asked. "Nothing," the Englishman replied. "I've just never seen Jews so free."[13]

Relief from *external* hostility, which has freed American Jews to a great extent from extreme self-consciousness, forces me to look more deeply at the many *internal* elements of Jewishness—the feelings of being part of a historic people, and the imprecise, sometimes critical, and sometimes proud sense of a unique Jewish identity that subtly influences family relationships and one's attitudes toward other people and indeed toward life itself. What is the psychology of the great majority of present-day American Jews, those who no longer follow most of Jewish tradition's practices of separateness in dress, food, and religious observance that had long reflected and reinforced the distinctiveness of Jewish life?

It is that great majority of Jews in the United States whom I study in this book. Forgoing long-held traditions, many such Jews still feel a strong sense of Jewish identity. They consider themselves part of a special historical people who, living in a special country, assert their right to be both the same and different. What are the nonreligious cultural essences of Jewishness about which Freud speculated; what gives the typical "Americanized" Jew a sense of Jewish "peoplehood"; and what are the forces, apart from anti-Semitism, that bind such predominantly secular people to their identity as Jews?

The unique context of American religious, social, and economic development has provided the soil in which Jewish-American culture has grown and been shaped for over 350 years. Throughout, two major factors have been active in all stages of Jewish cultural fusion in America that are not to be found in Jews' European past. The first is the particular governmental structure in America and the political actions of its leaders; the second is the enormous scale and diversity of its immigrant population. These elements not only have shaped the environment in which American Jews live, but also inform us about the future, providing probable answers to questions of assimilative life for Jews in overwhelmingly Christian countries. Is America truly different for its Jews than other predominantly Christian countries? Or will its government and leaders eventually fail them, as in Germany and in France, by not protecting them? Can what happened in Europe happen here? Will the advances made in the last fifty years be reversed in part or in whole? What is the likelihood that the broad increase in American tolerance for all "differentness"—which has benefited not only Jews, but other minorities and women—will be diminished by a backlash against change?

In the coming chapters, I will analyze themes such as the social integration or separation of Jews, the social hostility or social acceptance of them, questions of legitimacy of their citizenship rights, and perceptions of Jews as a race and not simply an ethnic culture. I will examine them through a framework of three major historical periods that reflect different levels of cultural fusion. The first was the Colonial period, stretching into the first eighty to ninety years of nationhood after the founding. With only small numbers of Jews, a relatively tolerant English Protestant population, and pariah status reserved only for African slaves, historians consider this a time of exceptional toleration in which Jews were granted full citizenship rights. It was a crucial formative period of Jewish integration, marked by the good fortune of the early Jewish immigrants in finding a land of predominantly English Protestants who embedded most of their Reformation ideas of tolerance, individual conscience, and pluralism into the new United States Constitution.

This initial period was followed by a second one extending from about 1875 to the mid-1950s during which anti-Jewish sentiment and social discrimination were prevalent. Anti-Semitism peaked during the Great Depression and the succeeding years of World War II, as sociologists and political scientists were able to discover using newly-developed survey research techniques.

The third stage in Jewish-American life saw another reversal, this time from anti-Jewish animosity and exclusion to acceptance and integration. The period from the early 1960s to the present can be considered an ongoing Golden Age for American Jews, and, importantly, the beginning of positive changes for other minorities as well. Changes in government laws and in customs and morality have worked astonishing transformations in American culture in a relatively short time. A rapid decline occurred in anti-Semitic attitudes among (predominantly Christian) Gentile Americans, alongside a somewhat less precipitous decline in anti-black prejudice. Why these dual trends developed so rapidly and so unexpectedly, what the sources of such changes were, and what it all meant to Jews and blacks—and to American life in general—is crucial to what follows.

Whereas detailed statistical surveys of non-Jews' opinions about Jews have been available for decades, far less information of a statistical nature (as opposed to anecdotally) is available about American Jewish opinion, partly owing to the Jewish-American population's very small size. In just the last seven years, however, two significant, large comparative studies—one by the National Opinion Research Center (NORC) of the University of Chicago, the other more recent one by the Pew Forum on Religion and Public Life which surveyed 35,000 Americans—now enable us to understand much more about certain specifics of Jewish-American culture, and how it compares to the changing culture of America itself.

I start with a look at the first Sephardic immigrants, who had fled the Catholic Inquisitions in Spain and Brazil, as they arrived in an America of exceptionally diverse Protestant denominations and started a new relationship with a Christian population that was unique for its time. As we shall see, the seeds sown at that beginning helped determine much of what is distinctive in the values and attitudes of present-day Americanized Jews.

Prologue to Chapter Two

The Thirty Years' War between Catholics and Protestants ended in 1648, but for those Sephardic Jews who had fled the Catholic Inquisition from Spain and Portugal to Brazil, the bloodletting between Christians had not ended. The tolerant Dutch Protestant colony in Recife, Brazil, was invaded by a Portuguese Catholic army in the 1650s, forcing the Dutch out, and, with them, any tolerance for the Jews who had lived there in peace for over a century. Again, the whole Jewish community boarded ships under pain of death and sailed to Protestant lands in North America, hoping to rebuild a tattered community and find peace, tolerance, and good fortune.

What forced their flight was the Inquisition's unwillingness to accept differentness. Forgetting how early Christians were treated by the Romans, the Catholic Church used deviation from its theology as warrant to punish Protestants. Catholic theology also laid the blame for the death of Jesus on Jews, despite the fact that Jesus was a Jewish rabbi and crucifixion was an exclusively Roman form of execution. The Church's theology, its power, and its long, continual demonization of Jews were the defining elements that literally chased the first community of Jews to America.

Once here, Protestant beliefs inspired the founding of a new nation that respected diversity of opinion and nontraditional religious beliefs. The culture of toleration of religious "differentness," and the Founders' insistence that private beliefs and individual conscience be protected by a secular government, brought freedom to Jews in America. The deliberate detachment of religious authority from government authority, unique in its time, was a giant step toward founding our democracy. The tolerance of the various immigrant groups for each other was crucial to America's development and to the acceptance of Jews in this country.

Chapter Two

The Protestant Reformation in America and American Jews

The roots of today's substantial Jewish integration into American life came not simply from Enlightenment ideas percolating in the new colonies of North America, but also from the original seeds of the Protestant Reformation in Europe. Protestant ideas of the rights of individual conscience and of opposition to a single church demanding conformity led to belief in religious freedom. It was Jewish good fortune that their first communal landing in the early North American colonies was to a predominantly Protestant group of colonies. The first Jewish settlers in New Netherland's city of New Amsterdam (later New York) were on the run from Europe. In the summer of 1492, Spain expelled Jews, on pain of death, after more than nine hundred years of peaceful coexistence, as did the Portuguese shortly thereafter. Some went to the tolerant Netherlands and others to Muslim lands in the Mediterranean. Others sailed to the distant Dutch colony of Recife in South America, now part of Brazil.

After living in relative peace in South America for many decades, the conquest of that tolerant Dutch colony by the Catholic Portuguese in the mid-1600s brought with it the Inquisition. Again, Sephardic Jews were forced to find a new haven from destruction. While individual Jewish traders and merchants from elsewhere had been to

New Amsterdam for short periods before, the bedraggled first group that arrived in 1654 was hoping to stay permanently and rebuild their community.

The clergy of the dominant Dutch Reformed Church in New Netherland was not initially happy with the arrival of Jews. It feared losing its position as the colony's only recognized faith. As the historian Jonathan Sarna has noted, Peter Stuyvesant, the director-general of New Netherland, petitioned the directors of the Dutch West India Company in Amsterdam to require the Jews "in a friendly way to depart" lest they "infect and trouble this new colony." He warned in a subsequent letter that, "giving them liberty we cannot refuse Lutherans and Papists."[1] Toleration of Jews, Stuyvesant wrote, "would serve as precedents and determine the colony's religious character forever after."[2] The acceptance of Jews (and others) of "differentness" thus became an early mainstay of the Protestant idea of accepted pluralism, later embedded in a new nation's Constitution.

Hostility toward and mistrust of Jews were not as prevalent among the Protestant colonists as they were among Catholics immigrating to South America. The Dutch West India Company sought a thriving economic base in the New Netherlands. It did not hurt, as they wrote to Stuyvesant, that "many of the Jewish nation are principal shareholders" of the company itself. The importance of economic growth was a key tenet of Protestantism thought in Europe, pointing Christianity to nonreligious matters and values. The directors of the company admonished Stuyvesant for banishing a Quaker from the colony who had earlier spoken in favor of the rights of religious "sectarians." The directors noted:

> We doubt very much whether we can proceed against [these faiths] rigorously without diminishing the population and stopping immigration which must be favored at a so tender stage of the country's existence. . . . You may therefore shut your eyes, at least not force people's consciences, but allow every one to have his own belief, as long as he behaves quietly and legally, gives no offense to his neighbor and does not oppose the government.[3]

Protestant ideas about the role of economics, individual conscience, and liberty in nation-building were prominent in the writings of Reformation European leaders and intellectuals in the seventeenth century, and such thought permeated the new colonies as well. It may be painful for present-day Catholics, who have done much to purge anti-Semitism from their Church over the last half century, to admit that their less tolerant forebears in religion played such an important role in driving Jews to America. But past realities remain important. The Protestant role in establishing religious freedom for American Jews and other religious groups, and its continuing impact on the Americanization of Jews, must be acknowledged. In fact, many of the values found among present-day Jews were likewise typical of early Protestant-Americans, and were embedded in the United States Constitution.

The Reformation's break with Catholicism produced translations of the Bible into the vernacular of many nations, and its reading of the Jewish Bible—the Old Testament—by many laypeople rather than just the Catholic clergy, produced a more profound and intimate connection between Protestants and the descendants of Old Testament Hebrews or Israelites. Protestantism clearly tightened the potential linkages between Hebrews and the American dissenters from Catholic Christianity; and Jewish biblical figures, particularly Moses, became prominent role models for early Americans, especially their leaders. Though still wary of Jewish colonists whom they saw as rejecters of Jesus as Messiah, a certain common respect for and connection to Old Testament figures made Jews more welcome in America than in Europe. Later I will delve more deeply into the differences between American and European relationships to Jews; here, it is enough to say that the unique values of American Protestantism vis-à-vis its European varieties were critical to the development of American values and specifically Jewish-American ones as well.

The new and different American form of Protestantism brought to the fore ideas percolating in Europe about pluralism, individualism, liberty, and a zealous commercialism that together produced a new kind of nation. From its beginnings, America was built on immigrants from other nations, with none of the feudal past of Europe, and this fostered a belief among its people that theirs was a new and different kind of country—a "new Israel" as the early Bible-oriented Protestant-Americans called it.

Deriving from the Protestant acceptance of a variety of religious pathways, America's national identity, its Constitution, and the eventual "American way of life" were based on a common political ideology. As the scholar Samuel Huntington put it:

> For most people national identity is the product of a long process of historical evolution involving common conceptions, common experiences, and common religion. National identity is thus organic in character. Such however is not the case in the United States. American nationality has been defined in political rather than organic terms. The political ideas of the American creed have been the basis of national identity. . . . The United States thus had its origins in a conscious political act, in assertion of basic political principles and in adherence to the constitutional agreement based on those principles.[4]

What clearly differentiates the early American national identity from that of the French, German, and English is that it is based on a political ideology with almost no historical component—no long-existent influence of a single dominant religion or form of government. It is not hard to see how much more easily Jews could be a part of America rather than of Catholic France, Lutheran Germany, and Anglican England. America had no citizenship restrictions with regard to religion or length of time lived in the new nation. Thus, Jews came to the most open and free land of the Diaspora, gaining national citizenship without its being grudgingly awarded. Their citizenship was derived from the United States Constitution, which separated the government from any religious institutional ties whatsoever, leaving religious influence to be exercised only through individuals. As a result, confidence in the new national government by American Jews showed itself early and continuously, and has much to do with why most contemporary Jews favor a strong and protective central government.

Reformation ideas of the seventeenth century spurred Christian philosophers and theologians to delve into Jewish writings, and not just the Old Testament. Christians cited the works of Maimonides and other rabbinic scholars. Hebraic studies flowered in the universities. As historian Eric Nelson noted, the Protestant belief that it was a Christian duty to study both the Hebrew Bible and the New Testament in their original languages was in marked contrast to the Catholic Church's ban on the lay reading of original Hebrew sources. Christian Hebraic centers were found in the Protestant United Provinces, particularly in the Dutch Republic where the thriving Jewish community of fugitives from the Inquisition provided Christian scholars access to many Hebrew documents and rabbinical scholars.[5]

Ideas of humanistic pluralism, tolerance, and the importance of individual conscience, which flowered later in the Enlightenment, were studied by Christian Hebraists: John Locke in his *Letter Concerning Toleration* (1689) stressed admiringly that the Hebrew nation of the Old Testament "practiced broad toleration, welcoming residents who did not obey the Mosaic law—and even tolerating idolatry outside of its borders." Locke continued, "Amongst so many captives taken . . . we find not one man forced into the Jewish religion . . . and punished for idolatry though all of them were certainly guilty of it."[6] The thread of tolerance for "differences" by Jews reveals itself in later studies of contemporary social attitudes in a significant way.

The ideas of the Protestant Reformation were carried into Dutch and English Protestant-dominated settlements in the American colonies, and the great diversity among the Protestant sects played a major part in the development of early pluralistic American values. While each church and sect believed its own ideas were true, the practical needs of early Americans required a certain respect for the right to believe otherwise, something rarely found in Europe. And the pragmatic acceptance of "the other" was a great benefit to Jews.

Anti-Semitism did, of course, exist in early America. But it is important in understanding the freedom of Jews, both in the colonies and after the country's founding in 1789, not to use present-day standards of nondiscrimination. In the Europe of the eighteenth century, Moses Mendelssohn was still pleading for Prussian Jews to be allowed out of the ghetto and for government to loosen its severe restrictions on everyday Jewish life. In the American colonies, Jews enjoyed freedom of movement and were integrated into society a full century before European ghettos were dissolved. American Jews became not only traders and merchants, but butchers and artisans who served the general population rather than just their own. While Leonard Dinnerstein's careful documentation of anti-Semitism has shown that it was part of the early Jewish experience in America, he pointed to the far more integrated aspects of Jewish-Gentile relationships. "Despite prevailing religious and cultural stereotypes of the Jew, in actual practice Jews and Gentiles had many pleasant and neutral interactions; the images both groups carried were rarely a hindrance to personal encounters among individuals."[7]

Letters from American Jews to families in Central Europe touched on two major themes: first, the great amount of freedom and opportunity for Jews; and second, the danger that the temptations of America might erode the morals, beliefs, and religious practices of traditional Jewish life.[8] Writing to his parents in Germany, Aaron Phillips of Charleston noted enthusiastically,

> How on earth is it possible to live under a government, where you cannot even enjoy the simple privileges that correspond to a human being. Here we are all the same, all the religions are honored and respected and have the same rights. An Israelite with talent who does well, can like many others achieve the highest honors. . . . America the Promised Land, the free and glad America has all my heart's desire. . . . Dear parents, if only the Israelites knew how well you can live in this country, no one really would live in Germany any longer.[9]

Compared to most European leaders, many American ones—almost all of them Christians—were more respectful of Jews, owing in part to the character of early American Christianity. As the sociologist Seymour M. Lipset observed:

> The European and Latin American nations have been domi-
> nated by the churches, the Anglicans, Catholics, Lutherans,
> and Orthodox. The overwhelming majority of Americans was,
> and still is, adherents of the sects: the Baptists, Methodists, and
> hundreds of other smaller denominations. The churches have
> been established and hierarchical. The sects have never been
> state related; they have always been voluntary institutions, and
> most of them have been congregational. . . . Protestant sectari-
> anism, which stresses the personal relationship of individuals
> with God, unmediated by church or hierarchy has contributed
> to the strength of individualism in this country. The competi-
> tive relationship of the sects with other denominations has en-
> abled the Jews to fit in, as one out of many, rather than as the
> only or principal deviant group.[10]

Though many early Americans did not link the Jews with the Hebrews of the Old Testament, many others, particularly in New England, did make the connection, and with admiration at that. They gave
their children Old Testament names such as Samuel, Isaiah, and Isaac,
and familiarized themselves with the stories, ideals, and history of an
ancient people. The initial granting of full federal citizenship to Jews,
unlike its withholding of those rights from slaves and Native Americans, was, at least in part, related to a unique biblical connection between Christians and Jews in post-colonial times. Early Americans saw
Jews as adherents to a non-Christian religion, not as a separate race.
The acceptance of differentness and respect for religious diversity (if
not for racial diversity) established a relationship of peaceful coexistence between America and its Jews. Such inclusiveness is captured in
an early letter from George Washington, who, upon his death, was
later eulogized and compared, as the first great leader of America, to
Moses, the "first conductor of the Jewish nation."[11]

In his 1790 letter to the Jewish congregation in Rhode Island,

Washington noted that, "All possess alike liberty of conscience and immunities of citizenship. . . . It is now no more that toleration is spoken of as if it were the indulgence of one class of people that another enjoyed the exercise of their inherent natural rights, for, happily, the Government of the United States, which gives to bigotry no sanction, to persecution no assistance, requires only that they who live under its protection should demean themselves as good citizens."

Washington concluded by welcoming all children of the Bible, all children of Abraham, to an America in which various religious groups could enjoy freedom, security, and the right to be different: "May the children of the stock of Abraham who dwell in this land continue to merit and enjoy the good will of the other inhabitants—while every one shall sit in safety under his own vine and fig tree and there shall be none to make him afraid."[12]

Even the rights of citizenship that Republican France later bestowed on its Jews—"everything as a Frenchman, nothing as a Jew"—differed markedly from American citizenship rights as Washington articulated them: the encouragement and *protection of difference* "as every one shall sit in safety under his own vine and fig tree." The French approach to being a good French citizen, then as now, demands a total assimilation that was not required of American immigrants. It would be politically unthinkable for an American president to state publicly, as the French president Nicolas Sarkozy did in 2011, "If you come to France you accept to melt into a simple community, which is the national community, and if you don't want to accept that, you are not welcome in France."[13] Thus the hybrid terms "Italian-American," "German-American," and so forth are often heard, but not "Algerian-French."[14]

Adherence to certain political principles and participation in republican life were thus the central basis of citizenship, not sameness of culture or religion. Our Founders believed, first, that ordinary men and women *could* govern themselves through representative government; and, second, that everyone in the political community (at that time adult white males) had equal votes; and, third, "that individuals who comport themselves as good citizens of the civic culture are free to differ from each other in religion and in other aspects of their private lives."[15]

Such thinking was more advanced than even that of Europe during the later Enlightenment, when greater freedom of thought did not result in the levels of tolerance and acceptance of *cultural diversity* fostered in America. From this country's beginning, its many immigrants have produced a unique stream of subcultures, hyphenated Americans, that has long distinguished the United States from Europe. Dynamic diversity runs throughout all three stages of American Jewish history and is a critical factor in shaping present-day Jewish values and attitudes. The early influence of a Protestant environment that formed the structure of government, and which set the initial attitudes toward the acceptance of Jews as American citizens, was crucial in providing a political underpinning of protection. When significant social anti-Semitism erupted after 1875, constitutional protections were critically important in limiting challenges to political rights and liberties for Jews—as did not occur in Europe.

The intense interest of the young country in trading and commerce also suited early Jewish immigrants from Europe. European monarchs like Fredrick the Great had banned Jews from agriculture and other related occupations, leaving low-esteemed trading and moneylending to Jews. But America encouraged all sorts of business activities in the early stages of its development. Usury, the making of money on money, had been barred in Catholic countries in both canon and civil law until well into the eighteenth century, and borrowing and lending money was considered disreputable for long afterward. Among American Protestant thinkers, in contrast, arguments were consistently made in favor of charging interest on loans, and the stigma of usury gradually disappeared.[16] Indeed, Benjamin Franklin all but endorsed usury when he wrote in 1748, "Remember, that Money is of a prolific generating Nature. Money can beget Money and its Offspring can beget more, and so on."[17]

Martin Luther stigmatized lending at interest, but other Protestant dissenters, like John Calvin, approved of it, assuming the rates were reasonably limited. In Protestant England, as scholar Jerry Muller has noted, "a similar distinction was drawn in the course of the seventeenth century between legal usury up to a fixed maximum rate of interest, and illegal usury."[18] While Max Weber, in his *The Protestant Ethic and the Spirit of Capitalism,* later attributed much of the capitalist or mercantile focus in America to cultural aspects of Calvinist Protestantism, he nevertheless defended it on the basis of economic efficiency. Against those who identify capitalism with greed, he noted that the impulse of acquisition had without question existed prior to the development of capitalism.[19] In any case, the hyper-development of and focus on commerce has been a critical aspect of America. It was, and still is today, an element of compatibility between America and its Jews.

Jews who immigrated in the nineteenth and twentieth centuries also had the advantage of bringing significant cultural capital. The occupational restrictions imposed on most European Jews which forced them into trading and moneylending also encouraged the development of numerical and analytical skills that were essential in a rapidly growing commercial nation. Widespread Jewish literacy—dating back at least to 64 CE when Joshua Ben Gamla decreed universal schooling for all Jewish males over six years old so they could study the Torah and its many commentaries—gave Jews a distinct advantage over other immigrants, most of whom were illiterate or semi-literate.[20] Studiousness and commercial trading—two cultural characteristics of Jewish life emphasized for almost two thousand years—were an important foundation for Jewish accomplishment and integration.

Although Jews continued to face some instances of local prejudice (such as being barred in certain states from holding government office) social interaction with non-Jews was generally quite common, and Jewish-Christian intermarriage has been estimated by historians at between 10 and 15 percent of American Jews, and by 1840 at 30 percent, far higher than the rates in the America of 1950 when I was married.[21] Even before the American Revolution had ended, New York state extended "free exercise and enjoyment of religious profession and worship" to "all mankind" whether Christian or not. As Jonathan Sarna has pointed out, however, the state still required those born abroad to subscribe to an anti-papist oath.[22] Fear of papal authority ran deep. Fear of Jews did not.

Jewish religious organizations borrowed heavily from dissenting sects of Protestants after the Revolution as well. They rejected the hierarchical form of Anglicanism and chose instead the congregational form—a form, both democratic and anti-authoritarian, that sharply distinguished it from the more closed practice of Judaism in Europe, England, and Mediterranean countries.

A number of historians have described various tensions and struggles *between* Jewish groups during the period from the country's founding until after the Civil War. This disharmony echoed the contrariness and decentralization of Protestant sects.[23] A Jewish people long oppressed in Europe, where they focused largely on group concerns and their insular communal and religious life, were now treated as individuals, with little if any rabbinical authority controlling their behavior. Prior to 1840, no ordained rabbi served in any pulpit in America. As rabbis did begin to immigrate and take their places in synagogues, the next half century was filled with debates between traditionalist Jews (the Orthodox) and the reformers who gradually shaped their own institutions.[24]

In Europe, Jewish religious life had been highly organized, hierarchical, and focused on the group, not individuals. Jews were often governed by the *kehillah*, a religious communal organization, and in some nations by Grand Rabbis. An effort to form such a top-down organization of Jews was, in fact, attempted in New York in 1909, but failed quickly.[25] The culture of sectarian Protestantism with its voluntarist, pluralist, and individualistic emphasis overwhelmed attempts at European-style hierarchy, profoundly Americanizing the practice of its Jews. America's welcoming of religion while opposing the dominance of any particular one has provided Jews with a special type of protection. Just as important has been the strength and stability of the American government, which has weathered the major economic stress of depressions, war, and huge population changes.

Anti-Semitism did crop up in federal laws during and after the Civil War. Although there were Jewish generals in the Union Army, in 1862 General Ulysses Grant issued a directive, Order Number 11, expelling all Jews from his military district, which comprised parts of Kentucky, Mississippi, and Tennessee. In his directive, Grant wrote that Northern carpetbaggers, whom he thought to be mostly Jews, "had descended upon the region, and in violation of governmental regulations were engaging in rampant cotton peddling and speculations."[26] President Lincoln canceled Grant's order immediately. Grant himself was later so embarrassed by it that he apologized for it, telling his wife that he deserved the censure he received. When he became president, Grant went out of his way to show sensitivity to Jewish concerns and appointed many Jews to posts in and out of the United States, even offering the office of Secretary of the Treasury to Joseph Seligman, who turned it down.[27]

America was the first Western nation to include its Jews as full national citizens by popular agreement. The first Jews residing in America, and the millions that immigrated after, owed much to the Founders, who not only provided individual rights but set in motion a new government that has protected Jews politically ever since. Simultaneously in France and Germany, on the other hand, and as I will show further, top-down political grants of citizenship and governmental promises failed to protect Jews from extreme social and economic stress. As Leonard Dinnerstein noted of this early founding period in America:

> Yet, despite . . . prejudices, Jews were generally left alone. They were not as victimized and as exploited as Irish Catholics; they were not pushed out of society as the Indians were. And they were not enslaved like the Africans. Thus while they were objects of prejudice in people's minds they were not thwarted in the United States in anywhere near the same fashion as members of other marginal groups. And while Jews were allowed to follow their own pursuits and receive assistance from one another, they often moved in elite circles and found friends and companions among respected Christians within both local and national communities.[28]

The early, relatively benign relationship of American Jews to their social environment lasted approximately seventy years; it was shattered by the anti-Jewish hostility that erupted in the last quarter of the nineteenth century and intensified during the first half of the twentieth. But it did not lead to political limitations on Jews, as it did in France and Germany, though it did lead to a certain social segregation, in response to which American Jews built their own social organizations, including charities, sport clubs, and other private-membership clubs. Some of them still exist.

This second major period in Jewish-American life, which I will discuss further, was a largely negative experience that shaped the psychology and attitudes of most American Jews for generations. But this period should not obscure or diminish the importance of the initial phase, which built a solid foundation of political protection and integration that was never pierced by later social animosity.

Prologue to Chapter Three

B efore the close of the 1800s, America's relatively benign environment for Jews was followed by an increasing intolerance that
brought social separateness. This lasted some seventy or eighty years,
into the early 1960s, and spanned my parents' entire lifetime. I, on the
other hand, lived only the first three decades of my life in the intolerant America of the 1930s, '40s, and '50s, and later enjoyed the renewed
tolerance of and respect for Jews (and other minorities) in America—
what has truly been a "golden age."

Our family had moved in the late 1930s from Brooklyn to Riverdale, New York, because of my mother's insistence that her children
attend the Fieldston School nearby—the route, she believed, to a good
college education. It was a deeply humanistic and progressive school
with ethical, but secular, values that were in accord with my own developing values and beliefs. The only problem, we found, was that
our rented house—situated behind the athletic fields of Manhattan
College, a Catholic school—was right in the middle of an anti-Semitic
community. No neighbors ever made any contact with my parents,
none of the children on the block would play with me or my two
brothers, and we were chased frequently by older students from Manhattan Prep across the street from our house. "There they are, get the
Jews," was their battle cry.

Unlike in the early decades of the country's history, social integration of Jews during this period of intolerance was severely restricted,
and they had to form their own golf, tennis, and other recreational
clubs, as well as build their own hospitals and create their own charities. Quotas were enacted strictly limiting the number of Jews who
could be accepted to colleges, medical schools, and social organizations.

So although there were not any attempts to limit the *political* rights of Jews, as there were in Europe, my parents' whole lives, and my own formative years, were lived in the shadow of severe *social* anti-Semitism, which strongly influenced the decisions Len and I were to make in our early years of marriage and parenthood.

My parents had struggled successfully to keep the tragic realities of the Great Depression from intruding into our family life. But it came at a cost. My father worked long hours, six days a week, and traveled often. In 1940, when Nazi U-boats were blocking British shipping but before the United States got into the war, he left home for a full month to seek entrepreneurial opportunities in blockaded Australia. It took weeks of island hopping to get there and back, and for me it was too long a period to be without a father. He would become my guide and mentor in later life, instilling in me the boldness to change my career from business to teaching, and inspiring my sense of close connection to the Jewish people.

The Fieldston School was, in retrospect, the single most important educational choice my parents would make, as the school propelled all three of us children into first-rate colleges, opening up many and diverse career opportunities. Without any formal education of their own past the eighth grade, my parents had made a wise and far-reaching cultural decision for their children.

Chapter Three

The Reaction: Industrialism and Mass Immigration Breed Intolerance

The last half of the 1800s produced changes that not only resulted in the rapid industrialization of America, but brought with it major disruptions of social and economic life. The first telegraph messages, sent in 1844, began centralizing communications, a change that helped initiate the greatest increase in industrialization and centralization the world had ever seen.[1] Because of the social stresses of that rapid transition from a dispersed, small-farm agrarian population to an industrialized and centralized urban society, American Jews found themselves in a growingly hostile environment—at both the top and the bottom of the social structure.

While politics remained local after the Civil War, economic forces centralized and consolidated industries like steel, oil, railroad, telegraph, and telephone. The growth and centralization of communications rapidly influenced the speed and penetration of mass opinion—magnifying the message of anti-Semitism. Daily newspaper circulation, for example, increased sevenfold between 1870 and 1900, and the use of telegraphs increased ninefold.[2] The number of miles of railroad track increased more than fourfold over a twenty-year period, turning agriculture, formerly confined to local markets, into a large national industry.

The continued drop in agricultural prices and income in the last third of the nineteenth century, the effect of modernized equipment and large-scale farming, forced much of the farming population into the cities. Among the other causes of this migration were government policies that put the rapidly industrializing Northeast in conflict with the primarily agricultural Midwest and Plains states. The Northeast, the center of manufacturing and finance, was politically supportive of high national tariffs to protect developing industry. As financial lenders, they were also supporters of gold and hard currency. But agrarian interests, which borrowed from Eastern banks to buy machinery and to support the growing cycle, were furious over the higher prices produced by tariffs. They also fought, ultimately unsuccessfully, to weaken the currency with the coinage of silver so that their debts would be softened by inflation.[3]

In short, America's transition in a mere fifty years from a largely agrarian society to an urbanized and industrialized one put enormous stresses on its social life. And the mass immigration needed to support rapid industrialization greatly aggravated those stresses, which eventually turned the tolerance and openness of America's early decades into angry religious conflict and regional strife—along with a changing attitude toward its Jews. The last half of the 1800s and the first half of the 1900s gradually raised the intensity of anti-Semitism to levels unthinkable to most present-day Americans.

The backlash to the pressures of industrialization and the mass immigration needed to support it produced the Populist movement, and with it long-dormant anti-Semitic stereotypes. It was, as one historian described it, a reaction of "provincials," small-town people, against the "cosmopolitans" of the cities. Such distinctions had scarcely existed in America before 1850. Now, tensions between urban-commercial interests and rural-agrarian ones had become major consequences of industrialization.[4] As political historian Everett Ladd Jr. later described the negative side of Populism:

> As the country industrialized and urbanized, the cultural gap
> between the big city and the farm, "the New Yorker and the

hayseed," widened. Populism was also nativistic, bitterly re-
senting of the "importation of foreign pauper labor" that was
crowding into the great cities, swelling the ranks of industry,
leading the assault on the style and traditions of an older America, the America of the small town and farm and the Protestant
church. Bryan the Populist was Bryan the religious fundamentalist, Bryan the prohibitionist, and Bryan the provincial.[5]

When William Jennings Bryan was chosen as the Democratic presidential nominee in 1896, polarization became full-blown. Although
scholars of Populism have found much good in the political goals of
the movement—such as anti-trust legislation and other governmental regulations to contain capitalism-run-amok—Populism's rhetoric
had a dark side for America's Jews. Frequent references by farmers
to "Rothschild," "Jewish bankers," "Shylock," and "international conspiracies" linked Jews to greed for money. Thus Bryan at the 1896
Democratic Convention famously thundered in biblical tones, "You
shall not press down on the brow of labor this crown of thorns, you
shall not crucify mankind upon a cross of gold."[6]

While anti-Semitism was never formally in the Populist party platform, as it often was in those of European political parties, the verbal
assaults on Eastern bankers—who were said to be ruining the farm
population with "conspiracies" of financial manipulation—played to
the stereotypes of Jews as greedy capitalists making money on money,
not by the sweat of labor. The animosity toward modern capitalism by
the farmers of "sweat," combined with the prominence of Jews both in
the Northeast, particularly New York, and in the "money businesses,"
intensified anger at "Jewish bankers" crucifying farmers on a "cross of
gold." The Jews can't farm, the sentiment was; they are parasites who
live off those who work the land.[7]

Resentment was only one of several reactions to the social and
economic stresses of the late nineteenth century and the first half of
the twentieth. The stresses of industrialization began to erode the social status of Jews at both the top and the bottom of the socioeconomic scale. While Jews of wealth and social standing had often been

welcomed into most clubs, resorts, and residential neighborhoods, anti-Semitism eventually pushed American Jews toward separateness. For example, a prominent Jew from Philadelphia, Jesse Seligman, a founding member of the Union League Club in the 1860s, was later unable to get a family member admitted because restrictions against admitting Jews had become part of the club's bylaws.[8]

As American group status destabilized with demands for social boundaries, American Jews became subject to more hostility than ever before. Joseph Seligman's exclusion in 1877 from the Saratoga, New York, Grand Union Hotel, where he had previously summered, began a trend toward social exclusion. Two years later, Austin Corbin's public announcement that "Jews as a class are unwelcome at Coney Island" extended and popularized restrictions that brought about a decline in the status of already integrated German-American Jews. Within a decade of such anti-Jewish hostility, there followed extreme anti-Semitic propaganda urging the end of the mass immigration of Jews from Russia and Eastern Europe on the grounds that they diluted American racial bloodlines.[9]

At lower levels of American urban social life, Irish and German Catholic immigrants were particularly resentful of Jews, largely because of religious differences and the vilification of Jews by priests in Catholic newspapers. Between 1890 and 1924 in Baltimore, all three Catholic newspapers portrayed Jews as Christ-killers and part of international conspiracies. Repeated acts of violence by the Irish against Jewish immigrants were one result.[10] The massive influx of at least two million mostly impoverished Jews from Eastern Europe in just thirty years provoked questions about whether they could ever become good Americans. Many were thought to have brought with them ideas of socialism, communism, and radicalism, exacerbating anti-Jewish sentiment. Even established and integrated Central European Jews, prominent in business, investment banking, and other professions, faced increased hostility. Jews were not only the victims of social snobbery by the upper class, but also the object of agrarian, populist anger at the lenders—supposedly Jews—who were calling in overdue mortgages. This despite the fact that Jews were primarily active in providing loans to corporate and governmental institutions, not in commercial lending to farmers.

The America of colonial times and the early decades of the nineteenth century was indeed a country of immigrants. But the population of the United States in 1820 was only 9.6 million, of which almost 2 million were slaves without citizenship.[11] The majority of white citizens at that time were of British descent, but by the late 1800s their numbers were reduced by mass immigration to approximately 40 percent of the white population. Also, the primarily English-Protestant religious basis of early statehood was diluted by, first, largely Catholic Irish and German immigrants in the 1840s, '50s, and '60s, and subsequently by many more Catholic immigrants from countries in Southern and Eastern Europe.[12]

In the half century following the Civil War, immigration per decade rose to an average of over 5.2 million, drastically changing the ethnic and religious composition of the American population. The immigration in the late 1840s and 1850s of Irish and German Catholics had already provoked a Protestant reaction, initiating a period of social and religious intolerance. Fear of alien ideologies, plus fear that the country's new Catholic population was controlled by the pope in Rome, increased doubts about the loyalty of Catholic immigrants to American values as interpreted by the country's native Protestants. The Know-Nothing movement, anti-immigrant and anti-Catholic at its core, won some local political victories but failed to curb immigration, which only accelerated as the economy grew.

The masses of newcomers fed anti-immigrant feelings, leading to the Immigration Act of 1924, which shut down large-scale immigration of what was considered "inferior stock." The effort to give "scientific" backing to anti-immigrant feelings, and the strong academic and social support for shutting off the immigration of supposedly less intelligent people, were reactions to the enormous change in the makeup of the American population. Jews from Eastern Europe constituted a large number of the immigrants and were considered by the Eugenics Movement part of the less intelligent, inferior "racial stock." Jews were subject to what became the redefinition of "race," one that departed from the accepted division of Black vs. White into new sub-racial categories that defined race by national origin.

Leading the opposition to the long-existing open immigration policy (for Whites only) were no longer just angry native workers, but many prominent Americans in the academy, professions, and business. The Eugenics Movement claimed that immigrants from Italy and Eastern Europe were diluting the stock of American intelligence and therefore weakening the quality of the original "Nordic" founders of the Republic.

Beliefs about inherent racial superiority and inferiority had, of course, already been reflected in the US Constitution's exclusion of Blacks and Native Americans as citizens. Later legislation entirely excluded the Chinese and restricted the rights of Japanese immigrants as well. The extension of "racially inferior" status to Whites of certain nationalities was a basis for the National Origins Act of 1924, one that severely limited immigration of Whites from the Mediterranean and Eastern European countries while favoring "Nordic" (or "Aryan") immigrants from Western Europe, England, and Scandinavia—largely Protestant countries.

Many among the academic and intellectual elite subscribed to the principles of the Eugenics Movement, which was voicing the supposed need to re-purify American intellectual stock, which they believed had been diluted by Negros, Italians, Slavs and, yes, Jews. The Movement was buttressed by the "scientific" research of Carl C. Brigham, a psychology professor from Princeton University, whose book *A Study of American Intelligence* gave "objective and statistical" legitimacy to already widely held beliefs about racial superiority. To understand the tenor of the times, one need only consider the 1896 Supreme Court case *Plessy v. Ferguson,* in which the seven-to-one majority (with one abstention) of justices cited the "acknowledged" intellectual inferiority of the African race as grounds for declaring racial segregation constitutional. The "clear statistical evidence" in support of such ideas provided by Brigham's 1923 book was widely hailed as proof of their scientific validity. Transcripts of legislative committee hearings show the frequent citing of Brigham's "hard evidence"; his writings were the intellectual and academic cornerstone of a movement that sought both to prohibit certain nationalities from entering America at all, and to lower immigration quotas for Slavs, Jews, and Italians in favor of the "superior" populations of Western Europe, England, and Scandinavia. Rep. Albert Johnson, chairman of the House Committee on Immigration and Naturalization, was also chairman of the Eugenics Research Association, an organization of leading citizens interested in making its so-called science into public policy.[13]

Brigham cited Memoir XV of the National Academy of Sciences, which measured the intelligence of over one hundred thousand World War I Army recruits. Brigham argued that "these Army data constitute the first really significant contribution to the study of race differences in mental traits. They give us a scientific basis for our conclusions."[14] But believers like Brigham in the intellectual superiority of the "Nordic" or "Aryan" races had to deal with the popular view that Jews, whatever their other defects, were nobody's intellectual inferiors. With a dexterity prompted by a foregone conclusion, Brigham handled that apparent contradiction:

> Our figures, then, would rather disprove the popular belief that the Jew is highly intelligent. Immigrants examined in the Army who report their birthplace as Russia, had an average intelligence below those from all other countries except Poland and Italy. . . . If we assume that the Jewish immigrants have a low average intelligence, but a higher variability than other nativity groups, this would reconcile our figures with popular belief, and, at the same time, with the fact that investigators searching for talent in New York City and California schools find a frequent occurrence of talent among Jewish children.[15]

This "assumed" variability transformed a few smart Jews into a large number of stupid ones. It was pseudo-science like this that buttressed the theories of the Eugenics Movement; but several years after Brigham published his book, his evidence was found to be fatally flawed, so much so that Brigham himself repudiated his own research.

But by then it was too late—the anti-immigration legislation of 1924 had passed.

The intelligence tests given to Army recruits were, of course, in English, and many recent arrivals spoke English only as their second language. The test given to adult immigrants was, of necessity, language-oriented, which disadvantaged them relative to native-born Americans and totally skewed the results. The translation of eugenicist racial theories into public policy was, of course, only a variant of the policies of slavery and segregation, which were themselves not possible without widely held ideas about racial superiority and inferiority. While beliefs in the superiority of one religion or culture to others can be held with relative impunity in America because of our sense of pluralism, the imputation of inherited racial traits treads on much more dangerous turf. The popularity of certain beliefs about racial groups has long been prelude to major public policy changes throughout American history.

The rise of anti-Semitism was fomented not only by the rhetoric (if not the programs) of Populism and the "science" of the Eugenics Movement, but also by efforts of the nation's mightiest industrialist of the early twentieth century, Henry Ford, who made anti-Jewish propaganda a principal focus of his nonbusiness zeal. In his newspaper, *The Dearborn Incident,* Ford published a series of articles from 1920 onward charging "the international Jew" with manipulating America into World War I, with corrupting the innocence of Anglo-Saxons through films, and with promoting African-American jazz (labeled by Ford as "Yiddish moron music"). Such claims, and his promotion of the debunked *Protocols of the Elders of Zion* as genuine, eventually were opposed by a petition signed by thousands of people—including hundreds of eminent non-Jewish clergy, intellectuals, and civic leaders, both progressive and conservative. Among them were Presidents Theodore Roosevelt, William Howard Taft, and Woodrow Wilson.[16]

In this period of change, Jews were caught between the challenge of modernity and traditional religious society. Unlike in Europe, the optimism and faith in progress that were common to a forward-looking America kept even critics of Jews from seeing them as permanently indigestible—that is, not assimilable. Even anti-Semites saw some valuable qualities in Jews that might sooner or later be "American-ized." From roughly 1920 to 1945, Jewish leaders focused on adapt-ing Jewish life to change. Mordecai Kaplan, for example, the founder of the Reconstructionist Movement, had much to do with reshaping Reform and Conservative Jewish life. While his "movement" never gained more than a small number of Jewish members, he nevertheless played a key role in the development of a cultural definition of Jew-ishness. In his writings in the *Menorah Journal,* and later in his major work, *Judaism as a Civilization,* Kaplan advocated a cultural rather than a racial definition of Jewishness, to great effect on non-Orthodox in-stitutions of Jewish life.

Originally trained as an Orthodox rabbi, Kaplan established com-munity centers where many cultural and nonreligious aspects of Jew-ish life could be more easily expressed; democratized Jewish ritual by having his daughter Bat Mitzvahed in the 1920s; and, importantly, rejected the idea of Jewish "chosenness" by God. A deeply religious person in his own right, Kaplan's impact on non-Orthodox Jewish life was significant, focusing it more on the cultural aspects of Jewish life, dispensing with some of the supernatural elements of Judaism, and bringing the self-definition of Jews away from race and toward cultural pluralism.[17]

During this same period, the "Red Scares" of the 1920s brought the Bolshevik Revolution closer to America. Communists, socialists, an-archists, and Jews were all part of the alien "un-American" conspiracy that Henry Ford and others wrote and spoke about. After the stock market crash of 1929 and during the ensuing Great Depression, scape-goats were sought on which to blame the economic disasters, adding impetus to the demonization of Jews.

Most prominent among the many who singled out the Jews for conspiratorial blame was the semi-populist, originally left-wing priest Father Charles Edward Coughlin, one of the first to use network ra-dio to reach a mass audience (his listeners numbered over 30 million weekly).[18] A supporter of Franklin Roosevelt in his first-term elec-tion in 1932, Coughlin moved steadily to the right as an apologist for both Hitler and Mussolini. As he turned against Roosevelt, Coughlin's broadcasts became suffused with anti-Semitic themes: the Depression was caused, he claimed in 1936, by an "international conspiracy of Jewish bankers." These same bankers, he said, were behind the Russian Revolution as well. By November 1938, the Jews were no longer "behind" the Russian Revolution, according to Coughlin, but in front of it: "There can be no doubt that the Russian Revolution . . . was launched and fomented by distinctively Jewish influence." In his magazine *Social Justice* he claimed that Marxist atheism in Europe was a Jewish plot against America.[19] Despite pressure from the Justice Department and the FBI and in spite of his making excuses for Hitler's Kristallnacht violence against German Jews in 1938, Coughlin solidified isolationist support. After America was attacked on December 7, 1941, however, the isolationist movement petered out. On May 1, 1942, the archbishop of Detroit, Edward Mooney, finally ordered Coughlin to cease all political activities and radio programs, and to confine his duties to being a simple parish priest.

One cannot underestimate the depth and breadth of social anti-Semitism in the 1930s and 1940s. Even liberal scholars aiming to eliminate anti-Semitism focused not on anti-Semitic discrimination itself, but on what its potential victims should and should not do to forestall it: deny differences; don't go into Jewish-dominated industries; assimilate fully, but don't be "pushy." The eminent sociologist Talcott Parsons, a liberal, advised that "generally speaking, any policy which tends to make Jews as Jews more conspicuous . . . would tend to be an invitation to anti-Semitic reaction." And nothing could make Jews more *conspicuous* than to press for legislation outlawing discrimination.[20]

In 1936, *Fortune* magazine devoted an entire issue to the subject of supposed Jewish control of the economy. Industry by industry, recounts Charles Silberman, "*Fortune* demonstrated that this simply was not the case; Jews were almost wholly absent from commercial banking and insurance; automobile, steel, petroleum, and chemical production; advertising and journalism; and, indeed, most other industries to which power adhered. Far from controlling the economy, American

Jews were confined to a few, mostly minor, sectors."[21]

Jews were, in fact, absent from most industries and certain professional groups, but not because of "clannishness and tribal inclination," as *Fortune* wrote; and the entry of large numbers of Jews into diverse areas of the economy during the later Golden Age is testimony to how mistaken theories of concentration and conspiracy were. As the sociologist Robert K. Merton noted, Jews would be seen as "pushy" if they tried to fully assimilate, and if they kept to themselves they were "alien and tribal." The systematic condemnation of the out-group continues, he believed, largely *irrespective of what its members do*.[22]

The spreading of anti-Semitism to huge radio audiences and by Nazi Bundists took its toll on the status of Jews during and after the Great Depression, so that popular opinion turned even more strongly against them. As Leonard Dinnerstein has noted, "By June 1944, almost a full year *before* the war ended in Europe, 24% now identified the Jews as the greatest menace [to America] with the Japanese at 9% and the Germans reduced to 6%."[23] This surge of anti-Semitic feeling, brought about by the war crisis, found its way into slurs from anti-Jewish US senators such as Theodore Bilbo of Mississippi, and from many economically and politically reactionary groups. The patriotic fervor of the war also increased suspicions of other "outsiders." The worst victims were Japanese-Americans on the West Coast, whose internment cost them businesses, professions and property—even while many of their sons were fighting in Europe for America. Other minorities suffered as well: African Americans, for instance, were attacked in a race riot in Detroit in 1943, and Mexican Americans were attacked in riots in Los Angeles.

For American Jews, there was a difference in the nature, stability, and strength of America's national political system during the Depression from those of France and Germany. While both European and American Jews were on the "scapegoat" side of anti-Semitism, different national governments diverged in their responses to social stress. In 1930s Germany, the collapse of the nascent democratic government of the Weimar Republic yielded quickly to the Nazi dictatorship with its demonization of Jews. Anti-Semitic governments dominated in

Austria, Hungary, and Romania. And in France, the extremes of Left and Right produced major upheavals, with far-right militia rioting in 1934, followed by government collapse—five national governing coalitions fell in just six months. Fascism, with its virulent strain of anti-Semitism, grew enormously throughout the 1930s as nationalist and ethnic-purity crusades served to isolate Jewish populations.

While America was under major economic stress and experienced significant outbursts of anti-Jewish sentiment, the national government not only acted as a deterrent to political acts of discrimination, but took positive steps to eliminate anti-Semitism. Franklin Roosevelt's New Deal coalition built even more than in the past on minority electoral "outreach," specifically seeking support from different ethnic groups, rather than pitting older "Americanist" groups against newer immigrants. During the 1930s, instead of yielding to pressure to isolate Jews as pariahs, Roosevelt brought over four thousand Jews into mid-level and senior positions in the federal government, a number unheard-of at that time in Western democracies, where the number of Jews in government service fell rather than rose.[24]

Roosevelt's welcoming of Jews was deliberate; indeed, reactionary critics referred to the New Deal as the "Jew Deal." In his book *Israel in the Mind of America,* Peter Grose notes the easy and close relationship of FDR and his Jewish subordinates, "teasing them in a manner that no one suspected of anti-Semitism could carry off." Grose quotes Nahum Goldmann, a diplomat of the Jewish Agency, about when he and Rabbi Stephen Wise were summoned to a meeting at Hyde Park in New York by Samuel Rosenman, a key Roosevelt aide and also Jewish:

> It was a sweltering day, and we were all in our shirtsleeves on the verandah when we heard the blare of a car horn and Roosevelt's car drew up in front of us, Goldman recalled. . . . "Carry on, boys. Sam will tell me what I'm supposed to do on Monday." The car was drawing away when Roosevelt stopped and called out: "Imagine what Goebbels would pay for a photo of

this scene—the President of the United States taking instructions from the three Elders of Zion!"[25]

Roosevelt dismissed the *Protocols of the Elders of Zion* as fraudulent, and his easy relationships with Jews extended throughout his presidency. In the crisis period of the Great Depression, his leadership tilted the political system against the social anti-Semitism of the time, not only in the liberal hiring of his administration, but in his opening of elective politics to minority groups. In addition, he nominated a Jewish professor of law, Felix Frankfurter, to the Supreme Court, in the face of noisy opposition from reactionary and anti-Jewish critics. It is therefore all the more difficult to understand his inaction in the face of Hitler's destruction of European Jewry.[26]

Anti-Semitism in America, while strong before the end of World War II, has always been weaker than in Europe. The multiple prejudices in this country both diverted and diluted specifically anti-Jewish enmity. For over 150 years, huge migrations have produced a country of minorities, where the original stock of New Englanders has become a small and diluted population. America is now, in fact, a minority-dominant political culture, long experienced in handling ethnic diversity and prejudices, though still in the middle stages of dealing with racial differences. For Jews included as white citizens from the country's origin, their status as absorbable and sufficiently assimilative was set by relationships in the early years of fusion and integration. Unlike Europe, America gradually developed an ethos of acceptance of ethnic differences, which could be celebrated without claims of alienness.

Over time, American Jews have developed a confidence in the values espoused by the national government that from Washington's time supported values of fairness and equality, starting with the pronouncement in the Declaration of Independence that "all men are created equal." That was quickly trimmed in the Constitution to apply only to white people, in response to sectional and local interests. The breakdown of the country in the Civil War was, in fact, the continuation of this crucial American argument, by means of weapons rather than words, over the primacy of a national or a state definition of social justice. Despite the anti-slavery amendments of Lincoln and the Republicans, the Supreme Court's narrow interpretation of the Fourteenth Amendment, and its ringing endorsement of state-mandated segregation in *Plessy vs. Ferguson*, frustrated those who had sought a broader and more expansive sense of justice from the national court. A long period of political inaction and deadlock followed, allowing segregation and Jim Crow laws to flourish in the South and in border states. The Republican Party lost interest in asserting its original racial liberalism, and the reunited Democratic Party became dominant in Congress through the seniority of Southern Senators and their control of the major committees. All legislative attempts at racial justice were easily thwarted, and discrimination against Blacks only worsened during the Great Depression. Lynching or "popular justice" in the South continued unabated, and even an attempt by Northern Democrats to insert an anti-lynching plank in the 1940 Democratic platform failed.

Jewish political interests were protected at the country's founding by the endorsement of freedom of religion (and also by their whiteness); the interests of Blacks were not. As dual Black and Jewish leadership activists in the National Association for the Advancement of Colored People (NAACP) Legal Defense Fund sought ways to break the hold of *Plessy,* efforts to counter discriminating behavior in the North also continued. The federal courts and the national government, particularly the presidency, kept up political pressure both during and after World War II, albeit with only minor success. The fight against social discrimination against Jews, and the greater struggle of black Americans against government-approved segregation, could only mark time. The start of World War II continued segregation in the armed forces, and anti-Semitism, particularly below the officer corps level, was notably strong.

The second phase of Jewish-American life came to a close in the 1940s. It was a period of intense discrimination and social ostracism, marked by quotas for Jewish admission to private colleges and medical schools, as well as restrictions on and broad exclusion from many types of employment—all of which I personally experienced in college and afterward when seeking a job. A new age for American Jews, and subsequently for black Americans, was about to begin, without any obvious foreshadowing. The formerly stymied national government—the Supreme Court, the presidency, and an initially reluctant Congress—would be transformed into an assertive and positive political force, demanding that the social system change its ways. It was accompanied by a remarkable and unexpected turnaround in Americans' political and social attitudes toward Jews, and subsequently toward Blacks as well. A moral reawakening took place both with the Supreme Court's 1954 decision in *Brown v. Board of Education of Topeka, Kansas,* and in the White population's change in racial attitudes. It was a transformation of enormous scope, one that would allow an assertive national government to push aside sectional resistance and impose a national definition of social justice as the norm for all its people.

This rapid change was the starting point of a Golden Age for American Jews, and with them all who felt the sting of discrimination. The Civil Rights Act of 1964 and the Voting Rights Act of 1965 were the most important *political* interventions in American *social* life in a century. Its reverberations are still being played out in American politics today. On the wings of that transformation—made possible by an attack on all forms of prejudice and discrimination by the president, the Court, and the national government—the age of Jewish freedom and accomplishment truly began.

Prologue to Chapter Four

I grew up in an unusual time for American Jews, personally witnessing the intolerant treatment of Jews in the America of my parents' generation, and then living through the transition to a new age of significantly diminished discrimination. In a country where social change is normally slow and incremental, the positive changes for Jews, Blacks, and women in the span of a single generation were both breathtaking and unexpected.

The mid-1940s through the early 1950s turned out to be the final decade of the "older" discriminatory life in which I had grown up. When a draft scare developed in 1948, I decided, prematurely, to join a US Marine Reserve program that would allow me an uninterrupted four years of college. My experience that summer in Marine Corps basic training made me realize how harsh anti-Jewish attitudes could be when linked with authority. At the end of our freshman year at Brown, I and my best friend Mac McDowell had driven down to the Marine Corps base in Quantico, Virginia, excited about the new and challenging experience facing us. We were in different platoons in different companies, and because of our religious backgrounds our experiences at Quantico were entirely different. At my orientation lecture, our platoon leader, First Lieutenant Guilford from Georgia, began by proudly detailing the high percentage of officer losses in the Pacific invasion landings he had participated in; then he turned to his evaluation of present-day Marines. They were, he said, "the best damn corps in the world until that goddamned Roosevelt let the niggers and the kikes in." I looked around at the group of college boys, who were visibly stunned by his vicious remarks. We had one black recruit in our platoon because, earlier in 1948, President Harry Truman had integrated all the armed services by executive order.

I had been aware of the extent of military segregation during World War II when the son of family friends came back from his tour as a bomber navigator in Italy. He had told me how only belatedly were the Tuskegee Airmen, a segregated Black unit, allowed into combat, flying fighter-pilot cover for his bomber group, and how effective they were. He had also described their humiliation in the South, having to travel in uniform in a segregated railroad car while German prisoners of war rode in the all-White car with the other Americans.

Lt. Guilford was certainly true to his regional prejudices. He waged his psychological warfare against his detested minorities from the start of training, and within four weeks he had broken the lone black Marine. I don't remember whether the recruit resigned from the program or was discharged. The remaining Jewish Marines in our platoon were solidified in their resolve not to let Lt. Guilford force them out—and we succeeded under duress.

Just before training camp was over, one other incident showed me that the world of the 1940s was not a tolerant and open era.

At Marine Corps Base Quantico, Fred S., a classmate at Brown and the only openly anti-Jewish student I knew there, was in my company, though not in my platoon. On the bus taking our company to the FBI pistol range, sitting several rows in front of me, he spoke disparagingly of Jews, loud enough for me to hear but not speaking directly to me. He was an athletic Midwesterner whom I had tried to befriend at school, to no avail. While he never said anything provocatively anti-Semitic directly to me, it did not stop him from speaking derogatorily and loudly within my hearing.

Shortly after the bus ride back from the range, our company was sitting outside in 105-degree heat watching maneuvers. We had finished a five-mile full-pack march earlier that morning, and the troops, myself included, were in sour moods. Fred S. was reclining about fifteen feet away and started again making loud, derogatory remarks about Jews. This time I reacted quickly and unexpectedly, rolling to my feet and springing on top of him, pummeling him with my fists. Flat on his back, he could barely extend his arms as I punched away enthusiastically until the non-coms broke up the fight. After I briefly explained to my superiors the reason for my attack, no punishment was meted out—the Marine Corps seemingly encouraged a fighting spirit. But the incident had a beneficial side effect: Fred S. never made a mocking, derogatory comment near me again, neither in Quantico nor back at Brown.

During this same decade, many hotels still denied accommodation to Jews, and most denied accommodation to Blacks. Sales of homes to "Jews, Negroes, and Orientals" could legally be prohibited. Many colleges and medical schools had quotas limiting the number of Jews who could attend, and most excluded Blacks altogether. Employment opportunities for Jews were limited in many industries, and even more so for Blacks. Two of my three roommates at Brown did not get into their first choice of school because of restrictive Jewish quotas at Princeton and Dartmouth. One of my roommates, Sam Goldenberg, was first in his class at his Midwestern military academy, and also the highest ranking officer there, yet he still failed to be accepted at Princeton, while the students ranking number three and thirty-three in his class were admitted.

In 1946, when I applied to college, the quota system became a personal reality for me as well. The principal of the Fieldston School, Luther Tate, brought each male student into his office to discuss the possibilities and appropriateness of each college in which a student showed some interest. My parents knew little about colleges. I knew nothing about their academic value, but I did have a slight preference for Princeton's football teams from having watched them at the many Columbia University home games I attended with members of our high school football team.

"Mr. Tate, I think I'd like to go to Princeton," I said with ignorant confidence. I was a good student, had received letters in football, basketball, and baseball, and mistakenly thought I was desirable. He responded quickly and directly: "Don't apply there, Richard. You won't be happy there." "Mr. Tate, I'm usually happy wherever I go," I answered. Realizing that I didn't get what he was really talking about, the pragmatic Gentile principal laid it out in detail: "There is a quota for

Jews at Princeton of less than two percent; there are eating clubs that do not accept Jews; and the school environment is not welcoming. No one has applied to Princeton as long as I've been principal, and, no, you would not be happy there!"

I was taken aback. The only response that I could muster was, "What would you recommend, Mr. Tate?" After a long pause, he said, "Brown University. A very good school, women in the classes just like Fieldston, a substantial Jewish population, and welcoming." I was surprised by the frankness of his recommendations. I went ahead and applied to Brown and was accepted, but I had begun to get a sense of what it meant to be a Jew in a Gentile America in the latter part of the 1940s. It was a time when the old prejudices were making a last stand against the coming racial and religious changes of the 1960s.

By the time my children applied to college in the 1970s, quotas for Jews were gone. Also by then, the Supreme Court had outlawed restrictive covenants on home sales, outlawed discrimination in hotels and other public facilities, outlawed segregation, and outlawed employment discrimination in all industries. In a single generation huge changes had occurred in both law and custom, and many Jews, already highly educated, were ready to take advantage of these new opportunities. I was one of them, changing my career from business to academics and earning a professorship in colleges that had been closed to me just a generation before.

Chapter Four

Toward the Jewish Golden Age in America

When World War II ended in 1945, there was little indication that a major political and social revolution would occur over the next two decades. In the typically incremental process of social change in America, the Supreme Court was preparing quietly to intervene in the American social system in a way that would completely transform the reality of discrimination. After World War II, discrimination against Jews was still active in academia, corporate employment, and in housing and hotel restrictions. It was worse, of course, for people of color. Southern segregation and Southern justice responded to any liberal agitation only by tightening its grip.

President Truman made an effort to improve the life of African Americans by proposing a civil rights plank in the 1948 Democratic platform that would advocate an African-American anti-lynching law, a peacetime Fair Employment Practices Commission, and voting protection.[1] However, there was no challenge whatsoever to the continued segregation of races according to the principle of "separate and equal." But even these modest reforms caused a walkout by some Southern state delegations and, shortly afterward, the founding of the segregationist States' Rights Democratic Party (a.k.a. the *Dixiecrats*).

In the ensuing stalemate, ensured by Southern control of Congress's agenda, there was little hope for any federal legislative action on civil rights. Then, without warning, the Supreme Court repudiated

its own ruling of fifty-eight years earlier in *Plessy v. Ferguson* by asserting in its unanimous *Brown* decision that the involuntary segregation
of races by state law was unconstitutional. How the Court came to
such a reversal is a fascinating story in itself,[2] but the ultimate result of
the ruling was to force the political, social, and racial transformation
of American life.

While the federal district and appellate courts were overriding local and state legal challenges to *Brown*, black and white civil rights
protesters had already begun sit-ins in the South, provoking the angry
responses of a white citizenry that was holding tightly to its claims
of racial superiority and its support for segregation. Attempts to racially integrate businesses or social institutions were met with violence by local vigilantes, and even by local law officers. Black churches
were bombed, and intimidation was used against local Blacks, and
any Whites, who sought to implement racial reform. As agitation for
change continued, the violent reactions of Southern white resisters
became a nightly story on network television, viewed by millions.
Violence against Blacks in the South had previously received only
occasional coverage in local newspapers; now such violence found a
much wider audience: all of us saw dogs and clubs and firehoses used
against civil rights activists.[3] Yet in spite of that, the percentage of the
public who believed in 1962 that "the most important problem facing
America is civil rights" was still only 4 percent. But after the massive
August 1963 civil rights rally in Washington, DC, at which the Rev-
erend Martin Luther King Jr. gave his "I Have a Dream" speech, civil
rights became the public's number one political concern, polling at
over 50 percent.

The Kennedy Administration had basically written the new Civil
Rights Act in 1963. But only after Kennedy's assassination, and with
President Johnson's fierce determination, did a broad new law have a
chance to move through Congress. Johnson's legislative skill enabled
him to pass the most significant law against racism and discrimination
in almost one hundred years. Breaking filibusters on the Senate floor
and stopping attempted vetoes at every level, Johnson and his liberal
and moderate allies prevailed against the forces of localism and states'

rights, and wrote themselves into American history as the most significant force for social justice in a century.

The close cooperation between Blacks and Jews in their long, mutual efforts to eliminate segregation in American life had begun after *Plessy* became law. American Jews had long played leadership roles in the NAACP in prior litigations and operations, and Jewish empathy, self-interest, and financial resources were a key part of the legal drive for social justice. The Supreme Court's *Brown* decision and the Civil Rights Act of 1964 were high points of successful Black-Jewish cooperation, later strained by new developments. The final language of the Civil Rights Act went far beyond righting the wrongs of racial discrimination: it guaranteed voting rights (Title I), prohibited segregation in all public accommodations (Title II), and called for the desegregation of public schools (Title IV). Focusing first on race, the Act also prohibited discrimination based on religion, sex, and national origin, enabling both Jews and women—the two most prepared groups educationally—to move to challenge their exclusion in employment and academia, which they did quickly and successfully.

Historically, in 1945, Jewish admissions to top colleges and universities were deliberately limited by quotas as low as 1 to 2 percent at Princeton and Dartmouth and only slightly higher ones at several other Ivy League schools. In that same year, the President of Dartmouth College, E. M. Hopkins, publicly proclaimed that "Dartmouth is a Christian College, founded for the Christianization of its students."[4] Lionel Trilling's appointment to the faculty of Columbia's English department helped shape the atmosphere in most elite universities at that time. As Trilling, a Jew, later wrote of his appointment, it was openly regarded as an experiment, and when his appointment was up for renewal, he was initially told that he would be more comfortable elsewhere. Only the intervention of Columbia's president brought about his reappointment. Trilling's wife, Diana, recalled that Emory Neff, his mentor in the English department, called on him after his reappointment and, after congratulating him, said he hoped Trilling would not use it as a wedge to open the English department to more Jews.[5] Discrimination in faculty appointment was not unique to

Columbia, as Professor Harvey Mansfield Sr. noted in a seminar of his that I attended as a graduate student in 1970. When he was a professor at Yale University in 1945, Mansfield said, the political science department intentionally excluded Jewish teachers. But the restrictive club of Christian gentlemen in academic life would soon be opened to Jews and others.

Law schools were generally open to Jewish students in the 1940s and 1950s, even if prestigious law firms weren't. Medical schools still had quotas, and many hospitals did not hire Jewish doctors. This restrictiveness was exposed when Jewish enrollments in Columbia University's medical school were found to have dropped from almost 50 percent in 1920 to less than 7 percent in 1940.[6]

Dan A. Oren, in *Joining the Club: A History of Jews and Yale*, has pointed out that until 1946 no Jew achieved the rank of professor at Yale College. By 1949, the Yale faculty still included only one Jew. Yet after the civil rights laws were enacted, the restrictions in academia on hiring Jews all but came to an end. By 1970, 18 percent of Yale College professors were Jewish. That same year, a Carnegie Foundation research project found that by then 22 percent of the biochemistry professors in America were Jews, as were 27 percent of all law faculties and 23 percent of medical faculties.[7]

By the end of the twentieth century, in the seventeen most prestigious universities, Jewish professors were between six and ten times *overrepresented* (in proportion to their percentage of the general population) in the departments of mathematics, political science, economics, sociology, and history. The gates of intolerance had opened in the 1960s and 1970s, in part by landmark antidiscrimination laws, and in part by a growing openness and fairness in the culture as a whole. Educated American Jews and women moved ahead. Social snobbery and intolerance had begun to give way for Jews in the professions and in business, leaving only a few private organizations to maintain restrictive codes.

At the administrative level of colleges and universities, aversion to hiring Jews held fast as late as 1966. Morris B. Abram, then President of the American Jewish Committee, wrote that while approximately a thousand presidents of public universities and colleges had been appointed in the previous seventeen years, not one Jew was among them.[8] The Protestant caste system was still in place in private elite colleges and universities as well, and Jewish exclusion was a big part of their academic culture. But change was happening fast, so that within a generation a *majority* of Ivy League schools had Jewish presidents. And, ironically, Brown University, founded by the slave-trading Brown family, chose as its president in 2001 Ruth Simmons, an African-American scholar.

The educational culture of the elite colleges and universities, before and just after World War II, was distinctively Christian. The aforementioned statement by E. M. Hopkins in 1945 that Dartmouth had a mission to Christianize its students may have seemed provocative, but it was, in fact, simply an acknowledgment that in most of these elite schools the Protestant ethos was dominant. Many of these schools had originally been established under the influence of a particular Protestant denomination—Brown University as a northern Baptist college and Yale under Congregational influence. Even though some religious formalities had fallen away by the late 1940s, compulsory Christian chapel services were still required for me and all other Jewish students. And the fraternity system helped perpetuate the dominance of the Protestant ethos, since most fraternities excluded "Jews, Orientals, and Negroes" in their national charters. The scholar David A. Hollinger, in his study of mid-twentieth-century intellectual history, has pointed out that by the 1960s elite colleges and universities had effectively been de-Christianized, ending a patrician-Protestant academic tradition that included snobbery and discrimination.[9]

The decline of anti-Semitic attitudes after World War II was surprisingly rapid (see Figure 1, next page). There had been a high point of animosity and fear in 1944, when almost one quarter of Americans saw Jews as a menace to the country, and just four years earlier, in 1940, 63 percent of Americans thought that Jews as a group had "objectionable traits."[10] The dramatic and rapid decline of anti-Semitic sentiment from over 50 percent of Christian Americans to less than 10 percent in a single generation is remarkable, particularly in light of the long period of intense anti-Jewish prejudices. The rapid reduction in American anti-Jewish feeling after World War II to the present produced, subsequently, a large increase in respect and admiration for supposed Jewish qualities. Terms like "energetic" replaced "pushy," and "greedy" changed to "charitable." The years following the war began a remarkable retreat not only of popular anti-Semitic feeling, but also (as a result of civil rights laws) of legal restrictions by social, academic, and business institutions. These decades were an exceptional time of rising integration and acceptance of Jews into the higher reaches of business and professional life; the level of Jewish accomplishment within these institutions has also been exceptional.

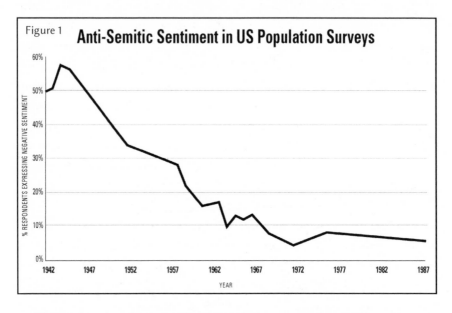

Figure 1 shows trend data detailing anti-Semitic responses to national survey questions from the period of 1942 to 1988. It is an agglomeration of a basket of three responses: affirmative responses to whether or not American Jews had too much power in either the business or political world, negative responses as to whether one would vote for a well-qualified American Jew for president, and negative ratings on where one would rate American Jews on a scale from 0 to 100, with 50 being neutral. Though the precision of the measured effect would be improved significantly if a single repeated question had been asked throughout, a comparison of the range of possible values at a 95 percent confidence level puts both the direction and rapidity of change beyond a reasonable doubt.

Such rapid change in a country of normally slow, incremental transitions deserves closer scrutiny. Why, in this particular period, did a step-level expansion of tolerance, openness, and fairness to Jews (and subsequently to African Americans) occur so quickly? Is it a durable change with genuine institutional support, or merely a trend easily reversed? What are the sources of such change, and why is it that Jewish Americans, when freed of restrictions, have been able to achieve disproportionately in the fields of business, medicine, science, academics, and the arts? What is it in Jewish culture and family dynamics that provides such fertile ground?

An answer to the first question—why did change in attitudes toward Jews come so quickly—can be answered by important, long-term studies of anti-Jewish bias (see again Figure 1, previous page), and is less speculative than the answers to the other questions, which I will address in a later chapter.

There are a number of different elements that can partially account for the rapid decline in anti-Semitism after World War II. Reaction to American claims of fighting discrimination in the world (while still being full of discrimination at home) is one. Increased levels of education, which correlate significantly with decreased levels of anti-Semitism and parochial racial attitudes, is another. Generational change is still another, as older generations, holding more intense anti-Jewish beliefs, die out and are replaced by younger, better-educated, and more tolerant people. Many other causes could also be at play, but all together they still could not have brought about such rapid attitudinal change toward Jews and other minorities, particularly Blacks. This extraordinary change can only be fully understood as a profound moral reaction to the ultimate result of discrimination—the Holocaust—which shook the Christian psyche in America and affected our national political institutions as well.

Horrific details of the death camps worked their way into American consciousness, not only leaving a deep wound in the psyche of American Jews, but also piercing the souls of an American public that had too easily closed its eyes to the rampant discrimination against domestic racial and religious minorities. Exterminating Jews, making the world *Judenrein,* was the goal of Nazi racial policies. Once that was understood, the reaction was swift: Americans, long blind to their own victims of discrimination, first readjusted their vision of Jews, and then, in a change of far greater magnitude, looked with a different set of eyes, a different morality, on American racism toward African Americans.

Even after slavery died, the stigmatizing of African Americans as an inferior race did not end. In fact, the legitimizing of those durable racial beliefs was legally enshrined in the *Plessy* decision in 1896, which made segregation the law of the land. When writing for *Plessy's* seven-to-one majority, Justice Henry Billings Brown noted that segregation of African Americans did not constitute "a badge of inferiority" except "in the minds of colored people." He went on to state, "If one race is inferior to the other socially, the Constitution can not put them up on the same plane."[11] Segregation was then legally and forcefully maintained in Southern states as well as in border states as far north as Delaware and as far west as New Mexico and Arizona.

When the Court overruled its own *Plessy* decision in *Brown v. Board of Education,* the Justices declared: "We have now announced that such segregation is a denial of the equal protection of the laws . . . for the policy of separating the races is usually interpreted as denoting the inferiority of the Negro group."

Justice Robert H. Jackson, the former presiding prosecutor at the Nuremberg Trials of Nazi criminals, made explicit in a memorandum to the deliberating Court the similarity of the genocidal Nazi anti-Semitism to racism against black Americans. He noted that public opinion had undergone a profound change and that "the awful consequences of racial prejudice revealed by . . . the Nazi regime" had caused "a revulsion against [that] kind of racial feeling." He then went on to confront *Plessy's* moral evaluation: "Whatever may have been true at an earlier period, the mere fact that one is in some degree colored no longer creates a presumption that he is inferior, illiterate, retarded, or indigent."[12]

Felix Frankfurter, the only Jewish member of the Supreme Court, took an active role in bringing unanimity to the Court's *Brown* decision.

Though once the activist jurist of Franklin Roosevelt's choice, in his later years Frankfurter had become a conservative who voted against major political change. But on this moral issue, Frankfurter, deeply affected by the Holocaust and its relationship to segregated life in America, was ready to jettison his restraint. Justice Frankfurter had once described his Jewish sensibilities thus: "One who belongs to the most vilified and persecuted minority in history is not likely to be insensible to the freedoms guaranteed by our Constitution."[13] He became closely allied with Thurgood Marshall, then part of the NAACP's legal team, and Justice Robert Jackson, both of whom aided Frankfurter's effort to bring forth a unanimous court ruling.

Nothing of the Court's judicial outlook had really changed. What was different was the awareness of a catastrophe, the Holocaust, that exposed the evil of anti-Semitism, and of racial discrimination in general, as nothing had before. It gave a clear example of racist ideas taken to their logical extremes, and shocked not only Justices Jackson and Frankfurter, but nearly all Americans.

With *Brown,* out went the ruling principle of "separate but equal" and in came a newly evolved, unanimously expressed principle that forced segregation was both immoral and unconstitutional. It does not require much imagination to see that the Holocaust had produced a sea change in the Court's attitude toward racism. Had the Court not declared segregation unconstitutional, legally enforced white supremacy would not have ended in the South and border states for many years.

The Supreme Court's ruling in *Brown* shocked the American public, including me. I had experienced segregation and discrimination personally—first, on a cross-country car trip after graduating from high school in 1947; and, as described earlier, again in the summer of 1948, when my commanding officer in Marine basic training made all too clear his anti-Black and anti-Jewish prejudices. Any threat to segregation in the South after World War II had been dealt with so harshly and quickly that, when I returned to college in the fall of 1948, I was sure that segregation would not end for at least fifty to a hundred years. Yet only six years later, the Court's ruling in *Brown,* without a single dissent from the three Southern Justices, spelled the beginning of the end of legal racial segregation in America.

Public opinion was also changing. Research from the University of Chicago's National Opinion Research Center, which had followed American opinion on important racial issues since the early 1940s, found an enormous change of White attitudes toward Blacks over the course of just two decades. For instance, approval of desegregating schools doubled from 32 percent in 1942 to 65 percent twenty years later; and support for equal job opportunity grew from less than half of Americans in 1943 to 80 percent by the 1960s. Additionally, there was a significant change in beliefs about the relative intelligence of the races. In 1944, only 48 percent of Whites believed that Whites and Blacks were equally intelligent, compared to 80 percent in 1956—only two years after the Supreme Court decision in *Brown*.[14] Figure 2 (in Appendix) shows a long-term decline in negative attitudes toward Blacks among white Americans, though it started somewhat later and was less abrupt than the decline in negative attitudes toward Jews.

The impact of the Holocaust can also be seen in the relationship between the Catholic Church and Jews. Before the Holocaust, the attitude of the primarily Irish Catholic hierarchs, parish priests, and laymen in America was often one of hostility, due partly to differences in culture, but more because of the deeply held belief that Jews were guilty of deicide. From the fourth century, when it was promulgated by St. Augustine, until Vatican II in the early 1960s, many Catholics believed in the doctrine of Jewish "witness," which held that it was God's will that Jews were not to be killed, but dispersed and kept in abject misery for rejecting Jesus; by their continued existence, Jews would serve as a "witness" to the truth of Christianity.[15] In the thirteenth century, St. Thomas Aquinas declared that "in consequence of their sin, Jews were destined to perpetual servitude." The "perfidiousness" of Jews was part of Catholic doctrine and liturgy. Some Catholic historians have themselves documented the Church's hostile treatment of European Jews during those centuries.[16]

The long-lasting Catholic hostility toward Jews came to an end after the Holocaust when, in 1965, the Second Vatican Council issued the document *Nostra Aetate*, which stated that "the Jews should not be presented as rejected or accursed by God, as if this followed from the Holy Scriptures," thus opening a new era of understanding between Jews and Catholics and a new respect for religious ecumenism.[17] This change in Catholic attitudes was echoed in an apology by the Lutheran Synod for the hostile and incendiary words of Martin Luther toward Jews; and most of the other Protestant churches developed a stronger ecumenical relationship with Jews and their congregations, seeking a closeness and respect absent before the Holocaust.

The Holocaust also had a major effect on Jewish self-identification, an issue I will discuss more fully in a later chapter. In brief, Hitler and the Nazi demonization of the Jews on the basis of race had moved most Jews away from seeing themselves in racial terms. Anthropologists had continuously narrowed the number of existing races, expanded the cultural differences within races, and weakened the idea that different countries were the source of different races. While the anthropologist Franz Boas had been unable to get the American Anthropological Society to discredit Nazi racial theories in the mid-1930s, by 1938 the Society passed a resolution stating that the terms "Semite" and "Aryan" had no racial significance whatsoever and identified only different linguistic groups.[18] Ethnic or cultural grounds for differences, rather than race, asserted themselves as key elements of a new and more appropriate definition of American cultural pluralism. After 1945, lay Jewish leaders and Conservative rabbis joined in moving away from racial definitions of Jews to concepts of "peoplehood," "cultural community," "ethnic group," and the like. Hitler's focus on race and his attempt to purify Europe by annihilating the Jews had a major clarifying effect on Jewish self-definition, and a great moral effect on American religious and governmental institutions. As a result, the belief among American Gentiles and American Jews themselves that Jews are a separate race rapidly declined from a majority view before World War II to that of a small minority in subsequent decades.

During the development of the Golden Age for American Jews, the enormous social changes precipitated by the *Brown* decision and the federal Civil Rights Act resulted, in turn, in the political realignment of the American electorate, particularly in the South, which was transformed from a solidly Democratic Party stronghold into an over-whelmingly Republican one.

When President Johnson signed the Civil Rights Act in 1964, he acknowledged that the Democratic Party, long dominated in Congress by Southern influence, would pay a severe price for the Democratic leadership's role in changing the face of racial relationships. The strik-ing turnaround in the alignment of the American electorate with the emerging identification of the Democratic Party with racial change was observed years ago by the scholar Gerald Pomper:

> In 1956, there was no consensus of the parties' stand on the issues of school integration and fair employment. Differences between the parties were less likely to be seen, and Republicans were as likely as Democrats to be perceived as favoring federal actions on civil rights. A startling reversal occurred in 1964; all partisan groups recognized the existence of the difference on this issue, and all were convinced that the Democrats stood more for government programs on behalf of Blacks.[19]

Senator Barry Goldwater, the Republican nominee for president in 1964, widened the polarization between the two parties by voting against the Civil Rights Act, squarely in opposition to federal pres-sures against "states' rights" in racial matters. In the next presidential election in 1968, the Republican nominee, Richard Nixon, adopted the "Southern Strategy" that made the South a Republican stronghold. In his overwhelming reelection victory over Senator George McGov-ern in 1972, Nixon won not only almost the entire South, but most white Democrats—except for American Jews. In fact, from the New Deal onward, American Jews were the only white ethnic group that supported liberal Democratic presidential candidates over Republican conservatives.

In the following chapter, I will go into more detail about Jew-ish political behavior, but suffice it to say for now that the back-lash against changing attitudes toward Blacks, and against the new antidiscrimination laws, did not affect Jewish liberalism and concern for social justice to the degree it did among other groups in the electorate. For the future of Jews in America, the new anti-racist attitudes and broader anti-discriminatory laws of the Civil Rights revolution, while still disruptive in parts of this country, bode well for the continuing decline in anti-Semitism that has typified the Jewish Golden Age. While the clear beneficiaries of anti-discriminatory laws are African Americans, Jews, and other minorities, the coalition of victims of prior discrimination has been joined by women. Their addition moves investment in anti-discrimination from small minorities to an overwhelming majority status for the future.

For American Jews, the Golden Age has meant significantly increased integration into the country's economic and social life, and an opportunity to excel and advance in careers unimagined sixty years ago. In the 1950s, for example, there was only one Jew in the US Senate; as of this writing there are twelve (mostly Democrats, as one might expect). Jews have also held top positions in the presidential administrations of both parties; for example, Henry Kissinger as Secretary of State during the Nixon and Ford administrations, and Robert Rubin and Lawrence Summers as secretaries of the Treasury in the Clinton years. This level of Jewish involvement in American politics has gone well beyond that of the pre-1960s. Not heeding the advice given in the old America, Jews today, including many former victims of discrimination, are politically very assertive, and empowered by Supreme Court rulings and national legislation. The Supreme Court, the presidents, and Congress have all moved from passive acceptance of racism and anti-Semitism to a pro-active government of anti-discriminatory morality guarding the freedom of, and opportunities for, its diverse peoples. The Jewish Golden Age, now very much a part of American life, reflects the increasingly intertwined relationship of Jewish and black Americans, beginning in the 1960s when their leaders joined forces in fighting segregation and racism, and continuing as they have benefited from the victories over prejudice and discrimination. While the election of Barack Obama does not tell us much about how far we have to go, it does tell us much about how far we have come.

With a few exceptions, American Jews have remained a significant force in the struggle for social justice, providing a liberal leadership cadre to benefit themselves and others. The next chapter, one that focuses on the distinctiveness of Jewish attitudes and behavior, points directly to the role of the past in forming these present values, and the important role of connective memory in present-day American Jewish life. The combining of Jewish and American ideas has produced a unique synthesis of thought and, as a result, a distinctively "Americanized" Jew who demands social justice and tolerance.

Prologue to Chapter Five

When I was in high school, sports seemed to be as American as apple pie. While I didn't actually like apple pie, I loved sports, and played football, basketball, and baseball. But though I was the starting pitcher as a high school sophomore, my father and mother never came to a game. My father worked six days a week and couldn't attend; my mother considered the games as "play," nothing more; and neither of my parents played any sport themselves. The role of sports in America had simply passed them by. For me, playing or watching sports was central to being American.

As I remember, the first game I pitched in high school was on a sunny day in the spring of 1944, and the first batter I faced was from the local Catholic parochial school, Manhattan Prep. As he stepped into the batter's box, he dutifully crossed himself—I assumed for heavenly aid—and I thought to myself, "It won't help. It won't help." I was also struck that day by how much my opponent and I were alike. We both loved baseball, and yet I remembered that it was his schoolmates who had, in earlier years, chased us as little boys with the cry of differentness, "There they are, get the Jews!"

I became aware that I was, indeed, different as a Jew—mainly, back then, because the vast non-Jewish world told me so, though I didn't understand why. The rest of my life as an adult, however, saw a growing awareness of how Jewish culture had quietly shaped my thoughts and actions. The following chapter demonstrates just how large are the differences are between Jews and non-Jews in the values and opinions they hold, even after four generations of substantial assimilation. The combination of Jewish values and ideas with American Protestant ones has profoundly influenced the thinking of the large majority of American Jews. It has made them distinct not only from Gentile Americans but also from Jews elsewhere in the world.

Chapter Five

Jewish Distinctiveness and American Pluralism

A merican Jews overall, as I've noted, are the most liberal group politically, the most progressive group socially, and the most secular
group religiously in America. But they have been generally reluctant
to make such attitudes clear. Assimilative American Jews, like similar
Jews in Europe, have often downplayed their group differences with
non-Jews, fearing that pointing out different attitudes or levels of accomplishment would open them to critical and prejudicial response.
Wanting the individual benefits that full participation would allow,
most Jews preferred historically to stay inconspicuous. Jewish accomplishments in science, law, medicine, and literature have been noted
on occasion, but the extent of differences in social and political attitudes, as well as in religious beliefs, are rarely discussed publicly.

American Jews give strong support for the constitutional and pluralistic values of the past, and they are, as I will show, also the most
vigorous proponents of liberal or progressive social change, particularly through federal government action. Research shows that, in
comparison with similarly affluent and educated Gentiles, Jews stand
more strongly for expanding the federal social-welfare safety net for
all people, and are disproportionately supportive of federal political

initiatives specifically to benefit black Americans. While there are
Gentiles who share these attitudes, Jews *as a group* believe in and support a number of positions that are far different from those of other
Americans. Showing just how different Jewish perspectives are can
be done with statistics. Explaining *why* such differences exist is more
speculative.

When it comes to evaluating different social, political, and religious beliefs, most national surveys of Americans as a whole tell us
little about small groups within the whole. Fortunately the National
Opinion Research Center at the University of Chicago, in its examination of differences of outlook among such American ethnic groups as
Italians, Poles, Scots, and Jews over thirty years, has combined a large
number of individual national surveys to produce sufficient samples
of each sub-group to yield some important conclusions.

For example, Nathan Glazer, in an article utilizing data from the
NORC database, sought to determine what had happened to the vote
of normally Democratic white ethnic groups during a conservative
Republican landslide led by President Ronald Reagan in 1984.[1] In prior
presidential elections, Catholic support of the New Deal coalition had
weakened, while still favoring the Democratic candidate overall. But
in 1984, over 60 percent of these voters supported Reagan. Among
Jewish voters, on the other hand, 68 percent voted for the liberal candidate, Walter Mondale, despite his promise that he would raise taxes
in order to preserve the social safety net.

This tendency toward liberalness is borne out by other research,
which consistently shows that American Jews are more progressive
on a wide range of sociopolitical issues than other groups of Americans. While there are, of course, individual Jews who are conservative, and individual Gentiles similar in their values to most Jews, the
percentage of Jews who are progressive in their political views and
behavior far exceeds that of other groups. The link between generally reformist Jews and the Democratic presidential vote has remained
strong, reaching 70–80 percent in the elections of 2000, 2004, 2008,
and 2012.[2] Even Republican Jews, who tend to be conservative on
economic issues, are less so on social-welfare issues.

The results of the 2012 election show the same continuing pattern, as Jewish voters went overwhelmingly for Barack Obama, although at a slightly lower percentage than they did for the Democrat in the three previous presidential elections. That Jewish Democratic majority of 2012 was accomplished despite the unprecedented interventions of Israeli Prime Minister Benjamin Netanyahu in favor of the Republican candidate. In addition, there were many multimillion-dollar expenditures directed against President Obama by billionaire Jewish conservative Sheldon Adelson, who claimed the President was anti-Israel. Despite such attempts to suppress Jewish Democratic voting, seven in ten Jews voted for Obama, while less than three in ten white Protestants and only four in ten white Catholics voted for him—a voting gap of roughly 40 percent and 30 percent, respectively.[3]

In congressional elections, American Jews give a far higher percentage overall to Democratic candidates than non-Jews, who are almost evenly split between the parties. In the critical 2006 congressional vote, for instance, in which committee control of Congress was at stake, the proportion of Jews voting for Democrats exceeded 83 percent, compared to only 53 percent of non-Jews.[4] But although Jewish voters are clearly more liberal than non-Jewish ones, to conclude that Jews vote under some form of direction would be wrong. Jews pride themselves on being informed, able to come to their own conclusions, argumentative, and even fractious. An old joke claims, "If you have five Irishmen you have two political parties; five Frenchmen, you have five parties; and five Jews, you have six parties!"

How is it that such highly educated and stubbornly individual people as American Jews just happen to vote similarly? Most reliable arguments for Jewish political behavior lie not in some knee-jerk loyalty Jews have to the Democratic Party, but in the fact that Jewish cultural beliefs and attitudes about important social and political questions are simply more in tune with Democratic policy positions. Examining Jewish opinion along many lines of division makes it clear that Jewish support for Democrats reflects the much more liberal and progressive beliefs and values of American Jews as compared to the beliefs and values of most other Americans.

In the 1950s, research done by the sociologist Gerhard Lenski on local politics found that on different measures of liberalism—regarding civil liberties, government activism for a social and economic safety net, and positive racial change—American Jews were the only group that consistently supported the liberal position.[5] In subsequent years, NORC has documented Jewish liberalism on many such social and political issues. More recently, a national study of American Jews found significantly more support for government-assisted healthcare among Jews than among non-Jewish Whites (only Blacks, the least medically-insured group in America, exceeded Jews in their support).[6] Along the old New Deal divide over whether an active federal government should intercede to help the less fortunate, Jews remain, despite their being disproportionately affluent, more likely to see the government as an important means of strengthening the social safety net. Although Jews and non-Jews share opinions on crime, capital punishment, enjoyment of life, and other matters, on most divisive social and economic issues—such as abortion rights, the science of natural selection vs. Intelligent Design, prayer in schools, sexual morality, and race—Jews regularly land on the liberal side. For example, the right of a woman to have an abortion in the first trimester of pregnancy is supported by approximately 80 percent of Jews; that figure rises to the mid-90s in cases involving birth defects or rape. Favorable support among various non-Jewish groups for *Roe vs. Wade* ranges from 35 percent among Hispanic-Americans to an average of 43 percent among all non-Jewish Americans. Whatever the way the questions on abortion are asked, American Jews are between 35 percent and 40 percent more pro-choice.[7]

In past surveys, when civil liberties issues are in question—such as the right of colleges to host speakers of communist, militarist, or homosexual background—Jewish support is notably higher. When civil-liberties issues involve Black-White relationships, the pattern of greater liberalness remains constant. In his recent study, "Jewish Distinctiveness in America," Tom W. Smith of NORC found evidence confirming that of other scholars that, by almost every measure, Jews look more favorably than non-Jews on racial equality, integration, and

inter-group tolerance.[8] Smith also found that 78 percent of Jews believe Blacks should push further for their rights, compared to only 56
percent of non-Jews—further evidence of greater Jewish support for
specifically Black rights, accounting in part for Jews' disproportionate activism for Black causes. Whether it comes to supporting more
government spending to improve the conditions of Blacks, voting for
a black president, or favoring open-housing laws, Smith found Jews
were consistently more favorable to Black interests than the public in
general. Such politically distinctive attitudes were translated directly
into the 2008 presidential election, when roughly 80 percent of American Jews voted for Barack Obama, compared to 47 percent of white
Catholics and only 34 percent of white Protestants.[9] This was despite
claims that Obama was a Muslim and that his election would mean
"the death of Israel." Indeed, the Jewish vote for Obama was three to
four percent higher than it was for John Kerry in 2004.

American Jews agree with libertarians on many questions of individual liberty, but disagree sharply with them on the proper role
of the government. Libertarians, with deep roots in the American
Protestant ethos of self-sufficiency, stand in sharp contrast to a Jewish
communalism that has not only sought to develop Jewish protective
organizations, but also looked to the national government to protect
themselves and less fortunate non-Jews as well. Americans know that
a disproportionate share of the expenditures on the socioeconomic
safety net will go to others, an idea acceptable to Jews but not to most
libertarians.[10]

Another major study, the 2004 National Survey of Religion and
Politics, which focused on religious sectarianism rather than ethnic
differences, gauged substantial differences between Jews and non-
Jews. Its findings support the NORC analyses of Jewish liberalism,
identifying a number of social and political issues where Jews and secular non-Jews hold different positions—principally on foreign policy,
support for minorities, and alleviating poverty. The National Survey
of 2004 found that on all questions of governmental support for minorities and the poor, even where tax increases would be required,
American Jews were significantly more approving than all Christian

denominations *and non-Jewish secularists.*[11]

Both these large-scale surveys, and another by Pew to be discussed below, identify a substantial difference of opinion between American Jews and Christians on the issues of prayer in schools, embryonic stem cell research, and equal rights for homosexuals. The evidence of differentness leads to the question of whether certain religio-cultural values and beliefs of American Jews, predominately secular and skeptical, have led them into distinctive positions in American life. Clearly, while assimilative Jews have acculturated in many ways, they have not, as the Orthodox have feared, lost a distinctive Jewish way of thinking. It may not be the Orthodox Jewish way of thinking, but it is the way most Jews regard important issues.[12]

Many American Jews have, particularly from their own long history, recognized the benefits of social equality and economic stability as societal ideals. The desire for social stability, enhanced by a strong welfare safety net for the less fortunate, and the protection of middle-class benefits of health and social security, offers at least a partial explanation of continued political liberality whereby Jews, as noted earlier, consistently support programs that appear to be against their own short-run interests. Perhaps the connection to the instability of their European past remains in a collective memory that makes present-day American Jews wary of the disruptiveness of excessive inequality, either economically or socially, especially because they are an easy target for retaliation.

About the time the neoconservative Jewish scholar and activist Irving Kristol lamented how "out of date" Jewish political concerns for social equality seemed to be, a *Los Angeles Times* survey of California Jews revealed its overriding importance among their political values. When asked about the relative value to their Jewish identity of (1) religious observance, (2) support for Israel, or (3) a commitment to social equality, social equality was, at 50 percent, by far the most important.[13] The impact of the past on present-day Jewish values remains clear in their sympathetic approach to the question of what should be done with illegal Hispanic immigrants. American Jews balk at immediate deportation and show a significantly greater willingness to allow a pathway to eventual citizenship.[14] Memories of their own past of unwelcomeness seem to be ingrained in the American Jewish psyche. Memory and history are a critical part of the present.

Jewish study and education, while initially focused on religious moral issues, long ago shifted that focus, under the influence of Greek and Muslim culture, to science, mathematics, and other secular subjects. Jewish intellectual life, not circumscribed by physical and material discrimination as it was in Christian Europe, and to a lesser extent in the Muslim world, became a sustaining and disproportionate part of Jewish life that bloomed with the freedom of the Enlightenment in Western Europe and still further with new freedoms in America. The study of medicine serves as a prime example of how the Jewish religious past reflects itself in the American present; how the Jewish religion and the historically "this-worldly" intellectual focus of Jews have contributed to their large presence in certain occupations today. Not only are Jews approximately eight times overrepresented in the number of physicians in America, but they have become approximately 20 percent of all teachers in medical schools.[15] The old bragging phrase, "My son, the doctor" (which now has the variant, "My daughter, the doctor"), has a long history in the focus of Jewish *religious* life. Dr. Sherwin Nuland, a physician and scholar of medicine, has pointed out in his study of the great rabbinical sage Maimonides just how deeply rooted the study of medicine was in Jewish rabbinical life as far back as the twelfth and thirteenth centuries CE, long before the Enlightenment. Approximately half the Jewish doctors then were also rabbis, Nuland noted, illustrating the Jewish connection of affirming, learning, study, and medicine.[16]

Jewish religious concern with health goes back to Leviticus in the Torah and to the Talmud, yet specific advances in medicine among Jews were dependent on rabbinical contact with Greek physicians. The importance of other cultures' influences on Jewish life, spoken of by Cynthia Ozick, is evident in Maimonides' acknowledged debt to Galen of Pergamon and other Greek medical scientists, and to Muslim physicians as well. As Maimonides stated, "Our Torah agrees with Greek philosophy which substantiates, with convincing proof, that a man's actions are in his own hands; no compulsion is exerted and he is constrained by nothing external to himself."[17] Nuland went further, noting that Christians at that time saw their lives as preparation for the next world, and regarded the body as merely a container for the soul, whereas "Jews lived for the time on earth, preserving health as the way to understand God."

Before the Renaissance, Christians had a long history of asceticism, of abnegation of concerns for the body. The Church held that disease is, in Nuland's words, "the work of the devil or a judgment from God, to be treated, if at all, by confession and prayer." At the Council of Rheims in 1135, for example, the Church forbade monks and clergy from practicing medicine because it was contrary to theological principles that it is Jesus who saves lives.[18] The Jews, believing in the idea of the "oneness" of body and soul, emphasized living for the time on earth (while waiting for the Messiah to finally reform it), and remained focused on health and staving off death, rather than the benefits of the next world, an emphasis that is still in place today. As Nuland noted, Maimonides himself said that the ascetic life weakens the body, which must remain healthy if the "highest purpose of the soul—to acquire wisdom and the knowledge of God—is to be realized."[19]

While Jews were not immune to the mysticism and superstitions of the Middle Ages, there has long existed in Jewish life, after its fusion with Greek and Arab culture, a strong scientific and analytic focus. The Enlightenment in Europe (the *Haskalah* to ghettoized Jews), and the Reformation and Enlightenment influences present in the founding of America, have all allowed for the surge of Jewish prominence in medicine. An intellectual intensity and a growing openness in the United States, over the last sixty years, to Jewish educational advancement in American universities has allowed Jews to become prominent in occupations, such as medicine, where intellectual analysis, "distinction making," and caring are goals.

Many Jews who have lost belief in God, and who think of themselves as "cultural" rather than "religious" Jews, are unaware of just how much of their "culture" has religious sources. Stemming in part from Jewish religious beliefs about life and death, in part from the negative experience of Jews in the European Diaspora, and in part from the influence of American life, the distinctive development of Jews in this country has special roots both in their religious-cultural past and in their secular American present.

The large majority of present-day American Jews are secular humanists, two words that are often hissed angrily by the Christian Right. Secular, a word initially meaning *worldly*, "of this world," as against the "next world" after death, has long been emphasized in the Jewish religion itself. The focus on life, how to live it properly, affirm it, and enjoy it was God's charge to the early Jews. "See, I have set before thee this day, life and the good, death and evil. . . . therefore choose life (Deuteronomy 30:15, 19). For early Christians the miserable conditions at the time of Jesus were to be accepted, and their Gospels focused on an individual's eternal salvation. For most Jews, the question of an afterlife—a subject of vehement disagreement among rabbis—was not of primary importance: the work of the world was theirs. Acceptance of misery in this world was subordinate to the duty to make the world better here and now, and lead a good life. As Rabbi Hillel commanded, "If I am not for myself, who shall be for me? If I am only for myself, what am I? And if not now, when?" His advice for mixing "good pride" and responsibility is still the basis for a Jewish life well spent.

Non-Orthodox Jews, deeply involved in modernity, have long been attracted to the secular connection. As Irving Kristol put it, "They find in the 'secular humanism' of this ideology an adequate approximation to the ideals of the 'prophetic Judaism,' which emerged in the nineteenth century and has infused itself into all non-Orthodox versions of contemporary Judaism." Kristol points out that secular humanism— impacted by the Renaissance and prophetic Judaism's moral thrust— has deep roots in Jewish values. It affirms "the possibility of humanity's realizing its full human potential through the energetic application of moral intelligence . . . and in the case of secular Jews, Prophetic Judaism merges into secular humanism to create what can fairly be described as a peculiarly intense, Jewish, secular humanism."[20] Jewish secular humanism, shaped by the Jewish past, is also distinguishable from non-Jewish secularism, as evidenced by the greater Jewish support for federal government programs that tax the wealthy to alleviate poverty, help the disadvantaged, and aid minorities. According to the *Fourth National Survey of Religion and Politics*, non-Jewish secularists support social-welfare programs far less than Jews, and at approximately the same level as most Christians.[21]

Although Kristol finds in liberal secular humanism a rational basis for Jewish political positions, his fellow neoconservative, Norman Podhoretz, sees it differently. Jewish liberalism, Podhoretz claims, is irrational, "a religion in its own right, complete with its own catechism and its own dogma . . . and obdurately resistant to facts that undermine its claims and promises."[22]

A humanistic focus on the self-development of the individual mind and a critical spirit has deep roots in Jewish tradition, particularly from the experience of Jewish life, long before the European Enlightenment that opened further secular life for both Christians and Jews. These religious sources of secular and humanistic values, plus the skepticism enhanced by Jewish history and by the intellectual and scientific focus of Jewish learning, has produced American Jews who, as a group, are relatively less religious, less God-centered, and more reformist of the life we lead. The emphasis on a skeptical, questioning culture—believing that study and knowledge will light the way of life—is a cornerstone of the non-fatalistic belief underpinning Jewish intellectual accomplishment.

Overall, American Jews are the least traditional believers in the biblical God of Abraham. An all-powerful, all-knowing, and all-merciful personal God is believed in by most Christians in America, but not by most American Jews. Jews remain more skeptical of the existence of a biblical deity, being one-fifth as likely to believe in one as mainline Protestants and one-eighth as likely as evangelical Protestants, with Catholics in between.[23] I will deal more extensively with the differences between Jewish and Christian beliefs about the nature and concept of God, the existence of heaven and hell, and the worldly activities of angels and demons in a later chapter.

Thus, American Jews, at least the great majority, are on the "enemies list" of the anti–secular humanist Christian Right. Not dominated by faith in God as much as by the experience of their history, their intellectual emphasis, and their skepticism, American Jews and others of similar value systems have been in the forefront of the modernizing, secularizing changes in America, challenging the moderate Protestant establishment whose dominance has only been challenged in the last sixty years or so. One does not have to accept all of the scholar Yuri Slezkine's provocative claims about Jews and the advance of modernism worldwide to see Jews as important factors, particularly in the later stages of modern secular movements.[24]

Jewish focus on knowledge, intellect, and distinction-making analysis, while clearly of religious and cultural origins, has fascinated researchers concerned with the innateness of intelligence. Jews, whatever they may think privately, are historically averse to claiming a genetic basis for superior intelligence as a group. Charles Murray, for example, claims that genetic inheritance accounts in significant part for the lower IQ scores of African Americans, and, conversely, for the above-average scores of American Jews and Asian Americans.[25] A large body of criticism, from conservatives as well as liberals (including many Jews), has countered Murray's methods, findings, and conclusions. But my interest in the issue of nature vs. nurture, heredity or culture, is that, for most of American history, different ethnic groups have been fairly easily absorbed into American society, while different races have not.

Jews have long tended to convert a physical or political liability into a psychological asset. Owing both to the studiousness of rabbinical Judaism and to the restrictive physical and material pressures of Gentile environments, Jews made the mind, the head, one's intelligence, a psychological province of their own. A *yiddisher Kopf*, a Jewish head, was a self-admiring attribute, a backbone of ego support among Jews in trying times, as opposed to a *goyish Kopf*, an uninformed Gentile head. Smart Gentiles were said to have a *yiddisher Kopf*, flattering the Gentile and the Jews at the same time.

While some Jews may think of their intelligence as inborn, most see the ability to think and focus as an outcome of their religious culture, their historic experience, and their families' nurturing of intellectual development. The greater emphasis Jews put on cultural as opposed to genetic inheritance is evidenced by the relative values they place on nurture vs. nature for *other* racial groups. For example, in the NORC study of the values or beliefs held by different American groups, only 7 percent of Jews agreed that lower results by Blacks vs. Whites is due to racial inheritance rather than cultural influences—far less than any other ethnic group, including Blacks themselves. On the question of whether or not Black-White IQ differences result from Black lack of education, almost two thirds of Jews say they do, a far higher percentage than any other group.[26]

What is present in American Jewish culture that predisposes certain kinds of thinking and action is, of course, complex and to some extent speculative. But certain elements deserve identification. Clearly the Jewish emphasis on the intellectual life has its roots in both religion and culture. But it is further cultivated by the texture of family upbringing, the emotional relationship within families, and expectations of one's children's future. While such culture-carrying factors don't lend themselves readily to statistical study, they nevertheless deserve an attempt to measure their impact. Clearly, how a child develops depends to a large extent on his or her family relationships.

Sociologists and psychologists have long known how much child-rearing patterns can vary, and how much they are affected by families and by the nature of emotional responses of parents to their children. While there is some evidence that the gap between Jewish and non-Jewish family patterns is closing, there remain significant differences, even as individual non-Jews have moved closer to traditional Jewish patterns. One clear aspect of Jewish child-rearing was identified in 1949 by the non-Jewish anthropologist Ruth Benedict, who, examining early childhood patterns of swaddling babies, found Jewish mothers were far more permissive of movement, wrapping their babies much more loosely than non-Jewish mothers.[27] The subsequent indulgence of parents in pleasing the desires of their children seems to result in the children having a sense of their own importance, on the border (or over the border) of being "spoiled." Such indulgence, however, seems to result in a tendency of Jewish children to be out-spoken rather than reserved, believing rightly or wrongly that their opinion has value.

The large number of Jewish respondents in the NORC study allows for some quantitative assessment of these perceptions about child-rearing. Asking parent-respondents from each religious and ethnic group what attribute they most wanted their children to acquire—obedience, thinking for oneself, working hard, or being popular—the survey found that 71 percent of Jews named "thinking for oneself" as their first choice, compared to an average among other groups of 50.3 percent (Asian Americans were at the bottom with 24.3 percent). Only 5.8 percent of American Jews rated obedience as most impor-tant, while most non-Jewish white groups were three to four times as likely to rate it first, and Asian Americans even more so.[28] The old saying that "children should be seen and not heard" does not seem to have found favor among American Jews.

It is important to understand what a child "thinking for his- or her-self" means. The skepticism and questioning in Jewish culture tends to lead to intellectual investigation, and intellectual investigation tends to promote multiple sources of knowledge. The religious and cultur-al emphasis on questioning can often bring about an unintentional weakening of Orthodoxy. Thinking means evaluating, using impor-tant existing knowledge from both religious and secular fields. Much of the "culture war" in American politics today depends on whether people rely on biblical or secular knowledge for their decision-making.

Although limited, the evidence lends credence to real differences in child-nurturing patterns, pointing to both the greater indulgence of Jewish children's behavior, and the higher expectations of "indepen-dent thinking." While a few Jews may agree with the Gentile scholar Charles Murray that intelligence-based accomplishment is due to genes, most Jews attribute it to culture and nurture. Genetic science shows that a great deal of non-Jewish DNA can be found in today's Jews—probably from conversions, conquest, intermarriage, or rape—suggesting that genetic inheritance is at best of marginal importance in accounting for Jewish intellectual differentness.[29]

Orthodox and traditionalist rabbis fear that the absorption by most Jews of American culture will dilute not only Jewish customs, rituals, and observances, but also a uniquely Jewish way of thinking. But far from being "melted" into the pot of American life—as Rabbi Abraham Joshua Heschel warned against decades ago—the evidence is overwhelming that a distinctive Jewish voice can still be heard. It is not the voice of Orthodoxy, but it is still a Jewish one, although perhaps more broadly inclusive and less reverent and God-infused. To most American Jews the connection to a "people," an ethnic and cultural linkage, is compelling. In the 2001 American Jewish Identity Survey, most Jews reported being of "no religion," but still defined themselves as Jewish. It points again to the ethno-cultural aspect of peoplehood, heritage, common destiny, and community of thought that encapsulates the way most American Jews think of themselves.[30]

The question of how to transmit such secular Jewish values to children and grandchildren in nonreligious families is a vexing one, and the "Americanization" of most secular American Jews is in many ways a serious threat to Jewish continuity. If the issue of continuity—exacerbated by both secularity and intermarriage—is to be resolved, it will probably not be by way of a return to Orthodoxy, but to other new religious institutions, or the mutation of old educational forms. The pluralism and individualism of America have a strong attraction for modern Jews, and while Orthodoxy and traditionalism can thrive and modestly expand its numbers, it is the future of the much larger body of assimilative Jews, some four to five million of them, that is the greater concern for maintaining the intensity and scale of Jewish involvement in contemporary American life.

One shouldn't forget that most Jewish families in America today originally came from Orthodox families. The Eastern European Jews who came to America in the decades just before and after 1900 were almost all from Orthodox families, and culturally and religiously quite different from the (mostly German) Reform Jews already in America.[31] Considering that the Jewish population of America was only about 250,000 before some 2.5 million East Europeans came here between 1884 and 1924, the inability of Orthodoxy to hold on to children from traditional Jewish homes says much about the seductiveness of a modern and relatively open country. Today's American Jews retain their distinctiveness, but will tomorrow's? Efforts to prevent the shrinkage of the American Jewish population must also focus on the 80 percent who are not traditional or Orthodox, but are more liberal, universalist, and secular. But will they and future generations be able to sustain a sense of connection to the Jewish people and the Jewish past without the discrimination that is now significantly diminished in America?

Orthodoxy, energetic and galvanized in recent decades, will survive and continue. To those religious Jews, Jewish law—*halachah*—is a matter of divine revelation, and its observance is not to be compromised. Will the 80 to 90 percent of other Jews continue to thrive as Jews without the unifying stimulus of anti-Semitism? Will increasing intermarriage and secularity among today's Jews result in later generations not thinking of themselves as Jewish? Will they continue to think and act as Jews with only cultural and intellectual connections to hold them? Will American Jews strive, as did many of the non-Orthodox and highly assimilative Jews of Germany and France in the mid-nineteenth and early twentieth centuries, to fully assimilate themselves even by converting to (nominal or sincere) Christianity and denying their heritage? Or does American pluralism offer a different social and political environment for an assimilative cultural Jew where he or she can be both alike and different, finding new ways of preserving an integrated, but still distinctive, American Jewish life? In the remaining chapters, I will try to answer those questions.

Prologue to Chapter Six

When we lived in Riverdale from 1939 to 1943, my brothers and I were chased regularly by a group of older boys from Manhattan Prep because we were Jewish. The leader of the group had the last name of Shapiro. At the ages of twelve and ten, respectively, my brother Bill and I did not know that the name Shapiro was a Jewish name; but to my mother, who did know, the presumably Catholic Shapiro was a mystery that was only solved when I was nineteen and in college. It was an experience that demonstrated some of the important problems of intermarriage and shaped my and Len's efforts to blunt its effects on our own family.

I knocked on the door of Rena G.'s apartment to attend a party celebrating her engagement to my brother Bill, and to my surprise Bill greeted me immediately. "Please. Please, don't start anything. Shapiro is here!" "Why?" I asked incredulously. "What is that Jew-hating bully doing here?" "He's related to Rena's family. Promise me you won't start anything with him!" I assured Bill I wouldn't make a "scene," but feelings of eager anticipation filled me. I could not wait to see what the Jew-hater of my early years looked like, and I relished the discomfort he must be feeling surrounded by all these Jews.

Bill pointed him out, sitting by himself in the library. I casually walked over to him and introduced myself as the brother of Rena's fiancée; in turn, he told me he was related to the family on Rena's side. The monster of the past was a frail young man with thick glasses, about 5'8" and 130 pounds, more than four inches shorter and forty pounds lighter than I was. I believe he already knew who we were, but to make sure I had the right person, I took him through a few questions. "Where did you go to high school?" "Manhattan Prep in Riverdale." "That's funny; we lived right across the street from Manhattan

Prep." "Really?" "Yes, and my brothers and I were regularly chased by students there because we were Jewish." "Oh."

After a few minutes of his squirming, I walked away to find out more about him. It turned out to be a pathetic story of an intermarriage gone wrong: a Catholic woman marrying a Jewish man who, before their child was two, was killed in an automobile accident. The child was then brought up as a Catholic by his mother, and spent his school years in the Catholic parochial school system before World War II. Unlike present-day Catholic schools, which make a point of ecumenism, the pre–Vatican II Catholic schools of our day imbued their students with hostility toward Jews, undoubtedly causing confusion for young Catholic Shapiro. To fit in with his schoolmates, he tried to be even more anti-Semitic than they were.

Learning more about Shapiro from Rena's family diminished my feelings of anger, adding an element of compassion for his confused, angry younger self. It also gave me a model of a life to *avoid* for my children, one that was resentful of Jewish roots, and filled with feelings of apartness, aloneness, and self-hatred. Len and I resolved early in our relationship that we would not live, when married, in an area where Jews were few and unwelcome.

As I've said before, I am not a religious person, having grown up in a nonreligious home of parents leading a secular life among largely Jewish friends. From my very early years, I had difficulty believing in miracles, or in the personal God of the Bible who was all-powerful, all-knowing, all-loving, and very angry at bad behavior. The Holocaust intensified my religious skepticism. I simply couldn't understand how such a God could allow six million of his "chosen people" to perish in the death camps. I am not proud of my lack of belief, nor ashamed of it—it's just a fact. And I am deeply respectful of religious people who do not harm others. For the Orthodox or traditional Jews, with whom I may disagree, I am nevertheless thankful to them for their strength of belief that has kept Judaism and the Jewish people alive for thousands of difficult and painful years.

Len has given me a happy life and has helped keep me a strong believer in Jewish culture, Jewish values, and the Jewish people. We have five children, four of whom have followed our Jewish cultural pathway, several of whom are somewhat more traditionally religious than we are. One of our children, however, became a devout Catholic, demanding sure answers about life that his parents could not give him. He has rejected our pathway of life and has very conservative political and social views, opposed to those of the rest of the family.

My own durable and happy marriage to a born Gentile, one who claims her Jewishness by cultural osmosis, does not blind me to the potential problems that might arise in an intermarriage, particularly when children are involved. That is because many loving couples are unaware of the depth of their own religious or cultural feelings until their children's future pathways become an issue. It is all too easy during courtship to push questions of religious identity into the future, which Len and I did not. Intermarriage brings both rewards and problems, but in today's America, the softening of religious attitudes makes intermarriage less "scandalous" than in the past.

Although the personal problems that come with intermarriage are lessened when both spouses have a secular rather than religious outlook, that fact does little to address concerns about the children and grandchildren of intermarriage. Worries about what their identity will be in the future—concerns of the Jewish community—are justified. That identity will depend on how they are educated at home and in religious schools—whether as cultural Jews or religious Jews, or both. For traditional Jews there are no problems; for secular or assimilative Jews—the great majority of American Jews—assimilation does pose problems. Not having religious or biblical anchors means that Jewish culture, peoplehood, and history must be taught, so as to differentiate Jewish meaning and its pathway to life. Learning and teaching through books have stood the Jewish people in good stead. New approaches to learning about their own history and culture will be crucial.

The concerns of Orthodox and traditional Jewry about the continuity of identification of grandchildren and great grandchildren are certainly understandable. But what is more difficult to comprehend is just what it is that keeps the larger numbers of less religious Jews, those without a traditional belief in the personal God of Judaism, to continue to identify themselves as Jewish. What are the reasons for cultural Jews, those who don't accept the teachings of the Bible, to remain Jewish?

Focusing on intermarriage rather than secularity as a cause for group losses moves the needle of analysis to what's wrong with Jewish life rather than to what's right. Why do Jews of little or no religious belief, even avowed atheists and agnostics, nevertheless continue to feel part of an ancient and contemporary "people"?

For centuries, those Jews who believed themselves to be "chosen" by God held fiercely to their faith in God's justice and mercy despite oppression and torture, such as they suffered from the Inquisition. But in an America uniquely pluralistic and democratic from its beginnings, what are the positive forces—the personal, communal, and cultural elements—that have kept nonreligious Jews part of a distinct people?

I believe that the need to feel a connection to a family, to a history, to one's forebears, to a community, to a culture, is a powerful one. Linked to that need is the willingness of Jews to accept difference, for themselves and for others, an affirmation of *choice* that shows itself in the Jewish past as a stubbornness in maintaining their religious beliefs, and, in the Jewish present, as holding tenaciously on to uniquely Jewish values and beliefs, maintaining a community of like-mindedness.

There is a marked difference between secularist Jews and secularists who come from a majority Christian culture, because the experience of the Jewish past has taught them a more defined and positive meaning of tolerance. Still, many of the less religious Jews are more comfortable with the worldly, life-affirming, less miraculous beliefs of their own culture than that of Gentiles with whom they have lived. Life, history, and religious principles have made a strong impression on Jewish culture, and many secular Jews are unwilling to give up the history, memories, and values that have been absorbed.

At the deepest level of transmitted continuity is the "family" and its extension back to grandparents and beyond, to the community of the present and past, to the history and the psychological identity of belonging. Called a "common mental construction" by Sigmund Freud and an "intense Jewish secular humanism" by Irving Kristol, what are those specific forces that bind? In the face of anti-Semitism's pressure, it is not hard to see why some nonbelievers leave the fold of Jewish identity. What is harder to understand is what the elements are that provide substantial *continuity* of Jewishness among the many self-identifying but nonreligious Jews. Rather than dwell on fears of Jewish decline, we must do more to understand the reasons for the *persistence* of Jewish life—and then teach those reasons and values to young and old alike.

Chapter Six

Threats from Within:
Intermarriage and Secularity

Changing attitudes in America tending toward greater tolerance of Jews and other minorities have been caused, by and large, by the interplay of laws protecting against discrimination as well as by the growing acceptance of "difference" by young Gentiles. These changes are apparent in the election of Barack Obama as president—an extraordinary event, considering that less than fifty years ago issues of racial segregation still dominated the American political agenda. America's Jews have clearly gained added protection by the increased numbers of other groups sensitized to discrimination who have also organized against prejudice. The addition of women to the ranks of anti-discrimination activists, as noted earlier, has vastly expanded the numbers of anti-discrimination warriors. Changes in American society in the last fifty years have worked to the benefit and protection of Jews, and external threats to the group's continuity seem to be reasonably contained. But an important question remains: will the continuity of a diverse, distinctive and influential Jewish community be undermined from *within*—weakened or "killed with kindness" by a more welcoming and tolerant non-Jewish population? Will Gentiles, more accepting of and even more willing to marry Jews, lead to complete Jewish assimilation into American life? The question that traditionalist Jews ask—whether the children and grandchildren of an intermarriage will still be Jewish—while not a priority concern of young people in love, is still troubling for those concerned with the continuity of Jewish values, religion, and culture.

The Orthodox, as well as other more traditional Jews, worry that, as the blurring of lines of religious definition continues, it will also accentuate differences of religious authenticity between Jews. Questions as basic as who is a Jew divide the Jewish community, and threaten group continuity. With the rate of intermarriage rising from approximately 6 percent sixty years ago to approximately 50 percent today, a serious challenge to the continuity of American Jewry may arise.[1] While Orthodox Jews are relatively immune to intermarriage, Jews who are Reform, Conservative, Reconstructionist, or unaffiliated lead assimilative lives of varying degrees of Jewish religious beliefs, customs, and observances. A large majority of them hold that patrilineal descent, whether or not a non-Jewish mother converts to Judaism, also provides validation of the children of intermarriage as Jews—but traditionalist Jewry does not, a deep source of division over the critical issue of just who is or is not a Jew.

The founding period of Jews in America has been viewed by scholars such as Jonathan Sarna as relatively benign, lasting until the last quarter of the 1800s. But the dislocations and tensions of massive industrial growth, the enormous immigrations to America by different groups, and the strangeness of the recently arrived Jews, set into motion a new "apartness" that culminated in the vicious anti-Semitism that lasted into the late 1940s. Jewish-Gentile relationships hit an all-time low by 1950. It was also the low tide of intermarriage, with most non-Jewish families strongly opposed to having their children marry Jews, and most Jews opposing marriage to non-Jews. I was one of the Jews who chose to cross the social and family barriers then that served to enforce social separateness and mutual distrust. My loving relationship with "the other" developed a full generation before intermarriage became common, and a decade before the substantial drop in anti-Semitism. Len had to learn to weather the social rigidities and anti-Jewish prejudices of the Gentile world, and, at the same time, the wariness and anger of Jews toward Gentiles.

For Len and me, religious differences were not a problem, but the environment of separateness and mistrust clearly was. Neither of us was traditionally religious, and Len had agreed enthusiastically that our children were to be brought up as Jewish. She had, early on, confided in me that her stepfather had run a cold and dysfunctional family, and that on the train coming to freshman week at Brown, she had resolved not to return home after college, but only to visit. Her intelligence and studiousness had created the opportunity for her to go to college, and a small educational trust from her biological father paid the way. Hers was an unhappy family, and she believed that she and I would make a much better family life together. My family, as the biblical Ruth said, would become her family.

Len's mother, her French grandmother who lived isolated upstairs, and her sister Frankie were all welcoming and supportive of our marriage. Her stepfather, whose vocabulary for describing minorities included "wops," "spics," and "coons," said little to my face, but did try to provoke me. "Hitler did a lot of good things," he told me. His best friend Karl, upon meeting me for the first time, remarked, "A Jew with green eyes?" I got the message. On her biological father's side, Grandmother Rice was appalled at the possible intermarriage and said to Len's mother, "Henriette, what are you going to do about it?" Her retort: "Absolutely nothing."

The Rice side was a wealthy, socially prominent Philadelphia family whose ancestors came over on the Mayflower. Grandmother Rice tried and failed to interest Len in both her long pre-Mayflower English lineage and in the Daughters of the American Revolution, in which she was an active official. Len's memories of dinners with her grandfather and family were of an aloof family, cold and impersonal. Her real father, Willard Rice IV, was to Len's distress only minimally involved in her life.

As for me, I was stunned by my mother's initial objection. There was no history to explain it. Her brother had married a Protestant woman from the Midwest whom she liked, and they stayed at our home when they came east. She also interceded ecumenically when a child of a close friend insisted on marrying a non-Jewish woman. Although our family was culturally Jewish and belonged to a Reform temple, God was not a word heard in our home, except in an occasional "Goddammit!"

For almost two years, resistance to our marriage hung over my family life, but I didn't tell Len about my parents' attitude. I hoped they'd change their minds, and I didn't want Len to resent them. The result for me was a neurasthenic stomach disorder I suffered for over a year, and a diet of Gerber's baby food. In the summer after my sophomore year at Brown, friends of my parents bombarded me with warnings about the distress that intermarriage would bring. I argued back that I understood their resentments and had no illusions about Jewish-Gentile relations in general, but that Len was different and not part of "them," that she wanted to share "our" life, bring up our children as part of "us," and did not have an intolerant bone in her body.

Finally, I decided that I had to trust my parents' fundamental tolerance and their love for me. They weren't religious, that I knew, and they knew I was not a rebellious or thoughtless son. When my father had a cancer scare, my mother told me I might have to interrupt college for the family's sake if the worst happened. It was only a scare, but it did tell me something of their expectations, my centrality in the family, and how responsible and mature they thought I was. They made me feel I wasn't just a twenty-year-old kid, but an independent young adult. With confidence but also trepidation, I decided to test my parents' trust in my judgment.

I sat down with my mother for a discussion of my future in the family. My father still had not voiced any resistance to my marital plans, and I didn't believe my mother's warning that my marriage to Len would "kill him," a phrase frequently used in those days. I began to express how I felt and laid out my plans for the future. First, I told her of the pressure I felt from her friends not to marry a Gentile, that it was making me literally sick, and that I had lost fifteen or twenty pounds. I said that we had no plans to marry for another two years, until after graduation, and that Len would be willing to convert if necessary, but that I couldn't accept their polite but unloving response to the woman I loved.

Calmly, I told my mother that if she couldn't fully accept Len that I would leave home that week, not return to college that fall, and would make my way with Len without them. Now, I told her, it was her choice; I had thought it over carefully. "Carefully" is what I said, but in truth I hadn't given any real thought to where I would go or what I would do if they rejected Len. I was gambling on the depth of their feelings toward me and the lack of religious bias in their objections. Their fear of losing a son to another community I could understand, but that wasn't the issue with me. I could also understand their fear of "losing face" with their Jewish friends, but that didn't compare to the loss I would sustain by giving up Len.

My mother listened quietly to what was, in effect, an ultimatum. It was in a sense a gamble, but at its core, a clear statement of how deeply and irrevocably I loved Len—and how far I would go to keep her. We did not argue further, and my mother retired for the night, presumably to speak to my father about the choices I had offered them. The next morning, my mother pulled me aside before breakfast and simply said, "It's over. We will love her like she was our own daughter. You are not going anywhere without us." And just like that, within scarcely twenty-four hours, a struggle of almost two years was ended for good. My parents opened their hearts to Len, and while she only learned of their resistance after the fact, she quickly succumbed to their attention and love. She was their biblical Ruth, too, and, as long as they lived, she was their favorite daughter-in-law, and the one they called for when ill health struck them in later life.

My experience of intermarriage had not been a typical one; it was much more traumatic for other Jews, particularly among the wealthy and socially prominent Jewish families in those decades of social hostilities. A significant number of prominent, originally Jewish families had "married out" of Jewish affiliation. The roll call of the families becoming at least nominal Christians was significant, and included the Belmonts (born Schönberg), the Schiffs, Treasury Secretary C. Douglas Dillon, and Eugene Meyer, grandson of an Alsatian rabbi and the financier who bought the *Washington Post* at a bankruptcy auction in

1933. His daughter, Katherine Graham, later the president of the *Post*, was brought up by her Lutheran mother Agnes, who deeply resented the social stigma that her husband's Jewish heritage brought with it in the period after World War I. As the biographer David Halberstam noted, "The Meyer home was made to seem thoroughly Protestant. Kay Graham was sitting with some classmates at Vassar when one of them asked her what it was like being Jewish. She had no idea because no one had ever mentioned to her that she was."[2] The social reality of the Christian world into which these Jews moved was captured by Otto Kahn, an investment banker and arts patron and himself a convert to Christianity, who reputedly said that "a kike is a Jewish gentleman who has just left the room." Intermarriage, as in Germany, was then usually perceived to be the first step on the way out, but it wasn't mine.

Starting shortly after the end of World War II, and accelerating through the 1950s, '60s, '70s, and '80s, changes in academic, business, and social institutions reopened genuine interaction between Jews and Gentiles. The rate of intermarriage increased approximately six-fold at all levels of society. From a semi-pariah group suspected of various types of character failings, Jews had become far more favorably viewed by the public, and many of the negative stereotypes Gentiles held about Jewish religion, culture, and character traits had been significantly reduced, though by no means eliminated.

Not only has a new social environment encouraged Gentiles to view marrying Jews in a new light, but similarly, Jewish family resistance has waned, partly because such marriages did *not* result, as they had generations before, in the complete assimilation of the Jewish partner into a nominally Christian culture. As the Reform rabbi James Rudin explained in 1947 at a lecture at Brown University (attended by my wife-to-be), intermarriage meant to him "one Jew less."[3] "Marrying out" was regarded by Jews sixty years ago as motivated by a desire to leave a Jewish life behind, or as a rebellion against the Jewish community's disapproval of intermarriage. A good deal of recent research has shown that this earlier pattern of leaving the community of Jews has been replaced in contemporary America by a much more mixed pattern of communal involvement and acceptance.[4] For example, the scholar Sylvia Barack Fishman found in her recent research that 38 percent of those intermarried now brought their children up as Jews and another 9 percent as "Jewish connected," meaning that almost half of intermarrieds were still tied to a distinctly Jewish ethos.[5] Intermarrieds under fifty years of age, she found, were *more*, not less, likely to bring their children up as Jews. Other research on intermarrieds has found that although only about 10 percent of non-Jewish-born spouses officially convert to Judaism, a much higher percentage of intermarried families live as Jews, often belonging to a Reform or Reconstructionist temple and/or living as cultural Jews by "osmosis." Some families live profoundly secular lives, recognizing both spouses' heritage while showing little interest in formal religion as a whole. Unlike earlier pressures to dissolve into a Gentile and at least nominally Christian culture, only a very small percentage of Jews actually convert to Christianity.

These figures do not speak to the issue of what will happen to Jewish identification in subsequent generations, diluted by participation in "American" observances such as Christmas celebrations and Easter egg hunts even when they have no religious content. The research on intermarriage has produced overall agreement on one count: that intermarriage by a group long held to be inbred has been steadily increasing over recent decades. There is disagreement, however, about what it means for the Jewish future. Some scholars and less tradition-bound rabbis believe in "outreach," efforts made to bring intermarrieds into the Jewish fold by welcoming them into religious and cultural life, even if the Gentile spouse has not formally converted to Judaism—and as long as he or she is willing to bring up any children as Jews.

On the other hand, Professor Jack Wertheimer, Charles Liebman, and Steven M. Cohen have found that the traditionalists, or "inreach" Jews, favor stronger ritual boundaries and less dilution to protect against intermarriage, which they believe represents a lack of solidarity with the historic Jewish people and a failure of will to survive as a religious culture.[6] Wertheimer takes an even stronger position on his own:

> It would mean speaking forthrightly and directly about where, and how, and why Judaism dissents from the universalistic ethos of the culture at large. And it would especially mean speaking on behalf of those commandments, beliefs and values for the sake of which Jews over the millennia—born Jews and those that have joined themselves to the Jewish people through conversion alike—have willingly, and gratefully, set themselves apart.[7]

Sentiments of "inreach," stressing sharper boundaries with clearer restrictions and obligations of "apartness," are clearly in opposition to those who believe in the softening of boundaries to prevent intermarrieds from being pushed away. While traditionalists argue for specifically Jewish customs and education, believers in "outreach," such as the sociologist Egon Mayer, find in their research that a more traditional Jewish education is unrelated to the frequency of intermarriage, except when there are at least nine years of attending a yeshiva or full-time Jewish day school.[8] Less than 75 percent of Jewish young people do so today.

Clearly, traditionalists want to resist rather than accommodate intermarriage, while their opposition assumes it is inevitable in an open and accepting America, even though it may divide some Jews from other Jews. Some researchers, among them Arnold Eisen and Steven M. Cohen, while seeking to slow the rate of intermarriage themselves, note that, from the perspective of many Jews and particularly their non-Jewish partners, certain deeply held beliefs of traditional Judaism are not easy to support. They find that while most nonobservant Jews—the vast majority of American Jews—accept and support the moral and ethical aspects of Judaism, some particular beliefs are either ignored or are unacceptable. It comes as no surprise to them, for example, that most Jews in an intermarriage (as well as their non-Jewish spouses) find the concept of Jewish "chosenness by God" difficult to accept. The authors point out that the beginning of the *Aleinu* prayer, for example, "[which] praises God 'who has not made us like the nations of the earth' does not reconcile at all with our interviewee."[9]

The Jewish belief that Jews are God's chosen people, elected to live up to high moral standards and be punished for failure, has eroded in America. A country with deep-rooted beliefs in religious pluralism, with its related ideal of equality, produces a natural tension with such an idea. The historic Jewish belief in "chosenness," one that had long provided an inner core of resistance to conversion to Christianity for many centuries, has been attenuated or reinterpreted by many American Jews. The questions raised by the Holocaust about God's protectiveness of His people have induced most assimilative Jews to reassess the meaning of "chosenness," and of God's very nature and existence. While most Jewish Americans can accept the concept of a "common destiny" for the Jewish people, only a small percentage, mainly Orthodox, can reconcile the biblical meaning of Jewish chosenness with the fact of six million Jews slaughtered in the Holocaust.[10]

Reaching out to a person of a different religious and cultural background in an intermarriage, needing to find common ground, seeking bonds of agreement—these require playing down ideas of Jewish particularism, and pose a difficult problem for Jewish leadership. On one hand, there are strong feelings among many less traditional leaders to try to keep intermarried couples and their children within the formal Jewish community. On the other, the increased acceptance of intermarriage that is linked to less traditional customs and beliefs leads to concern that intermarriage will weaken the dedication to, and durability of, Jewish life in generations to come.

The fear is that without the formal underpinning of religion and traditional custom, and without overt anti-Semitism creating a kind of defensive cohesion, the transmission of primarily cultural Jewish life will not suffice to retain most children, grandchildren, and great grandchildren as part of the Jewish community. The question is whether the bridging of difference, even more necessary in an intermarriage than in an "in" marriage, leaves sufficient "distinctiveness" in Jewish life that can be passed on to future generations.

The traditionalists may be right about the status of grandchildren and beyond, particularly if there are no profound changes in Jewish education. What kind of education that is, of course, remains key. If the "outreach" believers are right that most American Jews would not consider having their children undergo nine or more years of traditional Jewish studies, and the traditional "inreach" Jews are right that present-day intermarriage dilutes and confounds Jewish life, then how can such a dilemma be resolved? There are problems with both positions, some of which come from not taking the dynamics of secularism among Jews into account. Indeed, some price for inclusion may have to be paid.

Research into American Jews and Gentiles reveals some profound differences over the extent of secularism as a guiding sensibility—which may be a core factor in greater intermarriage. It also reveals how vast is the difference in the degree of secularity between Jews and non-Jews. Without understanding how nonreligiously guided (as against ethically and scientifically guided) most Jews are today, resolving the question of Jewish continuity is all but impossible. Without understanding how widespread the uniquely Jewish strains of secularism are, it becomes immeasurably difficult to educate Jews to develop their sense of distinctiveness. Most Reform, Conservative, Reconstructionist, and "unaffiliated" Jews simply do not give to the Talmud, Torah, and Hebrew language the same educational focus as do the Orthodox.

It is stunning to realize how little interest there has been among many Jews in the study of Jewish history and culture. Even more remarkable is the ignorance most present-day American Jews have of their ancestral history in the many lands of the Jewish Diaspora throughout the last two thousand years. These Jews are likewise ignorant of the many transformations that Jewish belief has undergone over those two millennia, going beyond the Bible stories that once were its primary focus.

An awareness of the distinctiveness of their religious and social beliefs, and of their attitudes toward life and death (and much in between), as compared to Christianity has been observed to be limited among Jews, reduced to such generalizations as "Jews are more focused on education," or "Jews tend to be more liberal than other groups." In my own talks with intermarried couples, the most detailed and accurate comparisons of Jewish and Christian differences were articulated by the non-Jewish spouse, who noted disparities in their individual early backgrounds, while the Jewish partner tended to press for a more common or shared past. The non-Jews found commonness of *present values and beliefs,* not necessarily those of their upbringings, and mainly those of a secular and ethical, rather than religious, emphasis.[11]

Writing decades ago about Jewish knowledge of Judaism and its culture, Nathan Glazer spoke of the ignorance that most Jews (excluding the Orthodox) have about their religion:

> Were we to limit ourselves to what American Jews say about their religion, or what they carry on the surface of their minds, how confused and banal a picture we would carry away! We would find, on the one hand, the clichés of liberal religion and, on the other, a kind of confusion in which loyalty to the Jewish people is identified with the Jewish religion.[12]

Clearly, not much has changed in the level of knowledge of most assimilative Jews. The failure of many assimilative Jews to understand even the basic differences between the Jewish religion and Christianity, beyond the issue of messiahship, partly obscures the very religious foundations of secular Jewish life. Jews are, in fact, more secular than Christians whether they are religious or not.

For example, while Jews and Christians both speak of heaven and an eternal afterlife, there is a difference in emphasis. The Christian "New Testament" (as against the "Old") is based on the idea of eternal life in heaven and individual salvation through Jesus Christ. The thrust of the Synoptic Gospels is that this temporal world is not the important one, that the material world is largely irrelevant, and that belief in Jesus as God the Son, as the savior of mankind, is the primary means of gaining everlasting life in heaven. This emphasis on the next life and de-emphasis on this one, particularly among early Christians, has been for most Jews unconvincing; they have always had an optimistic, this-worldly outlook. And the foreshadowing in Isaiah of a coming Messiah who would bring peace on earth, and the lion lying down with the lamb, was to Jews a prediction of change to come in this world, and a command for Jews to be agents of such change.

Although the relative emphasis on the "next world" as against "this world" of early Christianity has been attenuated over time, many (if not most) self-identifying Christians in America still believe that faith in Jesus is necessary to gaining eternal life in heaven, and believe in a personal God who intervenes in individual life and in the universe. Most present-day American Jews, when it comes to perceiving this world and how it is controlled, differ in their beliefs about the existence of heaven and hell, and how this world and the next are interrelated. As recent large-scale Pew opinion surveys show, American Jews are far more secular, and their sense of the meaning of the word "God" is also different.

Greater secularism among Jews has both a direct effect on the number of intermarriages and a diluting effect on the extent of religiousness in the actual intermarriages. Though the present education of liberal or intermarried Jews may be insufficient to produce Jews into the third or fourth generations, will a formula of simply more traditional Jewish education stem such a tide? Or do assimilative Jews need a different kind of education that focuses clearly on understanding the differences between Judaism and Christianity and how these differences play out in personal, social, and political values? While the Christian New Testament is not shy about criticizing Jews (often harshly), Jewish teaching about comparative values of Judaism and Christianity is all but nil, such that many of the comparatively positive values of Judaism in modern life remain little-known, and much of how Jews are seen derives from Christian sources.

It is important to understand just how secular Jews have become compared to other Americans, keeping in mind that while secularity requires the separation of issues of government from the province of spirituality, it does not necessarily mean one is an atheist or an agnostic. Although the Christian Right has tried to define it that way, a significant number of secularists in social and political life actually believe in God and/or have their own spirituality unlinked to organized religion. The author Susan Jacoby rejects right-wing Christian efforts, for political purposes, to portray all secularists as atheists or agnostics. "To call our Constitution 'atheist' rather than 'secular' turns it into something else," she notes. "Our Constitution is secular because it ascribes no governmental power to God." But the usage has nothing to do with a lack of personal belief in the spiritual elements of God. Jacoby goes on to point to a particularly Jewish aspect of secularist meaning: "People since the 19th century have said, 'I am a secular Jew' to mean 'I am a Jew but not a religiously observant Jew.'" In contrast, she notes, "You never hear someone say 'I am a secular Christian.'"[13]

In one of the few large surveys of the American religious landscape, the *Pew Forum on Religion and Public Life* examined 35,000 respondents, using a significant number of Jews in its sample. It explored issues of secularity and religion in the life of the American people, and in doing so revealed the depth, breadth, and uniqueness of the values and opinions of the American secular Jew. While intermarriage may tend to dilute traditional Jewish life, strong waves of secular life may be the larger threat to the question of "will my grandchildren be Jewish," whether intermarried or "in-married." What the evidence shows is that, intermarried or not, American Jews have moved much more than other religious groups to nonreligious beliefs about their own identity.

Assessing the belief in an afterlife, for example, three quarters of Christian Americans (75 percent) believe in life after death. By contrast, only about half as many Jews (35 percent) do so. Although most Protestants and Catholics say they believe in heaven, less than half as many Jews do so, their attitudes offering them a somewhat less sunny future. On the other hand, since only a fifth of Jews believe in hell compared to three quarters of Christians, the "downside" of the future seems to be better protected. Approximately seven in ten Americans still believe that angels and demons are active in *this world*. In stark contrast, the large majority of Jews do not.[14]

There are strong links between Americans' views on political issues and their religious affiliation. For example, on two issues that have been prominent in the political culture wars of recent decades, abortion rights and homosexuality, the survey points to secular Jews taking a much more tolerant and nonreligious approach. Although almost half of Protestants and Catholics believe that "abortion should be illegal in all or most cases," only 14 percent of Jews agree. Considering that Orthodox Jews also hold religiously to a slightly less rigid but similar antiabortion view, it is clear that among non-Orthodox Jews, most are in substantial *disagreement* with America's Christians.[15]

In responding to the question of whether "homosexuality is a way of life that should be discouraged by society," over 40 percent of Christians agree, against only 15 percent of Jews. The evidence does not mean that Jews have a greater preference for a homosexual "way of life"; it shows, rather, that America's Jews are more tolerant of "difference" than other segments of society. The source of their beliefs is not in religious principles, but in the Jewish experience of being different, and of being frequent victims of intolerance. While there are many less divisive issues than abortion and homosexuality, such as the environment and aid to the poor, about which the differences between Jewish and non-Jewish opinion are narrower, Jewish culture and experience engenders a distinctively Jewish voice in American social and political life. The secular attitudes of most Jews are a major factor in the marked increase in intermarriages, which occur largely among those who are not religiously devout.

Usually religiousness in a mixed marriage does not matter if one member yields to the feelings of the other. In the cases where the sharing of both traditions occurs, they usually involve couples who are not deeply connected to either of the religious backgrounds. Most intermarriages are, in fact, between primarily secular individuals reaching out beyond any religion into which they may have been born, to a world that is less religiously infused, and one that is highly tolerant. It is easier to become a cultural Jew, by way of "Jewish osmosis," because the religious demands are more limited.

The losses of Jews to other religions are relatively small. Losses to a secularism that is without a Jewish cultural dimension are more numerous when the elements that contributed to cultural Jewishness—its particular social and personal beliefs, its skepticism and intellectuality—fade away. To prevent the erosion of Jewishness among assimilative Jews, a greater consciousness and awareness of the distinctiveness of Jewish *cultural* life must be developed among non-religious Jews. While dress and customs were used by Jews histori-cally to reinforce that they were "a people apart," only the Orthodox maintain a visible separateness. To most assimilative Jews, eager to be seen like others are, what remains distinctive resides not in exter-nal reminders of difference, but in their internal and cultural sense of themselves—their ideas, their history, and a way of looking at life that is more defined, in reality, than most Jews suspect.

The Orthodox have external and internal means of protecting their religious beliefs, which they will sustain in an America that will protect their difference—despite the normal losses they will suffer over time from America's temptations. Assimilative Jews, however, are under great pressure to preserve their future links to the Jewish people and Jewish culture. To the extent that some assimilatives are religiously Jewish, that itself provides at least a part of retentiveness. But for the great majority who are cultural rather than religious Jews, they and their progeny remain at risk.

Future educational efforts will be needed to redefine, clarify, and imprint a clear sense of that distinctiveness of peoplehood, of culture, whether or not Jews are God-directed. Today, Jewish education deals little, or not at all, with comparisons between Judaism and Christian-ity on issues relating to God, original sin, asceticism, faith vs. moral law, and the linkage of the temporal to the eternal. Even differences in secularism between the two religions are not defined. Jewish secu-larism, spawned by the worldly focus of the religion itself, is further affected by the experiences of living as a small, vulnerable minority. Thus secularism in the Jewish mind encompasses memories of the de-structive effects of religious intolerance that is not afforded to those secularists who came from a *majority* religious tradition. The history of Jews as victims of intolerance, culminating in the Holocaust, has produced among most assimilative Jews just what the survey research finds: a people whose history has produced a highly developed level of *tolerance for difference.*

The underscoring and reinforcing of distinctive and positive elements in Jewish life will have to be part of future Jewish education, and of a defined cultural consciousness. Samuel Freedman, when looking at the future, saw the Jewish religion as a critical carrier of peoplehood. Fair enough. But what happens to the future of the other 70–75 percent who are not religious in any traditional sense? They have lost the immigrant sense of *yiddishkeit,* of a common Jewish ethos and history, and future generations of Jews will be even more disconnected from it. Freedman is only partly right when he says, "Jewishness as ethnicity, as folk culture, as something separate and divisible from religion, is ceasing to exist in any meaningful way."[16] But what about those Jews who have long ago lost the culture of the Yiddish past, but still share, as we have seen, distinct Jewish family values, social and political beliefs, and a common view of this world and the next? Although their mindset is not yet easily understood at present, the clarity of their "differentness"—politically, socially, and personally—leads me to believe that such distinctiveness can be taught and made clear.

On his seventieth birthday in 1926, Sigmund Freud said that being Jewish meant to him the sharing of "many obscure emotional forces, which were the more powerful the less they could be expressed in words, as well as a clear consciousness of inner identity, a safe privacy of common mental construction."[17] Freud also saw his Jewishness as a spur to his originality: "Because I was a Jew I found myself free from many prejudices which restricted others in the use of their intellect; and as a Jew I was prepared to join the Opposition and to do without agreement with the 'compact majority.'"[18] It meant maintaining a deep respect for differences.

American Jewish secularism grafts upon itself the long experience of difference from the homogenous populations in Europe and North Africa, so that it has become adamant in its belief in the separation of the governmental and religious spheres. At the same time, the process of Americanization has heightened Jewish understanding of the contribution of other cultural groups. This acceptance of the positive aspects of diversity was not historically a major part of traditional Jewish life, but has been fused into Jewish life by American culture.

Going beyond toleration of difference to the belief that differences can produce a greater good is a very American belief about the benefits of diversity. As George Washington's letter to the Touro Synagogue noted, we, as a new government, must go beyond mere toleration to the celebration of the very positive contributions of difference. The long history of Diaspora life for Jews definitely made these new American ideas easier to accept.

Jews in the past came in contact with great non-Jewish cultures—the ancient Greek world of philosophy and medicine, the Arab golden era of mathematics and astronomy, and the European rationalist world of the Enlightenment. As a result, they came away with something added and something unchanged. While long a people holding fast to their traditions in the Diaspora, the Jews of the world were still able to absorb and accommodate other cultures in which they lived. The Americanization of most Jews is but another example of such cultural fusion.

Building on a Jewish religious culture already deeply focused on a "promise-centered" messianic worldliness, Jewish optimism joined that of the Protestant Founders who believed they were establishing in America a "new Israel." The strong sense of Protestant individualism, a typically American ethos, has been absorbed by a historically inward and protective group-minded Jewish people, fusing that individualist spirit with a Jewish collective empathy. There is, of course, a price to be paid by those assimilative American Jews in terms of the cohesion and solidarity of Jews overall, on which pluralism and individualism have intruded. But it seems to be a price a great majority of American Jews are willing to pay.

Within the American experience alone, the profoundly secularist Constitution and the distinctive Jewish experience of being a defender of that secularism, yet vulnerable to the political pressures of an assertive Christian population, have also shaped American Jewish culture. Far more insistent than many Christians in distinguishing government from religion, most Jews also lead a less mystical, more secularly-oriented personal life. Even among the Orthodox, there is less contempt for doubt than among faithful Christians. Indeed, probing and skeptical questioning is embedded in Jewish life, an outcome of the intense focus of the intellect on religion.

As the late Rabbi Abraham Joshua Heschel said, the key word in Christianity is "salvation," which requires the proper faith, while in Judaism the key word is "mitzvah"—the deed, the action in fulfillment of one of God's commands.[19] The greater emphasis on how you live, on deeds rather than doctrine and faith, has made the transition to secularism easier for America's Jews. One of the major weaknesses of assimilative Jewish life in France and Germany in the nineteenth and early twentieth centuries was that Jewish secular-oriented communities, unlike those in America, did not develop in a pluralistic society but in one with a homogeneous culture demanding conformity. European secularist and rationalist impulses of the Enlightenment produced among its secular Jews greater absorption into Christian culture, often with at least nominal conversion to Christianity. In Germany, Reform Judaism attempted to fill the gap, but culture without religion did not maintain its secular Jewishness as it did in an avowedly pluralistic America. American Jews built more nonreligious organizations of social and political community, running from fraternal groups like B'nai B'rith, Workmen's Circle, and the Jewish Bund to a variety of socialist-oriented political organizations.

In an American Jewish future, nonreligiously motivated Jews, a driving force of accomplishment and activism, should, I believe, know more about their own culture and their religious heritage, and, in addition, how to educate their children and grandchildren about the extent of positive qualities such as tolerance, and the other specific reasons for such distinctiveness. A "common mental construction" as Freud speculated—and a sense of a common destiny—may still be enough to curtail damaging losses from within. Yet for a people who have maintained their distinctiveness for thousands of years, fears of dissolution seem unwarranted. Jonathan Sarna has written:

> Over the centuries, Jews have survived one doomsayer after another—not by ignoring or belittling predictions of gloom, or by succumbing to despair, but by instituting selective

discontinuities that have, in the end, proved the predictions wrong. There, perhaps, lies the real secret of Jewish continuity in the Diaspora.[20]

The so-called "People of the Book" are, in fact, worshipers of books, thus worshipers of learning and knowledge as the guides to life. It would be both fitting and poetic that in learning anew the dimensions of their own distinctiveness, assimilative American Jews could "educate" themselves into a more cohesive future.

Prologue to Chapter Seven

When I was seven or eight years old, new information about my family brought me a sense of wonder. My mother told me about her Texas family: her grandfather Lewis Hammer; a woman she thought was her mother, whose married name was Engelhardt; and a boy she thought was her brother, whose name was Max. But in fact Mrs. Englehardt was my mother's aunt, and Max was her cousin. Grandfather Hammer had brought them from Vienna to Texas, leaving behind his other daughter, my mother's actual mother. In 1908, that other daughter emigrated from Vienna to the United States with her new husband, reclaimed my mother as her own child, and brought her from the open spaces of Houston, Texas, to the poor and densely populated Orthodox Jewish section of Brooklyn.

Years later, in 1937, my father went to England on business, taking my mother who, through her Texas family, had somehow made contact with her real father. My father yielded to my mother's desire to find and meet her real father, so they traveled by train through Nazi Germany to Austria a year before the Anschluss in 1938. They arrived in a Vienna that was brimming with Nazi agitation and overt anti-Semitism.

My father told me that anti-Jewish feelings expressed themselves everywhere; and as a result, Mom's father did not show up for their meeting, either from fear of exposure by associating with American Jews, or from the inability to face my mother and explain his early desertion of her. His failure to meet his daughter kept my mother in tears for three days, while Europe headed for war and Jewish communities everywhere on the continent began a fearful flight from Hitler and Fascism. The governments of Western Europe, fragile themselves, could not or would not protect their Jews from an onrushing Holocaust. My mother's loss was only one more failure of Europe to treat its Jews fairly and tolerantly. Europe was surely, I thought, not like America—but why?

Chapter Seven

Anti-Semitism: Is America Different?

In a provocative comparative study, political scientist Benjamin Ginsberg focused on the outcomes of the relationships between different Jewish communities and the governments under which they lived. His pessimistic view is reflected in the title of the book, *The Fatal Embrace: Jews and the State.* The question Ginsberg raises is one that many of today's assimilative Jews pose for themselves: Is America really different from France and Germany, where Jewish citizens could not be protected from anti-Semitic violence? Would American protection also fail in times of extremism, or does the "exceptionalism" of America extend to its relationship with its Jewish population? Is the belief of many American founders that they were forming a different kind of government, a kind of Promised Land, likely to be proven true?

That *social* anti-Semitism from Christian Europe reached America is a fact made clear in my earlier discussion. The question is whether America's political institutions, and its people, are ultimately different from those of the democratic countries of Western Europe. Is the freedom and opportunity of Jewish life in America simply a phase of American history that won't last, or is it a durable consequence of a growing ethos that is something particularly American? Such questions guide our inquiry into the relationships of the English, French, and German governments and their people to their Jewish populations

123

in modern times. The intent here is not to examine the different histories of these countries—they are, indeed, rich and variable—but specifically the relationship between each country's government and its Jewish population.

In examining Jews as a group in these Western countries, all deeply influenced by the Enlightenment, I'm struck by the consistent effort of assimilative Jews to participate in the opportunities of their host countries. Indeed, some scholars see the Enlightenment itself, in its emphasis on likeness and universalism, as producing a different set of problems for Jews because of their separatist beliefs and history.[1] While Orthodox and other traditional Jews moved more slowly into professions and businesses, more assimilative Jews were pushing to expand their rights and gain full citizenship and acceptance.

The German environment for Jews, however, was anything but consistent. Restrictions on Jews varied from region to region and from one period to another. Jews in Germany consistently sought the rights of full citizenship, but were largely denied such rights until the late nineteenth century.[2] In Prussia, where most German Jews lived, pressure for emancipation was exerted on the king, Frederick William III, which resulted in a temporary edict of emancipation in 1812. As the Israeli historian Amos Elon observed:

> The liberating act was the result not of a popular revolution, as in France or the United States, but of a command from above. The difference would prove crucial. Through [its] vague and contradictory language . . . [it] still enabled the exclusion of Jews from government positions and from teaching posts in public schools and universities pending future decisions by the king. Few German liberals of the time saw anything wrong in that; like the conservatives, they felt a need to preserve the nation's Christian character.[3]

Despite the pride that assimilative nineteenth-century German Jews had in their "Germanness," and despite their patriotic zeal against the French, the German "Volk" and particularly the German government resisted granting many rights that "racial" Germans took for granted. While Jewish doctors could practice in many hospitals, other professions like the law were restricted.[4] German Jews were first allowed to enter law school in the early nineteenth century without having to convert to Christianity, but they could not actually practice law until several decades later. With restrictions on positions for Jews in the faculties of the universities, in the bureaucracies, and in the highly influential officer corps of the military, many assimilative Jews gravitated to publishing and journalism as well as to trade. The restrictiveness of professional opportunities and the periodic surges of anti-Semitism were both the cause and the result of the lack of citizenship, which lasted from Napoleon's defeat in the early 1800s until after the Franco-Prussian War in 1870, when a new emancipation law was passed that applied to the entire Reich.[5]

Unlike in France, the republican spirit of democracy had little force in Germany even as its various regions were unified into one imperial state under Bismarck. In the euphoria of victory over the French in 1870, the regime finally gave its Jews equal citizenship. For Germany's Jews, however, despite their exemplary service and heroism in the war, the sun did not shine for long. In October 1873, a stock market crash caused a financial panic, and in the ensuing depression many middle-class and aristocratic families lost everything. The crash was blamed on the Jews and produced another wave of anti-Semitism, this time much worse than earlier ones. Racist attacks were launched by well-known and respected academics such as Heinrich von Treitschke, by a prominent Protestant clergyman in Berlin, Adolf Stöcker, and by many populist pamphleteers. Though Jews constituted less than 1 percent of the population, an onslaught began, shocking the nation's Jews, who couldn't understand how they could be blamed for so much influence over the entire economy. Within a year, the number of conversions to Christianity doubled.[6]

The intensity of anti-Semitism subsided as the depression came to an end in 1880, and Jewish confidence in their social position correspondingly rose. But the German Jewish psyche had developed a strain of self-hatred aimed at certain supposed negative Jewish characteristics arising from the constant stereotyping in public discourse.[7] Jews remained excluded from the senior officer corps and from high positions in the government bureaucracy. The country's leaders maintained a far less sympathetic approach to Jews than the more democratic French and English. As the Jewish historian Fritz Stern put it, "Imperial Germany was a strange hybrid, a magnificently disciplined modern society with an antiquated political order."[8]

The period of calm for Jews in Germany lasted a mere two generations before the Hitler era, although some families had enjoyed decades of relatively peaceful private life amid public scorn. But hanging over them was the growing racialism of the German people, who were coming to believe that Germans and Jews were divided not just by religion or culture but by blood. Racist views took hold even among prominent intellectual, governmental, and cultural leaders. Werner Sombart, for example, a well-known political economist at the University of Berlin in the early 1900s, and later an outspoken academic apologist for the Nazi state, acknowledged the high intellectual abilities of the Jews in dealing with abstract ideas, but claimed they came at the expense of "diminished emotional depth and empathy of character." The "purist form of capitalism is that wherein abstract ideas are most clearly expressed," Sombart wrote, "and that they are part and parcel of the Jewish character we have already seen . . . there is no occasion to labor the close kinship in this respect between capitalism and the Jew."[9] Writing at almost the same time in *Mein Kampf*, Adolf Hitler saw the exact opposite characteristic: "The Jewish doctrine of Marxism rejects the aristocratic principle of nature and replaces privilege of power and strength by mass of numbers and their dead weight."[10] The two contradictory claims about innate Jewish character could only be reconciled by a common anti-Semitism, which made Jews out to be inherently capitalists and communists simultaneously.

Racist German criticism of Jews followed along a similar path, exemplified by the writings of such men as the composer Richard Wagner, who, while conceding Jewish intelligence, nevertheless claimed for Jews a racially-based deficiency of emotional and spiritual understanding. The Jew, he felt, could not truly understand the great depth of German music, and he characterized the music of the composer Felix Mendelssohn, the Lutheran grandson of the great Jewish philosopher Moses Mendelssohn, as unable, because of race, "to take the shape of deep and stalwart feeling of the human heart."[11] Wagner warned that if a Jew intermarried with a German, the "impure" qualities of the Jew would contaminate the purity of the German partner. Later, in 1882, the revered composer added, in a letter to King Ludwig of Bavaria: "I hold the Jewish race to be the born enemy of pure humanity and everything noble in it. It is certain that [the Jews] are running us Germans into the ground, and I am perhaps the last German who knows how to hold himself upright in the face of Jewry, which already rules everything."[12]

In reaction, many assimilative Jews, such as historian Fritz Stern's family, became part of a large group of Germanified, non-Orthodox Jews (or former Jews). Several generations of Jews converted in great numbers to Lutheranism, often intermarrying. They lost their particular dialect, *Judendeutsch*, delighting in the language and other elements of German culture. Nevertheless, as Stern wrote, "still, they carried a memory of past apartness. I think they thought of Jewishness as both stigma and distinction."[13]

Prior to Adolf Hitler's rise to power in 1933,[14] the drumbeat of public German anti-Semitism never ceased. As Wagner and other Germans insisted, Jews were subversive of most good things German. Hitler's race-based ideology of Nazism had, then, fertile ground in which to grow, and in their desire to become Germanized, the tiny population of Jews underestimated the depth of anti-Jewish hatred and overestimated the protectiveness of German "Kultur." The race-based ideology spread to Vienna. There, too, the inferiority of the Jew was a constant theme in intellectual, artistic, and academic circles. The scholar Sander Gilman has carefully documented the insidious effects of such blatant anti-Semitism at the turn of the twentieth century on aspiring assimilative Jews. The prevailing view granted that there were smart Jews, cunning and shrewd, but that the race could not advance from being just "talented" to being truly "creative," from having a parasitic "reproducing" intelligence to having an "originating" one.[15]

Spinoza, Heine, and Freud did not count in this cultural view; and neither would Franz Kafka, Albert Einstein, and other Jewish geniuses still to emerge. The stigma on assimilative Jews, converts to Christianity, and the "racially mixed" (the *Mischlingen*) was deeply damaging in the self-hatred it generated. Although there has always been some racial element in the American variant of anti-Semitism, it pales in comparison to the German version. While many different ethnic groups in America, including Jews, worked hard to demonstrate their "Americanness," none had to work harder than the Jews in Germany and Austria, who had to prove they were *echt Deutsch*, that they really belonged.

The combination of misplaced confidence and denial in the early Hitler years was exemplified by Victor Klemperer, whose autobiography, *I Will Bear Witness*, speaks of his initial confidence in the power of German culture to right the wrongs of the national government's persecution of Jews and dissenters. Klemperer, whose family converted to Christianity, was a bemedaled veteran of World War I and a professor of Romance languages at Dresden Technical Institute. Concerned though he was about the evil of Nazism, his idealistic view of "his" Germany forestalled his escape until it was too late (though he managed to survive the Holocaust). A new and weak democratic national government had given way to a totally authoritarian one, whose people readily accepted the demonizing of its German-Jewish citizens. The weakness of the democratic government, the intense and widespread belief in Jewish inferiority and wickedness, and the favorable German responsiveness to strong authority, among other factors, permitted the rise of Hitler.

In France, citizenship was granted to Jews in 1791, after the French Revolution, and enshrined in the Napoleonic Codes in the first decade of the nineteenth century. "We must refuse everything to Jews as a nation and accord everything to Jews as individuals," said the code, recognizing no distinctiveness within or beyond citizenship in France.[16] As the first European grantor of Jewish citizenship, France subsequently opened the state bureaucracy, the national and regional ministries, and the military's officer corps to Jewish participation. As the scholar Pierre Birnbaum defined them, these "state Jews," consistently supportive of the secular and universalist Republic, were, however, constantly condemned by the anti-Semitic newspapers, such as *La Libre Parole*. Jewish support of the secular state and Republicanism elicited similar condemnation from Catholics, who had lost the dominant institutional position they held under the monarchy.

In the back-and-forth conflict between anti-clerical supporters of the secular Republic (nominally Catholic) and the monarchist-supported Catholic Church and traditional Catholics, the small numbers of Jews and Protestant *préfets* who oversaw the diminution of Church control over education and family relations came in for constant Church criticism.[17] Frightened by what they considered threats by the "Jewish Republic" (of whose population Jews actually constituted less than one percent) to its earlier dominance of French life, Catholic traditionalists condemned France's Jews for helping to build a secular republic free of religious dominance. Tension grew between French Jews and Catholics, eventually exploding in a venomous and slanderous attack on the patriotism of Captain Alfred Dreyfus—and through him all Jews—in the early 1890s. When major doubts arose about the accusations of treason, the publication *La Croix* (The Cross) denounced efforts to retry and rehabilitate him. In the end, his innocence was vindicated.[18]

The "Dreyfus Affair" was a turning point in French Jewish life. The court-martial of a Jewish officer on charges of spying for Germany unleashed an explosion of anti-Semitism, long latent, that not only set off violent demonstrations against Jews countrywide, but produced brutal anti-Jewish riots in Paris, the Republic's center of tolerance and enlightenment. These outbursts lasted for years, during the ebb and flow of the case, marginalizing Jews to a greater extent than they had been in almost a century of citizenship. After the initial verdict of guilty was reversed, even the most assimilated of Jews, such as the eminent sociologist Emile Durkheim, despaired over the impact of continuing protests and attacks. Writing in 1898 to a Jewish academic friend almost four years after the initial trial, he gloomily advised, "Let's do what we can and resign ourselves to the rest. I feel like an internal exile. I've almost completely withdrawn from academic life. What I see going on there is just too painful to watch."[19]

The tension between an avowedly secular Republic and the dominant Catholic Church reflected an argument about the separation of church and state that America had resolved over a hundred years before in its constitution. Efforts to return France, whose citizens were overwhelmingly Catholic, to Church dominance and power in civil affairs, was at the heart of a long period of political instability and an ongoing source of tension between traditional Catholics and French Jewish believers in Republicanism and secularism in government.

At the end of the nineteenth century, it was commonly accepted that Jews were part of a separate race. Their citizenship, accepted by French Republicans, was, however, constantly questioned by writers Edouard Drumont and Charles Maurras, by the anti-Semitic national press, as well as by traditionalist, anti-secular Catholics. As the French historian Pierre Birnbaum noted, "The new nationalism was largely responsible for . . . inciting social groups to construct an organic, dreamed-up French identity that was largely mythical: throughout the entire Third Republic, it was this nationalism that pushed for the rejection of the Republic, which was perceived as artificial and imposed by the supposed enemies of Catholicism, namely Protestants and especially Jews."[20] The "nationalistic" belief that the racial and religious core of "French" was Catholic stock and Catholic history was only partially accepted by French Jews, who, in European fashion, still granted race much importance. So while many French Jews acknowledged they were a different race, they nevertheless claimed the rights of citizenship.

In the Chamber of Deputies in 1923, Léon Blum, subsequently prime minister of France, rose to address his Jewishness. "I am Jewish . . . That is a fact. It is no insult to me to be reminded that I belong to the Jewish race, a race I have never denied, and toward which I feel only gratitude and pride."[21] This accepted role of race in European political and social life, and its quick substitution for what were different cultures, should be noted. Why? Because of essential differences, as we will find later, in the divisions in America; particularly in how racial differences, as against religious or cultural ones, divided the American people and how that division distinctly and decisively affected its Jews.

For French Jews, Republican government support was often open and strong, though periods of monarchical and nationalistic influence interrupted periods of democracy, and ultimately the state's benign relationship toward its Jews was severed. When, in 1940, a weakened and divided France was quickly conquered by the Germans, the collaborationist Vichy government that was formed in the South led to the rejuvenation of the Catholic Right and of the anti-Semitic nationalist press. As noted in Birnbaum's exhaustive research, "Without a doubt the two *Statuts des Juifs* enacted by Vichy on 3 October 1940 and 2 June 1941 were decided on voluntarily, not [as newly opened archives show] in response to a pressing demand from the German authorities, who were amazed by such speed."[22] The new statutes about Jews were clear and unequivocal: Citizenship was immediately stripped from Jews, even retroactively going back three generations, and all Jews in the armed services—including more than twenty generals and hundreds of commissioned and noncommissioned officers—were expelled from the military, as were all Jews from the public schools and civil service. In great distress, and in words typical of many other Jews in government and the military, Max Hymans, a député of Indre, wrote to head of state Marshal Pétain in February 1941:

> I have the honor of informing you that "more than two of my grandparents" practiced the Jewish religion. The French law of 3 October 1940 uses a new terminology. What does the word "race"—which it does not define—mean? Is race determined by religion? . . . To respond to the question of the office of the Chamber, I maintain that I am subject to the consequences of that law of exception and that forfeiture must affect me, as it has affected French professors, magistrates, and officers reputed to be "of the Jewish race."
>
> I will bear it without shame, for I am not of the Jewish race, but of the French race, or rather quite simply French as much as anyone else . . . How distressed my grandfather would be if he

were here to see those of his descendants who were not killed
in action and who were all, or almost all, wounded, cited, deco-
rated with the Médaille Militaire or the legion of Honor, today
reduced to second-class Frenchmen.[23]

So often at the forefront of most progressive social change, including the separation of church and state, Jews found themselves in the
middle of the arguments of a modernizing state. The French Jews,
particularly their assimilative segment, were eager to take advantage
of the new opportunities in government, administration, and military
that were denied to fellow Jews in Germany. Nevertheless, the weakness of the French state ultimately led to disaster for many Jews who
had believed it would always protect them.

The German and French Jewish populations were the largest assimilative groups in Western Europe. England's Jews, although less
than 1 percent of the population, nevertheless had a distinctive experience. Unlike France, which had a Jewish population throughout the
Middle Ages, England had expelled all Jews on religious grounds in
1290, an exile that lasted for 350 years. After royal promises of protection were made in 1674 and 1685, the 1698 Act for Suppressing
Blasphemy finally made it legal again to practice Judaism in England.[24]

Like fellow Jews in Germany and France, English Jews in the early
1800s pushed for full legal equality. An emancipation bill, passed in
the House of Commons in 1833, was defeated in the House of Lords,
and though Jews won some local offices, full emancipation came only
in 1858. In that same year, the Christian oath required for sitting in
parliament was eliminated, allowing Baron Lionel de Rothschild to be
seated. The temporary openness of England at that time allowed immigration from Russia, and by 1914, 250,000 Jews lived in England,
approximately two-thirds of England's present-day Jewish population.

England offered government stability that neither France nor Germany could provide. Though maintaining a class and ethnic snobbery
socially, and despite deep-running currents of anti-Semitism among
the population at large, the English government remained resistant to
large-scale attacks against Jews. There was, as in France and Germany,

both the popular and elite sense that Jews were an alien body—people, as the scholar Robert Wistrich put it, who could never be fully English. *The Protocols of the Elders of Zion*, purported proof of a Jewish conspiracy to control the world, was widely accepted by the London newspapers until Philip Graves, a London *Times* correspondent, exposed it as a forgery.[25] (It still remains a widely published and influential book, particularly in Muslim countries.) Attacks in the 1930s by Oswald Mosley's fascist Blackshirts did occur, but government action to keep order and protect the Jews was swift, and the 1936 Public Order Act banning political uniforms helped contain potential right-wing provocation and violent demonstrations.[26]

The English historian Anthony Julius, in his thoughtful study of anti-Semitism in England, has identified the difference between English and continental anti-Semitism. In France and Germany, he wrties, fear and hatred of imagined Jewish power was popularized by an explosive social element that periodically intimidated their governments. In England, anti-Semitism stemmed from condescension or contempt, rather than apprehension or fear.[27] English confidence in itself during and after the nineteenth-century Enlightenment was immune to fears of supposed "Jewish Power." In modern times, as Julius points out, "English Jews' civil liberties have never been threatened, nor has their security been even put in jeopardy." The way Jews are mistreated, he noted, is by social exclusion, not political limitations or mob action. It is a story of anti-Semitism "that shrinks from being named anti-Semitic," and prefers a thousand cuts. "The way in which Jews have been harried in England," writes Julius, "is by indirection, by means that permit a certain distance between bully and bullied."[28] Jews who sought a more assimilative life faced social inequality and condescension. Unlike America's heterogeneity and emphasis on equality and pluralism, English social stratification and its snobbish view of "differentness" has kept English Jews, despite political security and protection, "looking up" in a society looking down with disdain.

It's worth emphasizing just how small the assimilative populations of Germany, France, and England actually were in the nineteenth century. Most dense concentrations of Jews were in Eastern Europe, where they had little opportunity to move into the mainstream of their societies. After the pogroms of the 1880s in Russia and Poland, small numbers of Jews migrated to Germany, France, and England, but the most popular destination for Eastern Europe's impoverished and restricted Jews was America. While less than half a million Jews lived in Germany, France, and England combined, the three decades from 1880 to 1910 found almost two and a half million Jews emigrating to America, fleeing poverty and a hostile social and political environment—and the tight constraints of religious Orthodoxy. Within a span of a few decades, the main locus of Diaspora Jewry became the United States. American Jews quickly found themselves at the center of wealth and importance, reaching a peak of integration, opportunity, and accomplishment in the last sixty years.

Germany's Jews in the decades before Hitler had also become disproportionately accomplished in science, business, medicine, the law, and the arts. What, if anything, was really different between these assimilative Jewish populations in the Diaspora and the deeply Americanized Jews in America? How do we know that they too would not fall into a "fatal embrace"? Those most worried about Jewish security in the United States point to the decimation of these highly assimilative Jewish populations in Germany and France and what happened to them under extreme economic and political stress. That there is social anti-Semitism in America as in those states is, of course, true, and it is also a fact that much of Jewish progress here, both institutionally and in personal relationships, has occurred in only the last sixty years. Social, not political, hostility toward Jews has always been part of the American narrative, as various groups from different national origins and religions have had to adjust to each other, often with considerable friction.

What is different here is also significant, and that difference offers some measure of optimism. The uniquely *heterogeneous* nature of the American people, and the sheer number and variety of its immigrant citizens, are a principal difference. The unique popular founding and protection of freedom is another. When the Jewish-British art historian David Sylvester said to the artist Robert Motherwell that he "had never seen Jews so free," he was speaking about the absence of English condescension, about unselfconsciousness, about a broad positive acceptance of "differences" by Jews and non-Jews alike, that has evolved over time out of a particular American history.

In a strange and unintended way, the racial divide in America benefited Jewish Americans, who were generally thought of as white rather than black or red. In Europe, while there was a religious divide between Christians and Jews, Jews were principally considered a different race of lower quality—not only in "Aryan" Germany, but in France and England as well. The digestibility of Jews into "Frenchmen" and "Englishmen" always had an element of presumed race that carried into modern times, evident in the critical speeches about Jews by Charles de Gaulle as well as in the favorable ones by Winston Churchill, both of which emphasized the "Jewish race."

Whereas race and nationality were intertwined in the three European countries, with Jews at the bottom rung, the founding of America by immigrants from different nations served to dilute the emphasis on national origin. Thus, from the beginning, Jews were not classified as a race apart, but as white and European in a country that divided itself by color alone. As a mostly Protestant country, as noted earlier, there was a religious interest in and sense of connection to the stories and ideas of the Old Testament, which gave a biblical flavor to the idea that America was a special nation among nations, a chosen people, a new kind of "light to the Gentile world."[29]

The Protestant ethos of the country's founding had a significant effect on its perception of its Jewish population. While some Puritans were intolerant of other Protestant sects, others, as in the Rhode Island of Roger Williams, were not. In the diversity of Protestantism in America, tolerance of difference was a pragmatic necessity, and that tolerance extended even to the Jews, because of the belief that there were many different pathways to God. The very differentiation of Christian beliefs *within one nation* forced a pragmatic tolerance and acceptance of differences, as was not the case in Lutheran Germany, Anglican England, and Catholic France. While early America could not accept the diversity of race, it managed to accept the diversity of religion—even, if somewhat grudgingly, for a peculiar (and small) Jewish community.

Even Republican France's bestowal of citizenship on its Jews—everything as a Frenchman, nothing as a Jew, as noted before—is different from the American concept of citizenship with which Washington identified the encouragement and *protection of difference*. The idea that differences did not have to be compressed into uniformity, so as not to be considered alien, was deepened and accentuated by the enormous immigration of different nationalities and ethnic and religious cultures that occurred over 130 years of American life. In just the five decades from 1870 to 1920, for example, some 35 million immigrants became citizens. For American Jews, the migrations of diverse nationalities and religions was a distinct advantage; in the mélange of immigrant groups, Jews were no longer the only aliens, as they had been in Germany, France, and England. The multiplicity of different people and cultures, and attendant nativist and inter-ethnic tensions, served to disperse and attenuate anti-Semitism, which, while a factor in the socioeconomic history of America, did not focus mostly on Jews as it did in Europe.

The American culture of sectarian Protestantism with its voluntary, pluralist, and individualistic emphasis overwhelmed any attempts at European-style hierarchy, thereby Americanizing its Jews. Welcoming religion, but opposing the dominance of any particular one, containing an enormous multiplicity of diverse nationalities and sects, welcoming immigrants of various ethnic and religious groups, America has provided Jews with a special type of protection unavailable to European Jews. But just as important, if not more so, has been the strength and stability of the American government, which has weathered the stresses of depression, war, and huge population changes. Only in the Civil War, when the American party system failed to deal peacefully with slavery, did the national government become unstable and threaten to dissolve.

America's governmental stability, as it benefited America's Jews, is in marked contrast to the lack of democratic solidity in the governments of France and Germany. The good intentions of French

Republican democracy were for many years threatened by instability, which eventually weakened its ability to resist German aggression. German democracy had little historical precedent and much instability in its short life after World War I, finally yielding to the authoritarianism of the Nazi regime. What is distinctive about America and its relationship to its Jews is the unique combination of religious pluralism and the belief in the separation of church and state stemming from its Protestant origins, its vast and diverse immigrations to its shores, and a strong and stable governing leadership. That leadership has not supported social and economic demonizers of Jews when disruption of society has occurred. While vehement anti-Semites like the populist Tom Watson incited the lynching of Leo Frank, a Jewish businessman from the state of Georgia, in 1915, and Father Coughlin spewed his racist and anti-Semitic diatribes for his National Union for Social Justice on national radio during the Great Depression, these movements gained little national support among governing elites or at the ballot box.

The consensus among American governmental elites not to take popular prejudice and discrimination too far evidences a long-run unwillingness of American political leaders to demonize Jews or other ethnic groups. There have been scattered public slights in Congress and the Administration over time, but tensions have been fought out at local levels of contact and government. Anti-Semitism, even before its significant decline in the last fifty years, never reached the intensity, scope, and racial animus of European levels in the nineteenth and twentieth centuries. It differed also, most notably, in that it was not connected to nationalism, nor was it part of a nation's "organic" ideology, as in France and Germany.

It was a uniquely American anti-Semitism that, in Jonathan Sarna's words,

> had to compete with other forms of animus, Racism, anti-Quakerism, Anglophobia, anti-Catholicism, anti-Masonry, anti-Mormonism, anti-Orientalism, nativism, anti-Teutonism, primitive anti-Communism—these and other waves have

periodically swept over the American landscape, scarring and battering its citizens. Because hatred is so varied and diffused, no group experiences for long the full brunt of national odium. Furthermore, most Americans retain bitter memories of days past when they or their ancestors were the objects of malevolence. . . . The American strain of anti-Semitism is thus less potent than its European counterpart, and it faces a large number of natural competitors.[31]

What has benefited Jews greatly in just the last fifty or sixty years has been the expansion of freedom and opportunity to racial groups, particularly to African Americans who did not share in the openness and opportunities afforded to white European ethnic groups. The recent strides made by Jews, and by women as well, in entering almost all professions, business organizations, and academia were greatly aided by the scope of the Civil Rights Act of 1964 and subsequent amendments that focused initially on race, but eventually made discrimination against all minorities illegal. Although prejudice persists in the hearts of many, the new laws against discrimination, and frequent threats to enforce them, created a society that, even at the top, was generally unwilling to challenge them. Those men and women who were prepared to compete had vast new opportunities in recent decades, and American Jews were in the forefront.

The extension of anti-discriminatory laws, along with the expansion of opportunities to Blacks and other racial groups, has not only created new openings for Jews occupationally, but has also offered potential safeguards for the future. The multiplicity of ethnic groups has been expanded to include non-Whites and women who, heretofore, were the objects of discrimination and exclusion. As noted, a large majority of the population has been formed of different groups who have in the past felt the sting of prejudice and the discrimination that followed. More people than not have an investment in opposing discrimination.

The ability of American Jews to take advantage of the opportunities in areas that were not open to Jews in the 1950s is documented in the work of Charles Silberman, Steven Pease, and others who have identified the disproportionate success of Jews in many professions. These achievements, however, point to a paradox in the psyche of American Jews. Research has found that American Jews, by a large majority, fear a coming (or existing) rise in anti-Semitism. Despite the extent of openness to Jews in the last fifty years, and the drop in social and economic restrictions against them, they still remain wary. Steven M. Cohen and Alan Fisher found that an overwhelming majority of Jews think that anti-Semitism is still a serious problem. At the same time a survey of contributors to the San Francisco Jewish Community Federation discovered that one third of those polled thought a Jew could not be elected to Congress from the San Francisco area—despite the fact that all three members of Congress from contiguous or adjacent districts were, in fact, Jewish.[32] The reluctance to accept the extent of decline in anti-Semitism is evidence of the role of memory and prior experience in the Jewish psyche. Fear or lack of confidence in the Jewish future is paradoxically not present in the mind of Jews individually when they consider their own lives. Indeed, Jews, more than non-Jews, are confident in their ability to build a happy and successful life in America.

To the question of whether America is truly different from other assimilative countries for Jews, the answer has to be yes. Whether it will remain so, whether the government will maintain the stability it has shown in past crises, cannot be answered with total assurance, but many indications are favorable. I'm not talking about the end of anti-Semitism, which in America is largely in the hands of the Christian churches, their parishioners, and American schools, but rather the continued growth in the acceptance of "difference."

Still in its early stages, America's political and social acceptance of the right to be different and the benefits that can accrue are still only an extension of George Washington's prescient idea of moving beyond mere tolerance to the dignity of differences so that each group could be protected "under [its] own vine and fig tree." The idea that differences can be a positive value has grown in acceptance. A new majority of Americans, all victims of discrimination because of race, sex, or religion, forms a protective element, not shared in Europe, which bodes well for American Jews. With a strong tradition of protection by national governmental elites, the expansion of acceptance of differences by the population at large should give America's Jews an increased measure of confidence that America is, indeed, different.

Prologue to Chapter Eight

I always wondered why I had such strong feelings about black people, especially anger at how they were treated in America. I was aware that Jews and Blacks both had suffered, at different times, pariah status, humiliation, and sorrow. And I felt that if Jews were not more sensitive to the plight of black people than White non-Jews, then they had learned nothing from their own history.

The pricking of conscience from history's lessons I knew was a key to my attitude, as was a shared adulation of Moses by black people that was uncommon among white Christians. How could Jews, venerators of law and justice in the Torah, not see the rank unfairness of segregation and racist behavior? Yes, I had learned from Jewish history and experience to respect "differentness" in all peoples. But where did the strong *emotional* connection come from, one that has stayed with me all my life, reflecting itself in my teaching and mentoring of black students and developing strong friendships across racial lines?

These powerful emotional connections came early and personally from a particular childhood that brought a young, loving, and nurturing black woman, Pearl Robinson, into the intimate life of my family. While Pearl functioned in various capacities in our family for over fifty years, the most formative for me was the first decade when, fresh from North Carolina during the Great Depression, she became a tender but firm second mother to the three Rubin boys—nothing like the obsequious black Southern "mammies" in the movies.

In 1942, during Christmas vacation, Pearl was taking my brothers and me to meet my parents in Florida—a testament to how much they trusted her. Just before we reached Washington, DC, the train stopped, although there was no station. I later found out that it was a line on the map, the Mason-Dixon Line, below which racial segregation was to be strictly enforced. The conductor came through the car in which we were seated, holding a long wooden stick, and tapped each seat where black people were sitting. Black soldiers moved to a segregated car, and the conductor tapped the seat for Pearl to move also. I rose to my feet, yelling at the conductor that he couldn't take her away—he realized quickly that she was taking care of us and moved on. Seventy-one years later I vividly remember that incident and the humiliation it caused Pearl. When I see racism, I always think of her.

At that time, my parents were struggling to get into, and then stay in, the middle class. And my mother entertained business people many evenings, leaving Pearl to care for the children. Particularly for my younger brother Larry and me, the feeling of her skin, her radiant presence, and her loving nature were my earliest connections to black people, and have remained so emotionally and intellectually. Before I had the courage to introduce Len to my parents, I had her meet Pearl— and got Pearl's encouragement and approval. After her death, my brothers and I started the Pearl Robinson Foundation to give young black people opportunities that Pearl never had.

Chapter Eight

Intertwined: Race and Jews in American Culture

In Christian Europe, Jews were seen as members of a religion apart, a nation apart—and a race apart. In the eighteenth, nineteenth, and twentieth centuries, racial prejudice deepened and became singularly important. While the European reaction to the "universalism" of the Enlightenment focused attention and hostility on Jewish "racial" differences, the American embrace of the Enlightenment focused on pluralism and the welcoming of different ethnic groups and religions. As noted, both friend and foe, even some Jews themselves, thought of the Jewish people in racial terms. "Jews as a race" was a concept, not merely of personal or social importance, but one that was embedded in a definition that severely limited Jews in the political and legal systems of both Germany and England until the late nineteenth century. The idea that certain stereotypical character defects could be "cured" by religious conversion was for centuries a lively point of argument among Christian leaders. The Inquisition, an inquiry into the authenticity of a Jew's conversion to Christianity, was steeped in the Catholic Church's fears of the remaining Jew "within," and was evidence of the "universal" church's unwillingness to accept "difference"—one cause, perhaps, of the Reformation. Catholic historians have noted that post-Inquisition limitations on one's rise in the Catholic hierarchy because

143

of Jewish birth or roots affirmed notions of Jews as a different race.[1]

The Protestant founding of America was a significant advantage to early Jewish settlers because of Protestant interest in the Jewish Bible—the Old Testament—and because of their fascination with the Moses story and the Jewish flight from Egypt to freedom. As the historian Bruce Feiler observed in a magazine interview:

> For centuries, the Catholic Church had banned the direct reading of Scripture. But the Protestant Reformation, combined with the printing press, brought vernacular Bibles to everyday readers. What Protestants discovered in America was a narrative that reminded them of their sense of subjugation by the church and appealed to their dreams of a Utopian New World.[2]

Furthermore, Protestants thought of themselves and their emigration from Europe to America as akin to the Israelites' journey under Moses' leadership out of Egypt to the Promised Land. As Feiler points out in his book *America's Prophet: Moses and the American Story*, by the time of the American Revolution the "theme of a beleaguered people standing up to a superpower" had become a critical narrative of early American identity. At President Washington's death, many of the eulogies compared the leader and father of the new American nation to Moses, the "first conductor of the Jewish nation."[3]

As noted, many American founders believed they were descendants of the "People of the Book." They took Old Testament names, stories, and ideals, which served to diminish racial and religious "apartness" for Jews that had been cultivated in Europe. The importation of African slaves also provided a racial separateness, which, when coupled with the settlers' beliefs in Black inferiority, and absent a direct historical linkage to a biblical people, directed prejudice and hostility toward them.

For example, in Rhode Island prominent Christian merchants such as the Brown family (founders of Brown University), were deeply involved in the slave trade, while still linking themselves to the "Old Testament" narrative.[4] Obviously they missed the lessons of the

Exodus story, the meaning of Passover, and the flight to freedom for Moses and the Jews. As a result, Jews benefited unintentionally from the "racial" animus against Africans, and, alternatively, gained from a perceived common history. Both the biblical connections and the displacement of negative racial stereotypes onto African slaves served to weaken inherent or racial characterizations of Jews, though still leaving religiously based hostility and their residual stereotypes with certain Christian groups.

While many white Christians may have passed over the full meaning of the Exodus, Christianized African slaves did not. Negro spirituals from the nineteenth and twentieth centuries were filled with the ideas of freedom from the Old Testament, such as "Turn Back Pharaoh's Army," "I Am Bound for the Promised Land," and the virtual national anthem, "Go Down Moses." These songs, with their words from Exodus—"When Israel was in Egypt's land, let my people go! Oppressed so hard they could not stand, let my people go!"—were cries for freedom. Although Jesus was seen as the spiritual savior, the stories of the Old Testament were the daily bread of the need to be free. "Justice, Justice shalt thou pursue."

Abraham Lincoln invoked the Exodus narrative in his Gettysburg Address and, after his assassination, was compared, like Washington, to Moses. Henry Ward Beecher declared: "Again a great leader of the people has passed through toil, sorrow, battle and war, and come near to the promised land of peace, into which he might not pass over."[5]

The theme of freedom and equality sustained the civil rights movement for generations, and later became the high point of a Black-Jewish alliance, both harmonious and conflicted. The founding of the National Association for the Advancement of Colored People (NAACP) was initiated largely by black and Jewish leaders, as was, to a slightly lesser extent, the founding of the National Urban League (NUL) in the early twentieth century. While many black leaders recognized Jews as strong opponents of discrimination compared to other Whites, the uneducated, poor former slaves did not have any reason to connect the Jews of America with the Jews of the Bible. Most simply absorbed the anti-Semitism of the white Protestant churches that brought them into Christianity. The church singing of "Go Down Moses," was just as likely to be followed by the song, "De Jews Done Killed Poor Jesus" in black churches.[6]

Jewish and black leaders shared the political objectives of social justice and the end of discrimination, but the people who followed them were different culturally and psychologically. As Cheryl Lynn Greenberg pointed out in her history of Black-Jewish relationships, "Both communities recognized reasons to cooperate, but also found themselves at odds given the asymmetries between them in class, historical experience, and racial identity."[7] In addition, there were tensions in northern ghetto areas, where Jewish merchants were frequently accused, rightly or not, of economic exploitation.

The high points of Black-Jewish cooperation came first with joint legal efforts in *Brown* and then with the success of the civil rights movement led by Martin Luther King Jr. American Jews not only supported him financially[8] but marched in disproportionate numbers with him, registered voters for him, and, with the murders of Andrew Goodman and Michael Schwerner, suffered with him. King did connect Jews of the present with Moses and a Jewish narrative of the past. A close friend of King's, Rabbi Joachim Prinz, expelled from Germany in 1937, was one of the organizers of the March on Washington in August 1963. His lead-in remarks preceding King's historic "I Have a Dream" speech compared Nazism and Jews, on the one hand, to American racism and Blacks on the other. He began his speech, "The Issue is Silence," as follows:

> I speak to you as an American Jew. When I was the Rabbi of the Jewish community in Berlin under the Hitler regime, I learned many things. The most important thing that I learned under those tragic circumstances was that bigotry and hatred are not the most urgent problems. The most urgent, the most disgraceful, the most shameful and the most tragic problem is silence . . . America must not become a nation of onlookers. America must not remain silent.[9]

Both nonreligious Jews and Jewish religious leaders encouraged Jews to engage in the battle against racism. Abraham Joshua Heschel, who later marched with King from Selma to Montgomery, Alabama, was a keynote speaker that same year at the National Conference on Religion and Race prior to the passage of the Civil Rights Act of 1964:

> At the first conference on religion and race, the main partici-pants were Pharaoh and Moses. . . . The outcome of that sum-mit meeting has not come to an end. Pharaoh is not ready to capitulate. The exodus began, but is far from having been com-pleted. In fact it was easier for the children of Israel to cross the Red Sea than for a Negro to cross certain university campuses.[10]

Speaking publicly in the tension-filled day before his death, pre-dicting freedom but also the likelihood that he, like Moses, would not be there when it happened, King said, "I've been to the mountaintop. And I've looked over. And I've seen the Promised Land. And I may not get there with you, but I want you to know tonight that we as a people will get to the Promised Land."

The 1964 civil rights movement, which produced the legal end to segregation in public facilities and the Voting Rights Act of 1965, was the zenith of Black-Jewish cooperation. The focus in the latter part of the 1960s swung to Black Power advocates, to Afrocentric leaders, and to a search for new militant ways of supporting Black interests, for little had changed economically or socially for Blacks after the laws were passed.

The Black Power movement gave greater voice to Afrocentric mil-itants and identified American Blacks with other victims of colonial-ism. Their demands for immediate change galvanized much of black America. Stokely Carmichael and Charles Hamilton's 1966 book, *Black Power,* was a *cri de coeur* against the slow pace of progress and integra-tion by the predominantly white liberal coalition. An affirmation of power by a part of America long subjugated resonated with the black community, even if it knew that its most extreme elements, such as the Black Panthers, would not survive.

I believe that there are moral connections that have been, and remain, the underlying historic and psychological basis for a continued but reorganized Black-Jewish alliance. Both groups have been victims of intense discrimination, the Jews primarily in Europe, African Americans in the United States. Both can rightly claim to have been victims of extreme intolerance and of society's unwillingness to accommodate human differences. And both have an enduring investment in social justice.

Part of the reason for tensions between political allies is accounted for by social and economic differences. But experiences of discrimination and hatred link the two groups. Many Blacks look at American Jews resentfully, seeing them simply as white people, high achievers in most areas of economic and professional life. They have little knowledge of how Jews were persecuted and almost annihilated seventy years ago. They do know, however, that whatever resistance American Jews faced in America, it was clearly not as fierce as what Blacks suffered. It is hard to argue with James Baldwin's assessment that "one does not wish, in short, to be told by an American Jew that his suffering is as great as the American Negro's suffering. It isn't."[11] The black scholar Gerald Early has pointed out:

> In America, the situation is no longer the same as it was in Europe. Although Jews insist that their suffering not be forgotten in the American context, to the African American it is largely irrelevant because the Jew is white. In the United States it is the black who is the Jew, victim of pogroms, the outcast, the American Ishmael.[12]

Militant Blacks describe American slavery as the "Black Holocaust." The result has been a useless argument over "comparative victimhood." The use of the term Holocaust allows both groups to speak past each other. Jewish memories are strong, the Holocaust frightening and unique to Jewish life in Europe: slavery and its racist aftermath are frightening and very much American—both different, both the residue of intolerance, both horrifying.

However, the economic condition of Blacks was static, and, as a result, change was slow. The strong new voices of Black Power, Afrocentrism, and militancy not only became louder, but offered a clear non-integrationist approach to making gains—promoting collective, not just individual, benefits for Blacks produced by economic opportunity alone. Group gains, not simply individual ones, were said to be necessary to overcome the residue of past racism. Community control of schools, fixed quotas in hiring in formerly restricted trades and professions such as police, fire, and schools were also declared necessary. For Jews, a fair opportunity to compete was sufficient for success; Blacks found the hurdle of prolonged denial of education and centuries-long exclusion too great without collective help. Jews, who had long been highly educated, had sufficient cultural and economic capital to make major advances despite social anti-Semitism. Jews were, in fact, the poster boys and girls for equal opportunity, which had been the original goal of the liberal and integrationist idea behind the civil rights movement.

As a result, there was a growing tension when the bars of discrimination dropped for Jews but not for Blacks. As President Lyndon Johnson noted when he first promoted affirmative action, "You do not take a person who, for years, has been hobbled by chains and liberate him, bring him up to the starting line of a race and then say, 'you are free to compete with all the others,' and still justly believe that you have been completely fair."[13] The paradigm of liberal integration—equal opportunity—worked for Jews who enjoyed far more cultural capital; but for many Blacks it just made Jews seem more like other Whites who had benefited from White/Black inequality. As James Baldwin observed in 1967:

> The Jew profits from his status in America and must expect the Negroes to distrust him for it. . . . In the American context, the most ironical thing about Negro anti-Semitism is that the Negro is really condemning the Jew for having become an American White man.[14]

Jews have mostly held to a belief in individual progress through equal opportunity—the integrationist paradigm. But the concept was severely tested a year later in the Ocean Hill-Brownsville school conflict of 1968, when the issue of group demands erupted. A community-control issue in Ocean Hill, New York, quickly led to a conflict between a predominantly Jewish teachers union and a black community group seeking to transfer white teachers, predominantly Jewish, out of the district, and to replace them with black teachers. Former allies screamed at each other across police barricades. Anti-Jewish rants exploded at group rallies and on black radio stations.[15]

Other breaches between allies opened at the national level. In a series of Supreme Court cases, the Court ruled against trade unions and fire and police departments in favor of black petitioners objecting to exclusionary practices—petitions supported by Jewish groups and other liberal allies. When opponents of the rulings stonewalled the Court's demands to open the hiring processes, the Court permitted the use of compulsory numerical quotas. In 1978, black petitioners brought the issue of quotas to a head in the *Regents of the University of California v. Bakke* case, which deeply split Blacks and Jews. Three leading Jewish organizations—the American Jewish Committee, the Anti-Defamation League of B'nai B'rith, and the American Jewish Congress—took the side of the plaintiff, Bakke, who was protesting his exclusion from medical school because of a quota that made Whites ineligible for a specific number of slots reserved for minorities; all black groups supported the quotas. The use of quotas, the severest form of affirmative action, produced a major rift between former allies, and though almost all white Americans opposed hard quotas for Blacks, the fact that Jews also opposed them created a serious, though not fatal, breach in Black-Jewish relationships.[16]

The use of quotas had historical and present-day implications for Jews. Quotas had been commonly used *against* Jews, limiting their numbers in various institutions, particularly colleges and graduate schools, and in employment. Although restrictions evaporated when Jewish quotas were lifted in the 1960s and 1970s, Jews remembered. Quotas in present-day America were frightening for Jews who were heavily over-represented in many professions. Should admission into these occupations be allocated by quota rather than merit, it would, many felt, curtail the ability of Jews to advance.

The closeness of the Supreme Court's 5–4 *Bakke* ruling against the use of hard quotas for college admissions indicated that the history of racism and discrimination against black Americans required a different remedy. The Court jumped into the fray with its endorsement of the Harvard Plan, a type of affirmative action that was short of quotas, but nevertheless endorsed *some* collective benefit for black Americans on admissions. On the theory that student diversity was an overall advantage to the university and to education in general, the Court essentially allowed some consideration of collective disadvantage as a meaningful factor in admitting black applicants.

Jewish neoconservatives, who had led the opposition in *Bakke*, objected to the compromise, claiming that promoting diversity through the Harvard Plan was just as much a discriminatory affirmative action plan as quotas. The stridency of this argument, appearing frequently in both neoconservative and conservative publications, had an effect on American public opinion. The idea of affirmative action is still disapproved of by 75 to 80 percent of respondents and is closely associated with quotas in the mind of the electorate. But claims made by Jewish neoconservatives that promoting racial diversity is really the equivalent of quotas is not wholly accurate. The goal of racial diversity is, of course, a collective benefit, but if it were a real quota, then after decades of application of the Harvard Plan the number of Blacks admitted to higher educational institutions would parallel their proportion in the population as a whole.

The stated goal for black admissions at Swarthmore College, where I taught for thirty years, was 11 percent of the entering student body in 1979, yet actual admissions at that time reached only about 7 percent. Similar shortfalls existed in other institutions. The results indicate that the Court's endorsement of the Harvard Plan has produced *a* collective benefit, but not *the* collective benefit of a quota.

Affirmative action divided Blacks and Jews in the early efforts to promote a legal quota system for educational advancement; but the compromise of taking the racist past into consideration as *one* factor in admission decisions as against *the* factor has eased tensions. I noted earlier that research showed Jews were willing to support policies and resources to remedy past discrimination, but not by supporting quota-directed policies. Other sources of tension, such as the ardent support of some black leaders for the Palestinian cause, nevertheless did not interfere with the alliance between black and Jewish members in the United States House and Senate, though they did in society at large. In Congress, the Black Caucus supports aid to Israel, and Jewish members support social welfare and economic policies important to African Americans. The alliance has had its troubles, but it is clearly still alive.

Recently, scholars such as Cheryl Greenberg and Eric Goldstein have published new research concerning Black-Jewish relationships over time. They identify the complex relationship of these two groups. For my purposes, the research directs further attention to the ambiguous and changeable basis of Jewish self-identification by race, as well as the perception of that identity by Christian America. Understanding the changing perceptions of Jews in America, and the changing basis of Jewish self-identification, can tell us much about assimilative Jewish life, and help to define the different elements that can do much to answer a key question: Are American Jews truly different?

There were periods during which some non-Jews considered Jews a separate race. Many Jews identified themselves as a race apart as well. Always aware that in America the crucial divide of opportunity was between Black and White, many Jews defined themselves as "a white race of a different kind."[17] Prior to the 1870s, Jews did not self-identify in racial terms, but rather described themselves as did the eminent Rabbi Isaac Mayer Wise in 1859: "We are Jews in the Synagogue and Americans everywhere." It was a clear statement of what Americanization meant in that early period of American Jewish life. Later, Jews were not immune from what became a redefinition of "race," one that departed from the main division of Black vs. White into new sub-racial categories based on national origin and prior nationality— that is, the German race, the French race, and the English race. While non-Jews focused increasingly on the supposed racial differences between Jews and themselves, Jews went further than other "nationalities" in accepting and promoting their own "racial" differences. It was a case, noted the scholar Charles Liebman, where Jews were trying to balance two competing impulses: wanting to integrate into modern American life, and wanting to survive as distinctly Jewish in an open and absorbing culture.[18] In the early twentieth century, rabbis and lay leaders alike, fearing that a lack of distinctiveness in an open society would eventually dissolve non-Orthodox Jews into generic Americans, moved away from their earlier claims that Jews were simply a religious denomination; even Reform rabbis, who had originally defined Jews by religion alone, did so. It was a time when national and cultural differences were looked upon as indicating deeper elements of difference, and claims of prior national distinctiveness slipped easily into claims of race.

Many Jews, religious or not, embraced the concept of a distinct Jewish race as a means of a distinctive emotional expression from battered pride, desire for self-defense, and because a simply religious definition was insufficient to express the Jewish sense of unity and peoplehood. Jews knew, however, that such racialism, while it could and did give Jews an opportunity to counter negative racial stereotypes with positive "racial" accomplishments, was a dangerous type of defense.

In this same period, the cities expanded tenfold, industry developed, and capitalism went largely unfettered, all of which challenged Jewish and non-Jewish communal life. Unlike similar modernizing nations in Western Europe, America in the period from 1870 to 1920 experienced a huge expansion of its population and a major increase in the diversity of that population. Not only was America leading in its development of democratic institutions, but it was simultaneously a modernizing state absorbing major additions of diverse nationalities—with the optimistic goal of "melting" them in the pot of "Americanness."

The combination of social stress from industrial change, the leap of immigration, the violent Bolshevist Revolution beginning in 1917 in Russia, and the "Red Scare" in the 1920s extended a long period of anti-Semitism. It was sustained by the seeking of age-old "scapegoats" for the cause of the Great Depression and continued through World War II. If a prolonged period of prejudice, lasting almost seven decades, could exist in America, how can one still say that America's attitude toward Jews differs from that of Western Europe? The difference lies in the distinction between prejudice and discrimination. Prejudice is a frequent emotion responding to social and personal disruption and perceived unfairness—whether true or imagined. Discrimination is government-imposed penalties or limitations on those who are the object of the prejudice. Governmental discrimination is meted out with severity and specific consequences. For those on the receiving end, the most important element is the level of governmental restraint that keeps prejudices, of which there are many, from becoming public laws.

While hostility toward Jews found social leaders who were willing to discriminate against Jews in private matters, the political system in the United States restrained attempts by the social system to let such attitudes penetrate public policy and curtail or inhibit Jewish rights. There were no efforts, for instance, to challenge the political rights of Jews, which were granted at the nation's founding. It is worth emphasizing that such steadfastness of the national government, even in the face of attempts to demonize Jews by anti-Semitic organizations, was a clear and sharp difference between Europe and American Jewish communities and their governments. Also, there were many more social, intellectual and political leaders who spoke out against anti-Semitism. When the German economic recession of the mid-1870s led to violent agitation against Jews, the violence went mostly unremarked by the nation's political leaders; whereas in the United States many non-Jewish leaders, including presidents, often raised their voices publicly in opposition to anti-Jewish agitation.

In the United States, American Blacks and American Jews have had a much more intertwined relationship than most other Whites had with Blacks over the last century. Although Jews in the South were generally cowed by vigilante violence if they stood up to racism, in the North, Jewish concerns were evidenced by their disproportionate participation in civil rights organizations and support for housing opportunities. In addition, Jewish philanthropists disproportionately supported the initial development of black schools and colleges in the South when it was segregated and promising black students had no educational alternative.[19]

While the Jewish fight against discrimination had a strong element of self-interest, it also had antecedents. At one level of religious life, Jews have had a strong focus on justice in the here and now. The Torah, the core of Jewish learning for thousands of years, is not simply "the law," but, more broadly, justice made clear in the commandment of Deuteronomy: *Zedek, Zedek, tirof*—"Justice, Justice, shalt thou pursue." That particular command hangs over the desk of Supreme Court Justice Ruth Bader Ginsburg, who has said that to do justice—to pursue social justice—was an obligation of her Jewish heritage. Felix Frankfurter, she added, the Jewish Harvard professor appointed to the Court by FDR in the Depression, exemplified Jewish support for black advancement by appointing William T. Coleman as the Court's first African-American law clerk. Justice Ginsburg, in a speech at the Touro Synagogue in Newport, Rhode Island, asked rhetorically: "What is the difference between a New York City garment district bookkeeper and a Supreme Court Justice?" Her answer: "Just one generation"—her own life.[20]

Over one hundred years ago, when the board of the NAACP elected a Jew as both a founder and the first president of the organization, Jews and Blacks had a deeply intertwined relationship, which eventually, despite short-term tensions, produced in *Brown* the most sweeping change in the status of black people in a century—bringing, finally, federal justice over sectional justice.

Not all Jews have been assertive in supporting black rights and interests. But lack of intolerance among most Jews and their more favorable attitudes toward African Americans are shown by their behavior. A National Election Day Survey, conducted by the *New York Times* and CBS in 2008, found that the first presidential election involving an African American revealed much about the willingness, in the privacy of the voting booth, to support a black man who had been born into an America riven by segregation. Although issues other than race were involved in the election, of course, there is evidence, mainly geographical, indicating that *some* negative racial evaluations were part of the vote. Figure 3 (below) clearly reveals that as one goes deeper into the formerly segregated South, the White vote for President Obama markedly diminishes. Thus, while the White vote in the northern regions of the East, Midwest, and West was 49 percent for Obama, it fell to 30 percent in the Southern region as a whole, to 19 percent in the deep Southern States as a group, and to as low as 11 percent in Mississippi, 10 percent in Alabama, and 14 percent in Louisiana.

That Jews voted overwhelmingly (80 percent) for Obama in 2008, 30 percent more than white Catholics and 44 percent more than white Protestants, is remarkable. It correlates strongly with more favorable Jewish attitudes about race discussed earlier—and also with more favorable Jewish attitudes toward federal governmental activism in

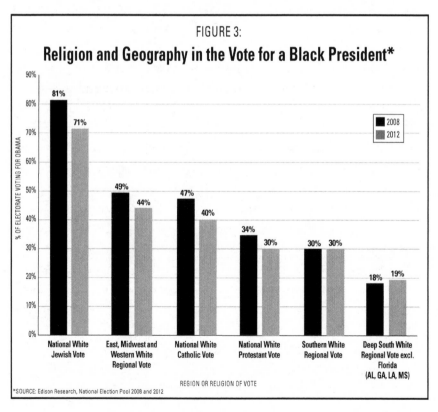

FIGURE 3:

Religion and Geography in the Vote for a Black President*

*SOURCE: Edison Research, National Election Pool 2008 and 2012

general. When one looks closely at Figure 3, the strength of residual racist feeling becomes increasingly apparent as one goes South. When the election of 2012 is specifically examined in Figure 3, the same distinctive patterns of past voting are clearly discerned. Despite the slight decline of Whites voting for President Obama overall, and the unprecedented conservative efforts in the United States and Israel to depress Jewish votes for Obama, the same liberal disproportion of Jews continues: approximately 70 percent of Jews voted for Obama, compared to less than 30 percent of white Protestants and 40 percent of white Catholics—a substantial and continuing difference between religious cultures.

For African Americans, the experience of the political structure working *for* them, as it had done for American Jews, instead of *against* them, is only decades old. Freedom from discrimination is an ongoing process, yet the country has begun to move toward George Washington's ideal, where the appreciation of diversity affords special benefits to the country and must be protected. While the election of a black president does tell us much about how far we have come, it does not tell us much about how far we have to go. Jewish life, entwined as it has been in issues of social justice, still has an important role to play.

Prologue to Chapter Nine

A fter the UN partition of Palestine into two territories, one largely Jewish and one Arab Palestinian, Israel declared its territory a sovereign state. The other territory did not declare a state, preferring to wait for the many armies of the Arab countries to sweep the Israelis out, leaving both territories for the Arabs to determine. America and other countries imposed an arms embargo, which did not, however, prevent either side from getting small arms by illegal gunrunning. My Jewish friend Bert Cooper, a pilot in the Pacific during World War II, was one of a number of pilots who flew clandestine missions to secret landing fields in Czechoslovakia to bring small arms and munitions to beleaguered Israel.

Six Arab armies invaded the Jewish state in 1948, but they were successfully fought to a standstill. Then, nineteen years later, seeking revenge for Arab failure, Egyptian President General Gamal Abdel Nasser removed the UN buffer troops between Israel and Egypt, blockaded an Israeli seaport, and announced on radio that his army would drive Israelis into the sea. Dread settled into the hearts of most American Jews, mine included, as a second Holocaust seemed about to happen. Fighting in 1948 had involved small arms, almost like sticks and stones; now, in 1967, Egypt had over 300 MIG fighter planes from the Soviet Union and hundreds of tanks. The American embargo of arms to the Middle East had deprived Israel of American planes and tanks, forcing Israel to purchase less-tested French jets and tanks as well as Czechoslovakian munitions.

Advised by their main armorer, General Charles de Gaulle, not to strike first, despite provocation and public threats, Israel struck anyway with force and accuracy, so that in a matter of hours Egyptian, Syrian, and other Arab air forces were mostly destroyed. A potential catastrophe had become an astounding triumph in just a few days, and the mood of American Jews turned from fear to euphoria. The Holocaust generations had seen redemption, and de Gaulle found out that the defense of Israel was strictly in Israeli hands, not dependent on any of the European nations who had failed Jews before.

Sometimes, however, a victory can be too great, setting in motion actions and attitudes that bring about new problems with old adversaries. Only six years later, in 1973, Egyptian armies surprised complacent Israeli intelligence by suddenly invading. Though the Israelis were victorious, it cost them over 4,000 casualties. The unexpected strike also led to the fall of the Labor government and to a new conservative dominance in Israeli politics.

The costs of war were driven home to me when I was teaching at Swarthmore College years later. A former Israeli tank officer came to the college as a visiting professor in economics. His tank had been destroyed in the surprise Egyptian attack, and he sustained severe burns. Despite many operations, his face was one enormous burn wound that could not be restored, which reminded me how vastly different Israeli Jewish life was from my own Jewish life in America.

The character of Israeli Jews, a product of European and Muslim anti-Semitism, has been indelibly stamped both by their pioneering efforts to build a country and by the constant hostility of the Muslim nations that surround them. Despite historic, familial, and religious linkages between Jews, powerful differences in their surrounding environments and the distinctive internal cultures of each country have worked to divide the characteristics and attitudes of the two largest Jewish communities in the world. It has produced a generational tension among American Jews about Israeli policies that stem from the two distinctive environments in which Jews live, and it has shaped the character qualities needed to advance each of the two societies.

Chapter Nine

The Promised Land: Here or There?

A merican Jews and American Blacks have something in common besides discrimination—their non-European roots—that
still shapes their lives and imaginations. For Blacks, it is their African homeland where they were enslaved and brought to America. For
Jews, their forcible dispersion from their land in Israel after their defeat by Rome in AD 70 led to almost 2,000 years of discrimination
against a people without a homeland. That homeland, however, was
kept alive in their imaginations, as evidenced by the traditional Jewish
farewell expression of hope to see one another "next year in Jerusalem."

The rebirth of Israel as a state in 1948 afforded American Jews, unlike black Americans, a realistic choice between returning to the land
of their roots or remaining in America. The reestablishment of Israel by the Zionist pioneers, an effect of the Holocaust, and American
political influence turned imagination into reality. Israelis implored
(and expected) American Jews to return from the Diaspora, wherever
they were, and live the only "authentic" Jewish life in the new Israel.
But it did not happen: American Jews heard the Zionist call to return,
but did not respond. Unlike many Jews in Europe and in the Muslim
world who did respond, the Zionist call to Jews in America, the evidence will show, resulted in a negligible net emigration to Israel for
over sixty years. Where is the Promised Land for American Jews, here
or there?

Many books examine the political and social events that led to the creation of a Jewish state. More still need to be written. This book, however, will focus narrowly on Zionism and Israel in the minds of American Jews. The very creation and rapid strengthening of the State of Israel has been an extraordinary and largely unexpected development of Zionist ideas that percolated in Europe in the last half of the nineteenth century. Fed by the notion of cultural rejuvenation through the rebirth of a Jewish nation, as articulated by men such as Achad Ha'am and Leon Pinsker, and galvanized into political organization by Theodor Herzl's *Der Judenstaat* (*The Jewish State*), published in Vienna in 1896, the Zionist idea came to fruition. After the UN voted to partition Palestine into two territories in November 1947, the Jewish territory declared itself the Nation of Israel in May 1948. The new nation was immediately granted formal recognition by the United States under President Harry Truman.

While Israel's safety and well-being remain a cause of concern for most present-day American Jews, the relationship between American Jews and the Jewish state has been complex and ambiguous. In fact, the thrust of Zionism's demand for the restoration of the Jewish nation was the direct result of European Jews' experience of hostility. Indeed, the most distinctive aspect of the Zionist response was its "Europeanness," created out of centuries of prejudice and discrimination, and the belief that Europe was incapable of changing its deep strains of anti-Semitism.

From Leon Pinsker and Achad Ha'am in Russia to Herzl in the more assimilative Western Europe, the Zionist responses to anti-Semitism galvanized Jews to consider the idea of self-emancipation in their own homeland. At its core, it proposed the reawakening of the Jewish character that had been muted by many centuries of ghettoized life. Writing about his fellow assimilative European Jews, Herzl noted, "They do not suspect it, but they are ghetto-natures, quiet, decent, timid. That is what most of us are. Will they understand the call to freedom and to manhood?"[1]

The historian Hasia Diner contrasts the intimidated and reluctant attitudes of European Jews with those of American-born Jews when, during the Civil War, General Grant expelled all Jews not in uniform from his district command (Mississippi, Kentucky, Tennessee). "Such things had happened to Jews before, in Europe. But the United States was different. European Jews affected by orders like Grant's had packed their bags and moved somewhere else. But the Jews of Paducah, Kentucky, knowing the Constitution and US law protected them, sent a representative to Washington to meet with President Lincoln, express their outrage, and demand a change in policy. Lincoln . . . immediately canceled Grant's order."[2]

The call of Zionism for the "new Jew" of Europe—the Eurocentric foundation of Zionism—was expressed by Herzl, himself a highly assimilated journalist and a nonpracticing Jew from Vienna. Writing at the time of hostile outbreaks of anti-Jewish rioting in Republican France in the 1890s, he exploded, "No one can deny the gravity of the situation of the Jews. Wherever they live in perceptible numbers, they are more or less persecuted. Their equality before the law, granted by statute, has become practically a dead letter. They are debarred from filling even moderately high positions, either in the army, or in any public or private capacity."[3]

While the call for a Jewish state had proponents and opponents, the idea had the effect of opening an emotional debate, producing high levels of Jewish reaction, while bringing the issue to the agenda of interested European governments. Some leaders in England, France, and Germany, vying for hegemony in the Middle East, initially saw an allied Jewish state as an advantage for their own economic interests. Others, particularly after the discovery of oil in the region, endorsed the Arab rejection of a Jewish state in Palestine. A few saw the establishment of a Jewish homeland as biblical redemption; even more saw it as a chance to rid their country of many of its own Jews.

In America, Zionism gained little traction. For one thing, Zionism was a *European* phenomenon. For another, American Jews believed that a good and full Jewish life could be lived in America, the *goldenah Medinah*. Zionism was rejected by Jews in America especially among Central European immigrants, native-born Jews, and even by the majority of immigrants from Eastern Europe. The rejection of Zionism by Reform Judaism in the last decades of the 1800s into the early part of the twentieth century was almost total, with their rabbis denying the principle that Jews could never be able to have a full and normal life except in a Jewish state. As Melvin Urofsky's study of America in this period noted, Zionist support was found mostly among some newly arrived Russian Jews—German Jews considered it an "alien" philosophy. Urofsky pointed out that Kaufmann Kohler, rabbi of Beth-El in New York and subsequently the head of Hebrew Union College, "identified Zionism as one of the 'oriental' aspects of the new immigrants, and called their prayers for a return to Jerusalem 'a blasphemy and lie upon the lips of every American Jew.'"⁴

When the Zionists held their first meeting of the Basel Congress in 1897, it provoked a stream of denunciation from the Central Conference of American Rabbis (CCAR) and the Union of American Hebrew Congregations (UAHC), both of which rejected the Zionist idea that American Jews were still in "exile." There was some support from Orthodox rabbis, but the most traditional among them objected to the Zionist goal of "return" as being a secular endeavor, to be pursued only after the coming of the awaited Messiah.

American Jews—in particular the wealthier Reform Jewish leaders—were sensitive to, and supportive of, efforts to alleviate the suffering of Jews in Eastern Europe, and of Russian Jews after the Tsar was assassinated in 1881, unleashing hundreds of pogroms. In 1903, the murder of a young Gentile near the Russian town of Kishineff, later found to be committed by one of his relatives, was said to have been committed by Jews needing blood to make Passover matzoh. The false accusation set off many more anti-Jewish pogroms and riots across Russia over the next three years. Despite petitions by both Jews and non-Jews, and the efforts of President Theodore Roosevelt and a joint resolution by Congress condemning Russian behavior, Russian authorities rejected any discussion of an issue they considered an internal matter.⁵

The German Jewish community in America never considered accepting Zionism, but they did take action after the Kishineff murder by forming the American Jewish Committee (AJC). The Committee was backed by the elites of the German Jewish community—Louis Marshall, Julius Rosenwald, Oscar Strauss, Cyrus Adler—and became active in defense against the anti-Semitic atrocities abroad and in aid of new, poverty-stricken Jewish immigrants from Eastern Europe. Jews fleeing poverty and pogroms in Eastern Europe resulted in a huge expansion of the American Jewish population in America, multiplying it more than nine times in just three decades.

Such rapid change in the size and nature of the American Jewish population created tension for highly assimilative and acculturated Jews, most of them from Central Europe, whose families had long before left behind the European ghettos and traditional Orthodox life. Nevertheless, America's German Jewish leaders did aid the new immigrants, in part out of genuine compassion for fellow Jews, but also to prevent them from embarrassing the older, assimilated generations.

The influx of Eastern European Jews enlarged the Jewish population in America to seven times the number of Jews in Germany, twelve times the number of French Jews, and almost twenty times the number of English Jews. Within a few decades American Jews became the largest concentration of Jews in the world, and within a few generations, those immigrants from the ghettos of Eastern Europe would turn themselves into successful and accomplished citizens.

American opportunity was clearly a reason for the initial rejection of Zionist ideas. But after the pogroms of the early 1900s, America's Jews began to see the value of a refuge for ill-treated European Jews. Yet Zionism preached more than refuge alone: its adherents believed in the redemption of Jews through a "normal" life from "exile" by a Zionist "return" to the Promised Land. But American Jews felt they had their own "promised land," and rejected the idea that living only in a Jewish state could provide the fullness of Jewish religious culture and freedom. Herzl claims in *The Jewish State* that "everything depends on our propelling force. And what is that force? The misery of the Jews."[6] And further, "The nations in whose midst Jews live are all either covertly or openly anti-Semitic."[7]

Until war broke out in 1914, American Zionism was a weakly organized and widely rejected ideology. Then one of America's most prominent nonreligious Jews, Louis Brandeis, became an ardent, dedicated Zionist, and his ideas flourished. Brandeis, then a prominent Boston lawyer, became the first well-known assimilative Jew to become an outspoken American Zionist.[8] At first, Brandeis saw the plight of the European Jews primarily as creating a need for a place of refuge, and he synthesized Zionism and Americanism into a common set of ethical standards. He ignored the cultural, religious, or nationalistic elements in Zionism and focused on building a homeland for European Jews, legitimizing and Americanizing the Zionist enterprise for its Jewish and Gentile supporters. He played down the Zionist ideas that Jewish redemption was only possible in their own state, and that American Jews were living in "exile." Brandeis's biographer, Melvin Urofsky, found that he "envisioned a secular society populated by Jews who lived according to American values that Brandeis conflated with those of the prophets."[9] To overcome the tensions of "dual loyalty," Brandeis embraced the writings of a young philosopher, Horace Kallen, who proposed a new approach to American immigrant absorption, replacing the "melting pot" idea with what he called "cultural pluralism." Urofsky described this concept of hyphenated-American pluralism as fully compatible with Brandeis's thinking about dual loyalty, concerns about which forestalled nearly all German Jews from supporting Zionism.

"Kallen believed that in fact immigrants, no matter how hard they would try, never lost the cultural traits of their home countries, and this is what made America great," Urofsky wrote. "Rather than discard their uniqueness, immigrants contributed to a unique American tapestry in which each ethnic group retained some of its own individual flavor while making the whole that much richer. The retention of Old World cultures, Kallen argued, did not lessen one's loyalty to America, but reinforced it."[10] The idea of cultural pluralism resonated with Brandeis. It enabled him to downplay the fervent nationalism of the European Zionists, as well as the Zionist idea of the personal return from "exile."

With the advent of World War I, the World Zionist Organization, headquartered in Berlin, was in disarray. European Zionists then looked for support to the then-neutral United States. At an emergency meeting of various Zionist factions, Brandeis announced the creation of the Provisional Executive Committee for General Zionist Affairs (PEC), an umbrella group for the organization and relief of distressed European Jews. As chairman, Brandeis became the leading American advocate of Zionism, giving it a new American definition and legitimacy. It marked an important turning point in the development of Zionism in America. For Brandeis himself, it began a lifelong interest in the creation of a Jewish homeland, which he believed was needed to save European Jewry.

In 1916, President Wilson nominated Brandeis to the US Supreme Court, and after a long and heated set of congressional hearings—there were some who didn't want a Jewish justice—he was confirmed as the first Jewish member of the Court. But he remained active in the organization of the Provisional Executive Committee, and became an advisor to President Wilson on many issues, particularly whether the president should approve Great Britain's efforts to establish a Jewish homeland in Palestine. But the famous Balfour Declaration (named for Lord Arthur Balfour, England's foreign secretary at the time) favoring a Jewish homeland would not have been made had it not fit in with Great Britain's colonial interests in the Middle East. And for a "declaration" its language was decidedly noncommittal: "His Majesty's Government view with favor the establishment of a national home for the Jewish people, and will use their best efforts to facilitate the achievement of this object."[11]

The Balfour Declaration was sent to President Wilson to secure his approval, but although Wilson was in favor of the principle he thought the timing was premature. Brandeis informed Colonel Edward M. House, Wilson's top advisor, of the need to act quickly—and Wilson's approval was duly sent. Brandeis's role was critical in expanding the growth of American Zionism, but he succeeded only by downplaying crucial issues of Zionist nationalism, including the required "return" of Diaspora Jews to the Zionist homeland. Until the early 1920s, Chaim Weizmann and other European Zionists, although chafing at Brandeis's American interpretation of Zionism, had deferred to Brandeis because of his influence with American Jews. But by the beginning of the 1920s, the deep divisions over the question of "exile" split the alliance between the European-oriented Zionism and Brandeis's American Zionism.

The underlying differences were real and long-lasting. The Misrachi, the religious Zionists, felt that religion had been ignored; the Hebraicists believed that Brandeis had underplayed the role of Hebrew as a living language, and that European Zionism's nationalistic commitment to Jewish "restoration" and "cultural revival" were not genuinely appreciated by the Americans. In 1921, the division between the Zionism of Europe and that of America came to a head when Weizmann accused the Americans of "lacking in historic understanding of Jewish life and wanting in the Jewish soul."[12] In a Cleveland meeting of the National Executive Committee (the Zionist group in America), Weizmann's Eurocentric wing defeated the American wing organizationally by a two-to-one margin, precipitating the resignation of its president, Julian Mack, who then read a letter of resignation from Brandeis himself. Then, after a stunned silence, Mack read a letter of resignation from thirty-six important Committee members, including Stephen Wise, Nathan Straus, Horace Kallen, and Felix Frankfurter. While all those who had resigned pledged to stay on as ordinary members and continue to fight for a Jewish homeland, the sounds of weeping resonated in the room. The Brandeis era of Zionism had ended. That division, though obscured by the growing need of a refuge for Jews both before and after the Holocaust, remains a source of potential conflict between American and Israeli Zionists.

While Zionist groups continued their activity during the rise of Nazism in the 1930s, Great Britain, with its growing interest in Arab oil, was gradually retreating from its Balfour Declaration. In a White Paper of 1939, the British indefinitely postponed the establishment of a Jewish homeland and sharply lowered quotas for Jewish immigration to Palestine. Though Zionist organizations and a few wealthy European Jews had fed the development of Jewish Palestine with purchased land, most American Jews turned their resources to the support of Jewish refugees, either for the few who could make it to Palestine, or for the larger number seeking emigration from Hitler's Europe.

In the post-Holocaust period, oil interests (two thirds of the world's proven oil reserves were underneath Arab lands when the war ended), the British government, and the US State Department were all opposed to the Zionists of Palestine and American supporters of a Jewish homeland, who included a varied assortment of non-Jewish supporters such as President Truman, congressional leaders, media figures, and sympathetic Christian leaders. With more than 100,000 Jews still in displaced persons camps two years after the war, and with the growing realization of the scope and horrors of the Holocaust, a consensus formed among non-Jewish Americans in favor of a homeland for displaced Jews. American Jews across the board—Zionists and non-Zionists—favored the creation of a Jewish state in Israel as a refuge from persecution.

In America, intense pressure was brought by David Ben-Gurion and other Palestinian Zionists for a United Nations decision in favor of a Jewish homeland. The British, who had renounced any role of trusteeship for their former mandate in Palestine, ceded responsibility for the area to the fledgling UN and promised to *oppose* the establishment of a Jewish state. In the spring of 1947, the UN formed the United Nations Special Committee on Palestine (UNSCOP) to investigate the issue and recommend an appropriate policy. The committee was composed of countries with no apparent stake in the outcome, so the United States, Britain, and the Soviet Union, among others, were excluded. The committee was led by Ralph Bunche, an African American, who organized the committee's travel, agenda, working papers, briefing, and testimony. Bunche's leadership was one of the decisive elements in the eventual creation of the state of Israel.

After visiting the displaced persons camps in Europe and meeting with the different factions in Palestine, Bunche took the initiative to secretly visit Menachem Begin, a Jewish revolutionary leader, in his hiding place. The historian Peter Grose describes part of that meeting:

> As he was leaving Begin's hideout, the no longer completely dispassionate diplomat said something that the future Prime

Minister of Israel never forgot: "I can understand you. I am also a member of a persecuted minority." Richard Crossman of Britain asked jocularly at one point if Bunche's exposure to Jews had made him anti-Semitic "yet." Bunche replied without humor, "That would be impossible." Caught-up short, Crossman turned equally serious, "Why?" "Because I've been a Negro for forty-two years. . . . I know the flavor of racial prejudice and racial persecution. A wise Negro can never be an anti-Semite."[13]

Bunche had developed two alternative proposals on which the UNSCOP Committee could vote. He managed to quell support for the first formula of a single unitary state combining 650,000 Jews with 1,200,000 Arabs. But he gained a majority—Canada, the Netherlands, Peru, Sweden, Uruguay, Guatemala, and Czechoslovakia—to support a *partition* into two territories, from which both a Jewish and a separate Palestinian state could emerge.

In addition to powerful economic and political interests, the personal and moral considerations of various leaders played a key role in the outcome. Arab oil interests and the goodwill of Arab leaders were important concerns, and Britain's diplomatic corps acted accordingly by opposing establishment of a Jewish state. On the other side, President Truman, against the opinion and machinations of the State Department and the advice of his Secretary of State, George C. Marshall, was the crucial force for the recognition of a Jewish state by the United Nations.

Angered by the persistent and aggressive lobbying by American Zionist groups, Truman would not meet with or take calls from the new and militant leader of American Zionism, Abba Hillel Silver, who had literally pounded on the president's desk in July 1946. Only a few Jewish friends could speak to Truman about the need for a Jewish state. Truman had long since decided what he wanted to see, and the partition idea served his purpose and beliefs.

The lobbying and infighting of different groups has been documented in excellent histories of the establishment of the Jewish state, but a brief look at the role of the Holocaust, the pioneering Zionist population of Israel, and American Jews is crucial to an understanding of the American Jewish reaction to Israel's founding. Surprisingly, many American Jews took no part in the fight for Jewish statehood. Even after World War II, there was apathy and confusion as to what was going on in Palestine. Acts of terrorism by the underground Irgun and other Jewish revolutionaries confused idealistic American Jews; even the *New York Times* opposed statehood. In addition, revered Jews such as the prominent Reform rabbi Judah Magnes supported a binational Palestine, dulling broad popular support for a single state and opening the door for activists. With militant Zionists excluded from hearings by President Truman, pro-statehood confidants of Truman such as Clark Clifford and David Niles fought the increasing pressure from the State Department, which was attempting to limit support for a single Jewish state.[14]

By the 1950s, approximately 94 percent of American Jews supported the state of Israel, but only two or three percent intended to emigrate to it. Division broke out over issues that Brandeis had papered over regarding Zionist demands for nationalism and authenticity. With statehood, what reason, committed Israelis asked, could American Jews have for not emigrating? At the twenty-third Zionist Congress in July 1951, Ben-Gurion's partisans led off with a slashing attack on American Jews, reopening the wounds of Eastern European Zionism's clash with American quasi-Zionists who saw a Jewish state as a refuge—for others.

Israeli speakers asked how a person could claim to be a good Jew if he wanted to live in despised exile rather than in the Israel of restoration. Quick and angry responses by American speakers followed: What right do you Israelis have to tell us we are inauthentic Jews and that we are not fulfilled in our adopted land? We support you in any way we can, but don't tell us we have to abandon our American loyalties and heritage! Ben-Gurion and other European Israelis could not let go of this issue for years, and, after many arguments and heated exchanges, Ben-Gurion demanded that anyone who claimed to support Zionism had "the duty of personal immigration."[15]

For travelers to Israel in 1960, such as myself, the question of where were the immigrants from America was part of almost every conversation. Although Israel was then only twelve years old, the patriotism of its citizens was strong, as was their disdain for American Jews who refused to emigrate. They believed, and would rudely express, that American Jews regularly accepted anti-Jewish scorn by Gentiles in order to live a soft, materialistic life. A 1962 study of *Sabra* (native-born to Israel) Jews revealed Israelis' opinions about how they differed from Diaspora Jews: Israelis saw themselves as physically exuberant, straightforward, and non-introverted; they saw the Diaspora Jews as weak, over-intellectual, and timid.[16] That view of Israeli toughness and American softness accords with the experience of many American travelers to Israel.

Israeli disdain for American Jews who would not emigrate reflected the European evaluation of how Jews lived in America. One had to acknowledge that there was still significant anti-Semitism in this country, though by the 1960s it had significantly abated. The case that American Jews enjoyed the benefits of the diversity of the American population was, however, hard to make to Israeli Jews. At different levels of Israeli society, the same themes were frequently sounded, and the same incredulity about the quality of American Jewish life manifested itself. Echoes of Ben-Gurion's insistence that good Jews must immigrate to Israel are still heard from some prominent Israeli leaders today.[17]

The early history of Israel had, however, a very positive psychological effect on American Jews, especially those who grew up believing in anti-Jewish stereotypes, such as Jews can't farm; Jews can't fight; Jews are parasites; Jews can't work with their hands. Israeli Jews proved all those stereotypes wrong. For religious Jews, the resurrection of Hebrew as a living language strengthened their sense that Israel had a uniquely Jewish cultural identity. For many nonreligious Jews, Israel represented either a homeland of choice or a choice of last resort.[18] It was a vibrant country, where almost everybody seemed Jewish, from the airplane pilot to the hotel porter.

During my visit there with my wife and friends, the differences were apparent. Israeli life exudes a culture of out-front disputatiousness that can shock even an American Jew used to a culture of argument. With a directness that can be disconcerting yet refreshing in its honesty, the level of customary self-assertion was extremely high. Writing fifty years later, David Brooks noted, "I find the place by turns exhausting, admirable, annoying, impressive and foreign." Brooks captures the Israeli essence when he writes, "They treat strangers as if they were their brothers-in-law and feel perfectly comfortable giving them advice on how to live."[19]

In 1967, Egyptian President Gamal Abdel Nasser demanded that the UN remove its buffer forces between the adversaries. He then blockaded routes to an Israeli port and publicly threatened to drive Israel into the sea, bringing a deep sense of dread to almost all American Jews, who feared another Holocaust. In response, Israel's air and tank assault brought quick victories over the collective armies of Egypt, Syria, Jordan, and Lebanon, which had other Arab support from Iraq and Saudi Arabia. The war produced euphoria not only in Israel, but among American Jews as well. The non-Jewish world was both surprised and awestruck by Israeli military prowess, which in less than three hours destroyed 300 of Egypt's 340 Soviet-built combat fighters. Syrians were quickly driven off the Golan Heights, from which they had periodically bombarded Israeli farming communities below; and Jordan lost the West Bank and the parts of Jerusalem they had secured in 1948.

What most Americans don't remember is that before the war of 1967, the United States did not supply weapons and fighter jets to Israel because of a United States embargo on arms to the countries of the Middle East. The Israeli air force consisted of French Mystères, and the French, along with Czechoslovakia, also provided most of the Israeli arms. Despite the Egyptian blockade of Israel, itself an act of war, French President de Gaulle insisted that Israel accept the first blow before fighting back. Israel's rejection of his advice brought about the end of French military supplies. In his press statement, tinged with anti-Jewish, not just anti-Israel, feelings, de Gaulle stated that the "Jewish people are elitist, self-assured, and domineering," reflecting one side of French opinion. Coming so soon after the Holocaust, de

Gaulle's remarks were considered a major insult not just to Israelis, but to all Jews.

The American government quickly became the principal supplier of arms to Israel, using the Jewish nation as an opposition force to Soviet intrusion into the Middle East. This began the close military relationship that has, with a few bumps, continued to this day. The victory of 1967, however, produced a laxity and overconfidence that resulted in Israel's being unprepared for the 1973 Yom Kippur invasion by Egypt. Before the Israelis could rally, and before they received American resupplies, Israel suffered over four thousand casualties, proportionately equivalent to America losing over two hundred thousand soldiers. The war ended with Egyptian forces still in the Sinai and Israeli tank commanders threatening Cairo. It was a frightening experience for both Israeli and American Jews, and it led to the fall of the Labor government, which had governed the country from its founding. Menachem Begin and his Likud Party took over, marking a conservative shift in Israeli politics and the beginning of divisions between liberal American Jews and a conservative Israeli government.

The alliance of the religious parties with Likud led to efforts to define who is a Jew. The new allies insisted that only Orthodox religious law should govern Gentile converts to Judaism. Proposed laws delegitimizing American Conservative, Reform, and Reconstruction conversions of non-Jews, and basically delegitimizing certain non-Orthodox religious practices, brought on fierce opposition from America's non-Orthodox religious leaders and nonreligious organizational leaders. Fears that American Jews would withdraw their support for Israel eventually led to a narrow defeat for the new legislation in the Israeli Parliament. America's "live and let live" attitude among assimilative American Jews pointed again to differences between Israeli and American Jews on the issue of the separation of organized religion and the state. The lack of such separation in Israel has long been opposed by many American Jews.

Although Israel's population is more secular than America's overall, its form of government is a European parliamentary system rather than America's presidential two-party system. A system that provides representation for small parties who gain as little as 2 percent of the total popular vote increases the possibilities for small Israeli parties to shape the coalitions needed to govern. No major party has ever had, even in Ben-Gurion's time of Labor dominance, a majority vote on its own; support from Orthodox religious parties has always been necessary to forming a winning coalition. As a result, Israel's religious parties have always been able to extract many concessions from the competing major parties. The different political system in America clearly separates organized religion from direct governmental power. American Jews discovered the difference when the minority power of the Orthodox parties almost succeeded in winning them control over American conversions to Judaism and the definition of who is a Jew. It reminded them of the different roles that religion plays in the two countries, and how deeply religion actually intrudes in the governing of the Israeli state.

Zionism has been exceptionally successful in its gathering of Jews from both the European continent and the Muslim lands from which Jews were, in effect, expelled. The establishment of Israel, and its success in defending itself, produced an emigration of almost 600,000 North African Jews, primarily to Israel but with some to Western countries, including America. The Zionist ingathering from Europe, the former Soviet Union, and the Muslim lands has helped to increase an Israeli population from 650,000 Jews at the origin of the state to approximately 5.7 million (as of this writing), edging out the United States as the home of the largest Jewish population in the world.

This has been offered as a prime reason for the source of Arab-Israeli conflict, but historians have documented strong Arab resistance to any Jewish settlements from early in the twentieth century. Still, the Israeli-Palestinian conflict results largely from two opposing but legitimate claims to the same land, where neither side can accept the position of the other. In large part it is a tragedy of two cultural groups, both with a long history of humiliation, struggling for redemption, and now intransigent. To Israelis, past anti-Semitism in Europe led to the extermination of a majority of Europe's Jews. That horror has produced a determination among Israel's people to make their own decisions about their own defense, regardless of the opinions of other nations who would not suffer the same degree of consequences from terrorism or the Iranian menace.

Arab humiliation came at the hands of a Western, Christian, industrial culture that replaced a once-powerful and dominant Muslim culture. In the last two hundred years, the Ottoman Empire—one that had advanced militarily deep into Europe—has been overwhelmed by the growth of Western nations, which have industrialized and modernized their economies and military, leaving behind a largely colonized, subordinated, and angry Muslim world. In Arab minds, the West deposited unwanted Jews in their midst as a reminder of colonial power over Arab lands. For Muslims who deny that Jews have any right to Israel as a historic Jewish land, Israel and its modern military power is a constant reminder of the triumph of modern, Western, and secular culture over a traditionalist and stultified Muslim culture. Arabs, conscious of their proud warrior tradition, have felt further humiliated by military defeats inflicted by a vastly outnumbered group of Jews, some of whom had lived peacefully in their midst for centuries as a tribute-paying people, "protected" by the Arab political *dhimmi* system.[20] Thus, reactions to past circumstances make opportunities for the future look dim.

By any standards, the Zionist idea of the return from exile has not won favor with American Jews. A review of actual emigration figures points to an overwhelming rejection of the Zionist principle of "exile" and "return." Immigration data from the Jewish Agency in Israel on the gross number of American immigrants to their country (including those who subsequently returned to the United States) point to a lack of success in fulfilling the Zionist principle. From the founding of the state of Israel in 1948 to 2010, the average yearly emigration of American Jews to Israel was only one-twentieth of 1 percent of the approximately 5.5 million Jews in the United States, for a total of roughly 123,000 emigrants to Israel over the entire 62-year period. Israeli sources themselves put the net immigrants, excluding returnees, at approximately 100,000 Americans. There is, in short, a negligible net movement of Americans to Israel.[21] A comparison of Jewish emigration to Israel from France and Great Britain during the same period only demonstrates further the special relationship between America and its Jewish population. Whereas Jewish-American emigration to Israel over the period from 1948 to 2010 amounted to just 2 percent of the American Jewish population, the corresponding statistic for Great Britain's Jews was 12 percent, and for French Jews 17 percent.[22] Since 2010, the pace of French Jewish emigration to Israel has only accelerated in response to an increase in French anti-Semitism and terrorism.

Israeli leaders from Ben-Gurion onward can only have been disappointed by the extent of American Jewish emigration; still, their belief in American "exile" has not diminished. In welcoming a recent group of two hundred American Jewish émigrés in the summer of 2009, Prime Minister Benjamin Netanyahu greeted them as a return of exiles: "Our whole history in the last two thousand years has been to come back to the land, reestablish our independent state, and our ability to control our fate and our destiny. And that involves the ingathering of the exiles," he said.[23]

Over two thirds of recent Jewish immigrants to Israel have been Orthodox; considering that the Orthodox of all kinds are no more than 15 percent of American Jews, emigration from the United States has clearly become skewed to the religious side of Jewishness. Such patterns of immigration to Israel work toward the increasing power and importance of religious Israeli Jews, increasing the tensions in Israel between secular and religious Israelis. The increasing role of religious Jews in the current settlement movement also produces tension between a liberal Jewish religious community in America and a fast-growing and powerful fundamentalist religious element in Israel. The rigidity of religious parties in Israel makes negotiation with the Palestinians more difficult, and the Palestinians have an even larger fundamentalist bloc to deal with. It appears that Conor Cruise O'Brien, an Irish diplomat and admirer of Israel, was right when he predicted years ago that militants on both sides would shape the future.[24]

The immigration of Jews from Russia and from Eastern European countries such as Hungary, Romania, and Poland has brought well over two million Jews to Israel. But the call for American Jews to leave their "promised land" for the biblical Promised Land remains unanswered. It probably will remain so unless American anti-Semitism becomes more prevalent and intense that it ever has been.

For almost fifty years, American foreign policy and Israeli national policy were synchronized, particularly when the Soviet Union was attempting to extend its military, economic, and political power into the Middle East. Military and economic aid bought significant influence for the Soviet Union, which re-armed Arab air forces and tank battalions after wars with Israel. The close ties of the American and Israeli military have remained firm, but with the disintegration of the Soviet Union, the need for this alliance lacks urgency. The decline of the Soviet (now Russian) intrusion in the Middle East is only one of several important changes that may impact the relationship between America and Israel: it may lead to a rise in tensions between Israeli Jews and American Jews. Differing assessments of the risks involved in an Israeli-Palestinian peace process, and differing views on Israel's push for military action against a nuclear Iran, are becoming more and more divisive.

There are other changes in the American Jewish population that, though rarely discussed, are also worrisome for the continued closeness of Israeli and American Jews. These changes are not those of foreign policy differences, but internal ones—a changing attitude of America's Jewish population toward Israel itself. Different perceptions of Israel by the generations of American Jews after Israel's establishment in 1948 can seriously affect the level of American Jewish support. The older generation's almost unanimous view of Israel as an underdog has been impacted by a series of military actions that allow younger Jews to perceive Israel as a military power. The sense of fear and defensiveness that adults of the post–World War II generation felt for a beleaguered country was altered first by the Israeli invasion of Lebanon in 1982, with its bombing of Beirut, and later by Israel's powerful and purportedly disproportionate response to terrorism.

Whether it is the greater secularity of American Jews, or the different perceived experience of younger generations, or the substantial increase in intermarriage that neutralizes the intensity of Jewish links to Israel, it is clear from new research that the recent generations of young Jewish adults no longer feel the same level of connection to Israel as the generation before them. Researchers Steven M. Cohen and Ari Y. Kelman have documented the "distancing" of young, non-Orthodox Jews from Israel. The authors produce evidence that a decline of support for Israel from *internal* elements, not just external policy differences, is already underway. Those who prefer comfortable thoughts might explain away such findings by claiming that the decline is simply a product of a "family life cycle" effect, and that younger adults, when they get married and have children, will then take on their parents' attitudes toward Israel. But Cohen and Kelman write:

> That each age group is less Israel-attached than its elders suggests that we are in the midst of a long-term and ongoing decline in Israel attachment. The age-related differences cannot be attributed primarily to family life cycle effects, if only because the age-related declines characterize the entire age spectrum from the very old to the very young. Rather, we are in the midst of a massive shift in attitudes toward Israel, propelled forward by the process of cohort replacement, where the maturing younger cohorts that are the least Israel-engaged are replacing the oldest cohorts that are the most Israel-engaged.[25]

Although there still is support for Israel by American Jews of all generations, the decline by generation could be problematic in the future because the growing distance between American Jews and Israel will provide a weaker platform for US support. Cohen and Kelman agree that the conventional notion that liberal or leftist identities are at the heart of the erosion of attachment to Israel is not supported by evidence.

Whatever conclusion one may draw from the actions of political elites or the writings of intellectuals, left-of-center political identity (seeing oneself as liberal and Democrat) in the general population exerts little influence on the level of attachment to Israel.[26]

Cohen and Kelman's study produces evidence that for each successive generation, experiential anchors support distinctive generational perceptions. For example, the growing extent of intermarriage has also resulted in significant declines in the level of attachment to Israel when comparing intermarried Jews with in-married Jews. There may be broad intellectual support for Israel by the non-Jewish-born spouse, but it is not the same visceral reaction to anti-Semitism that produced Israel. Interviews I conducted with many non-Jewish-born spouses of Jews have confirmed Cohen and Kelman's findings. Even those non-Jews living in a predominantly Jewish environment revealed that, because they were not Jewish in their formative years, they did not feel the same depth of emotion as their Jewish spouses did about anti-Semitism and the state of Israel.[27]

Along with the growing secularity of each succeeding generation of Jews and the personalizing and privatizing of religious experience, intermarriage itself usually produces families with more open and fluid boundaries. The worldly experience of each succeeding generation makes a different imprint. For older generations, the Israeli War of Independence in 1948, fearful memories of Egypt's Nasser threatening Israel's existence in 1967, and the tensions and destructiveness of the Yom Kippur War in 1973 shaped those generations' attitudes and feelings. Those born after 1974 know little of these fears, yet they are aware that Israel possesses major military power, including, almost certainly, a significant arsenal of nuclear weapons. They see the asymmetry that seemingly makes Israel the "overdog." The rightness or wrongness of Israel's policies of disproportionate military response may be arguable, but the reaction of the younger generations of American Jews is not. External and internal events have clearly weakened the emotional solidarity of support that older generations held fast.

Concern for the future is twofold. Israeli leadership seems less aware of the strength and devotion of American Jews both to America and to American Jewish self-definition. From Ben-Gurion on the left to Netanyahu on the right, the Zionist ideology of the centrality of Israel was needed to succeed in order to build a state from nothing. This not only undervalues American Jewish belief, but overvalues the certainty that American Jews will follow Israeli policy without question. American Jews see the Promised Land "here," the kind of normal Jewish life advocated by Zionists and Israeli leaders as "there." Although Israel is an important place of refuge and the source of a valued collective spirit, a full and normal Jewish life does not necessarily mean living in a Jewish state.

Most American Jews do not look favorably on the intrusion of Christian fundamentalism into American government, and they find Jewish fundamentalism in Israeli government likewise troubling. Israel's acceptance of religious power in government has affected secular Israelis and has alienated many American Jews. The policy leverage of AIPAC (American Israel Public Affairs Committee), in its all but automatic support of conservative Israeli policy, is also dependent on an older generation of supporters, and should not lead Israeli leaders to believe that such strength transcends any future generational opposition. In fact, the other American pro-Israeli lobby, the "J Street group," which has criticized some Israeli governmental policies, is largely composed of activists of a younger generation. A *Los Angeles Times* survey noted that the quality cited by most Jews in normal times as most important to their identity as Jews was social equality, not support for Israel. It should give pause to past assessments of the emotional primacy of Israel in the minds of many American Jews.

What Israeli Jews sincerely believe is not only good for Israel but for Jews everywhere is a conception that may lead to future divisions. American Jews, particularly the younger generations minimally exposed to anti-Semitism, do not consider themselves self-hating and timid; they see security and safety for their families as more important than social anti-Semitism. They consider freedom from violence and hate to be a critical element of "normality," and do not see normality in building protective walls needed to keep out violent neighbors.

On the other hand, Israeli Jews continue to live in constant fear of hostile neighbors, organized terrorism, and Iran's nuclear ambitions. The Israeli mentality has also been shaped by the past tyrannies of Europe. A large number of Holocaust families live in Israel, as do over one million immigrants who fled the Soviet Union's limits on Jewish opportunities. Both groups are now a force in Israel. Most American Jews understand this and are pleased by the continuation of American military and political support. The nuclear threat under which Israel lives is real; Israel alone among nations has been publicly threatened by other nations. Thus, Israel will require the patient support for its safety by American Jews, many of whom believe that Israel's settler policy is destructive, and that their political system is overly fragmented and dysfunctional.

The security and opportunity in American Jewish life is unparalleled. When Israel had its own land and its temple in Jerusalem two thousand years ago, the Jewish nation was in constant danger, eventually falling to Rome. America, however, has been a country of durable safety since its inception. The Jews who have made the United States their home are happy to yield to its Constitution, which limits religious power. Thus, American Jews are distinct from Israeli Jews, just as they are distinct from non-Jewish Americans in other ways. The fusion of Jewish and American culture has left its mark on American Jews, just as the fusion of Jewish culture with Greek, Arab, and European cultures did in the past. Whereas other nation states have carved themselves out of common history, common religion, or common ethnicity, only America has attempted to gather in so many different nationalities, races, and religions into one diverse yet stable nation. And with a government protecting those differences, American Jews have thrived. A normal life, one of safety and security, was an American promise that has so far been fulfilled.

Prologue to Chapter Ten

To my role as a mentor to my students, I brought my experience of two typically Jewish worlds: the world of business, law, and risk-taking on the one hand; and on the other, the world of intellect, teaching, and study. While each field requires different personal qualities for success, both require the ability to learn. Cultivating the mind, educating it for the work at hand, is essential—and that is the story of Maurice Foley. He was one of the students I mentored at Swarthmore College. I helped to change his life—and he changed mine.

Child of an intact family, son of an enlisted Army man, Maurice was a star student in a minority high school in Sacramento, California. Believing himself well-qualified for Swarthmore, he came with exaggerated academic confidence and a deep hostility toward white people, both students and faculty. On some of his father's military postings in non-black areas of Utah and California, prejudicial violence required police escorts to get Maurice to school and home safely, and his resulting hostility toward all white people was evidenced in his militant dress and in a fiercely angry attitude in school. Within his first year, he was suspended from school for behavioral as well as academic reasons, and his confidence wilted on the fast track of well-prepared white high-achievers.

Maurice was allowed to return to school after a year of course work at Temple University, and he entered my class on American Political Parties dressed in a military jacket and a bandana around his forehead, seemingly ready for a Black Panther meeting. Back then, in 1979, it was impossible to foresee that this bright but under-skilled and very angry man would graduate Swarthmore and go on to a distinguished career in law. Before he was forty years old, he became the first black judge on the Federal Tax Court, nominated by President Clinton on the advice of a white mentor, Secretary of the Treasury Lloyd Bentsen of Texas.

Maurice had benefited from having both a mother and a father in his life, parents committed to his education. These advantages, however, failed him in his first year of college—because of his lack of preparedness, a lack of academic skills that did not match his high level of intelligence. A bright child who had learned to read before he entered kindergarten, he was underserved by a ghetto high school that required little reading and writing. Pushing Maurice by affirmative action to Swarthmore had an initially deleterious effect on him, by jumping him ahead too fast. But he, like other survivors who have had the inner strength to overcome such shocks to their self-esteem, was eventually able to gain the benefits that came from attending a superior educational institution, one that was well above the level for which he had been originally prepared.

While each similarly unprepared black student had his or her own individual response, what they all had in common was having to deal with poor initial grades that not only disappointed them, but made them question their own intelligence. The single most important concept for these students to internalize was the difference between weak skills and low IQ. All the successful affirmative action students were those who struggled through the initially disheartening experience, learned the important distinction between skill and intelligence, and worked very hard to build the skills common to better prepared students. Regaining their confidence in their intelligence and working hard to repair old problems, all while dealing with new academic challenges, was the only way to success. And Maurice Foley, with great willpower and perseverance, made the effort to become the man he really wanted to be.

After five weeks in my class, Maurice had taken an exam whose outcome indicated good thinking but poor writing, and he had shown a willingness to work hard. He came to my office in his "black militant" uniform and a hostile demeanor, and opened the conversation with a challenge. "I want to be a lawyer. I know you know something about

the outside world, and I want to know if you can help get me there."
I responded by asking him what kind of law firm he wanted to work
in—a predominantly white one with a broad practice, or a predominantly black one catering mostly to black people. "I want to be in the
big game, not just the ghetto," he said.

I said to Maurice that if that was where he wanted to go, I would
help him, but that there were some things he had to change, and he
would have to accept criticism. I said that my criticisms were not
meant to put him down, but to help him up; nevertheless, they would
be criticisms coming from "Whitey." Seemingly appreciative of my
directness about the tough love that was coming his way, he allowed a
faint smile and said, "I'll get back to you."

Two weeks later he returned with the words, "I think I can take
it," and we began a journey of, first, allowing affirmative action for
improving skills; second, accepting me as his personal mentor; and
finally, taking me in as his close friend. When he agreed to take criticism—not always easy for black students to accept from white teachers—I told him in a kindly but firm tone the three things he had to do
to reach his goal of succeeding in a predominantly white America.
First, I told him he had to write properly—no big flowery ninth-grade
words that didn't quite belong, but sharp, concise, communicative
sentences. I could be of direct help in that area, and we would work
closely together. The second thing needing change was his speech patterns: he needed to learn how to speak with clarity and sharpness,
since that was a requisite skill of the law profession. Since Swarthmore had no public speaking courses ("our students don't need them"),
I encouraged Maurice to listen to himself on tape, to listen to other
well-known Blacks, and to take public speaking courses, if he could,
over the summer.

Maurice initially protested that his friends would think his new
speech pattern was "acting white." I answered that he then needed to
speak two languages, one for his friends and the other for the practice
of law in a predominantly white firm. I noted that many children of
immigrant parents also had to speak two languages, and that it was essential to reaching his career goals. Visibly discomfited by the thought

of the "makeover" I was prescribing, he said, "And what's the third thing I have to do?" I answered: "That one may be the most difficult to accomplish because of your history. You must learn not to hate all white people on principle, as if they're all the same. There are many Whites who are racists, and there are others that don't even know they are touched by racism. But there are also some Whites who will try to help you get ahead. But if they feel the same hostility toward them that comes through to me, they won't. I'll help you even if you hate my guts because I'm white—that's my job—but you have to work on the problem. We're not all alike, and you'll need other white mentors later."

With possibly some slight racial preference involved, Maurice was accepted at Harvard, Stanford, and the UC Berkeley School of Law. After deciding to study on the West Coast, he planned to visit both schools after graduation from Swarthmore. Before leaving, Maurice handed in a sixty-page research paper on political aspects of taxation for a joint course I was giving with an economist. It was so perceptive and well-written that it literally brought me to tears. He had cured the writing problem, and was halfway through developing his second language. As for his anger at Whites, however, he made little progress at Swarthmore. He had not had friendly words with a single white student while there, and I may well have been the only White he trusted.

We talked about his need to be more trusting of Whites, both students and faculty, while at law school, and to encourage teachers who took a special interest in him. He chose Berkeley over Stanford, feeling less comfortable on the suburban "white bread" campus in Palo Alto. He did well at law school, and upon graduation was offered jobs at several major "white" law firms. He called to ask my advice about whether his interest in tax law would be better served by taking one of the job offers or getting a master's degree in tax law instead. Maurice found out that if he worked for the Internal Revenue Service for three years, they would pay for the costs of a master's degree at Georgetown University Law Center. I recommended the IRS route on two grounds: first, because advanced knowledge in taxation would help him in his chosen career field; and second, because it would give him more experience of interacting with white people in the workplace before he would move on to bigger and better things.

Maurice got his master's degree and became the IRS's point man for explaining to lawyers and accountants the intricacies of the new (1986) tax overhaul. His role as that law's reigning expert brought him to the attention of Senator Lloyd Bentsen, who subsequently hired him for the Senate Finance Committee. When, years later, President Clinton selected Bentsen to be Secretary of the Treasury, Maurice was chosen as one of the few tax lawyers Bentsen took with him from the Finance Committee to serve on his personal staff at the Treasury.

Some years after leaving his job the Treasury, Maurice heard about a federal tax court judgeship vacancy that, as he told me, might be filled by a minority lawyer. He asked if I thought he had the appropriate judicial temperament, and whether he should write Senator Bentsen to seek his support for the judgeship. I told him he did indeed have all the qualities and temperament for the job, but no, he shouldn't write Bentsen. "You should go to see him personally, and tell him forthrightly that you are confident you can do the job." Maurice did what I advised, and as it turned out Bentsen said it was his privilege to sponsor him. After being approved by the Senate, Maurice was formally inducted into the court in a ceremony at which both Secretary Bentsen and I addressed the court on Maurice's behalf. I spoke first of the great transition Maurice was able to make from an angry, untrusting, and ill-prepared young student to the man he was that day: the loving husband of his supportive wife, Sandy, father of their three children, and a man about to become the first black judge on the United States Tax Court. I spoke about how his confidence in his intelligence, his hard work, and his willingness to change had enabled him to be what he wanted to be. And I said how proud I was to have helped him on his extraordinary journey from initial failure at Swarthmore to the success and acclaim he sought in "the big game."

Bentsen followed my speech, saluting me for my role as a teacher and mentor, and speaking glowingly of Maurice's intelligence, talent, and work ethic. This was followed by a twenty-five-minute address to the court by Maurice, who, speaking without notes, traced his own development and thanked those who had contributed to it, from his parents, to me, and to Secretary Bentsen, his crucial white mentor for the court appointment.

While public policy arguments have continued about the large-scale effects of affirmative action, for me it has been more individual and personal. Could I help my affirmative action students overcome their inadequate training? Could I help change a life for the better, open new hopes and careers? It required finding a different role for myself—as teacher, mentor, secular rabbi—in my chosen life. As the Talmud reminds us, "Whoever saves a life, saves the world entire."

I never quite realized, over my many years mentoring Maurice and my other important "mentees," just how much my own sensibilities were influenced and formed by my Jewish background. Certainly I knew that my knowledge of prejudice and discrimination in Jewish history had made me particularly empathetic to Blacks. I had, on occasion, even quoted some well-known Jewish saying or words of wisdom from a long-ago rabbi such as Hillel. But only many years later, at a special reunion of my mentees, did I fully realize the extent of the Jewish side of my role.

After many years of meeting at my home for summer reunions, Maurice and my other mentees decided to treat Len and me to a weekend at a resort in Pennsylvania's Pocono Mountains. We went for what we expected to be a recreational weekend, only to be surprised at dinner when each one of the seven mentees present—four black, three white—thanked me for mentoring and shaping their lives. When Maurice, a devout Christian, spoke, he told of how important to him had been Rabbi Hillel's famous words: "If I am not for myself, who shall be for me? If I am only for myself, what am I? And if not now, when?"[10]

That saying, which had resonated deeply with me early in my teaching career, was a particularly Jewish aphorism, a guide to living in this world. In its first sentence, it defines a positive aspect of pride, a pride of accomplishment and self-affirmation, of worldly ambitions. Its second sentence emphasizes communal responsibilities and charity, a necessary counterbalance to personal ambition. And the third sentence criticizes passivity, being silent instead of speaking out, and waiting instead of acting on one's moral values. It was a saying with deep roots in human psychology, self-affirming rather than ascetic, and a guide to how to live in this world—educating and cultivating the mind and its values.

I had to struggle to maintain my composure. After the dinner was over and Len and I went to bed, I spent almost the entire night sobbing. While I knew I had had some influence in their lives, I did not know how much; I had not realized how their image of me encompassed a teaching, mentoring and, yes, a fatherly relationship. It was a night of transmitted memory: the words of a rabbi dead over two thousand years, relayed by a Jewish secular humanist to a young black man affirming a new life. That night I realized my calling, for it became clear to me that I had, in fact, recapitulated the relationship I had with my own father. Without the pressure of material needs that I had felt as an entrepreneur, I had become a rabbi like my great grandfather, a student, a teacher, and a mentor, only this time without the rituals, without an open Talmud—but with the lessons deeply learned.

Chapter Ten
Facts and Speculations

It may be helpful at this point to summarize briefly what we have learned about the Jewish past in America, particularly the fusion of Jewish and American ideas, before proceeding in the next and final chapter to a discussion of the Jewish future.

Have American Jews remained distinct from other Americans, even after four or five generations of assimilative life? The answer, as we have seen, is yes. The evidence is clear on many counts: social and political values and preferences, levels of tolerance for others, racial and sexual issues, differing beliefs in God, heaven and hell. Also, American Jews remain distinctive in their stronger progressive attitudes and their tendency toward secularity—that is, a gradual loss of belief in the all-knowing, personally intervening biblical God of traditional Judaism. While there is a steady but modest trend toward secularity among non-Jews as well, the trend among Jews is far more pronounced. Will an increase of secularity among American Jews continue in the generations to come? That question is unanswerable.

The powerful strain of Protestant individualism in American culture has been broadly absorbed by Jewish immigrants. They have also become vigilant defenders of the uniquely American and Protestant idea of the separation of government from religion. American Jews have a greater respect for pluralism and diversity than one would expect from a group who traditionally has been "a people apart." For most Jews the impact of American diversity has actually gone beyond respect for differences to a welcoming receptiveness of other subcultural modes of expression. Eagerness to respond to the music of black America, and for Jewish composers to incorporate it into their idea of "American" music, is one example of such receptiveness. Jewish openness to other than their own ethnic foods is another indication of how distinct America's Jewish population is from that of Europe, and from the apartness traditions of Orthodoxy as well. The separateness and inwardness of Orthodoxy, designed to protect religious holiness from elements of modern life, have been challenged by the temptations and diversity of pluralistic modern America.

However, the individualism absorbed by Jews has been tempered by their collective history and by the socially oriented policies of Europe, which, more than in America, encouraged a belief in a social safety net. Though Jews share with libertarians a fierce adherence to the rights of the individual, they believe more strongly than libertarians in a federal government willing to protect and support the weaker elements of society. The modern amalgam of its influence of group concern—the morality of prophetic Judaism—and the influence of Protestant individualism has, as Irving Kristol noted, infused itself into all non-Orthodox American Jews. Kristol rightly claims that Jewish secular humanism affirms the possibility of humanity realizing its full potential through the energetic applications of moral intelligence—*learning*—and he argues that this attitude is provided by a "particularly intense, Jewish secular humanism." Again, such thoughts lead to optimism about a future that is both Jewish and American.

To the question, Is American assimilative life significantly different from the experience of French, German, and English acculturated Jews, the answer again is yes. The stability, strength, and protectiveness of our leaders has been substantially greater than in France and Germany; and the multiple prejudices of the different nationalities and races that make up America—again, the result of pluralism—diffuses the level of antipathy toward any one group. Unlike Europe, America has had many "others." And the different groups who have all felt the sting of discrimination now form a new majority, more sensitive to prejudices, who accept the dignity of differences. American pluralism has changed the nature of assimilation and the very process of integration of groups into society. Americanization, incomplete assimilation, is therefore the specific American way of absorbing different groups by imposing fewer obligations. Demanding *political* allegiance as the path to citizenship, but not social or ethnic conformity, along with the growing acceptance of differentness, has made the combination of diversity and stability possible.

A defining aspect of European history, its treatment of the Jews as a pariah race, was not duplicated in America. There never was an enforced ghetto. African slaves took the role of the racial "other," since Jews were considered white within the Black/White racial division. Only after World War II and the demonic racial focus of the Holocaust did American Jews fully reject the lingering belief that Jews were "a white race of a different kind." Only then did American Jews come to see Jewish difference as a product of cultural pluralism and not as a partially racial construct. The Holocaust also played a major role in diminishing Jews' long-held belief that they were a people "chosen by God," and also weakened their belief in an all-powerful, personally intervening God. God's failure to protect "His people" from destruction has reshaped the beliefs of many Jews and cannot be underestimated as a cause of American Jews' becoming more secular in orientation. For Jews, the Holocaust was a deeply personal event: loss of families, loss of links to the past, loss of confidence in others, and, for many, loss of religious faith.

The impact of the American experience has also shaped the Jewish view of Zionism and of Israel itself. One Zionist principle, the founding of a Jewish state for historically distressed European Jews, was embraced by Jewish Americans in the aftermath of the Holocaust. But another principle of Zionism, that American Jews are in exile until "return" to Israel, and that a normal and authentic Jewish life cannot be lived except there, was rejected, as proved by the emigration figures showing that the net difference over sixty-two years between the migration of American Jews to Israel and of Israeli Jews to America was effectively zero. The calls of Israeli leaders for Jews to return from "exile" have gone unanswered by the vast majority of American Jews, who continue to demonstrate their belief that a normal and authentically Jewish life *can* be lived in America.

Events of the last thirty years, and media interpretations of those events, have not only increased the isolation of Israel in the world outside of the United States, but have weakened the intensity of the connection between the younger generations of American Jews and Israel. Two other elements have also contributed to this decline: tensions created by the growing strength of religious and conservative parties in Israel, in contrast to liberal and increasingly secular younger generations of Jews in America; and the significant increase in intermarriage, which, while not necessarily weakening favorable attitudes toward Israel among non-Jewish spouses, has affected the degree of emotional attachment of younger Jews. While efforts to reconnect younger generations to Israel by Jewish philanthropists, such as Michael Steinhardt, have been partially effective, more is needed to bring young Jews near the level of connection with Israel felt by their parents. The fusion of cultures, which is at the core of assimilative American Jewish life, is achieved at the price of some group solidarity. What is also new in the Jewish-American equation is the diminished anti-Semitism of the last two generations. Earlier, reaction to anti-Semitism fostered Jewish cohesion and solidarity. Hostility by Gentiles against socializing with Jews, their abhorrence of the thought of intermarriage for their children, produced a wall against the dilution of Jewish solidarity.

But over the last two generations, the American Jewish world has changed. Anti-Semitism has largely disappeared, intermarriage is now common, and the outward distinction between Jews and non-Jews is minimal. What has not disappeared is the inward sense of distinctiveness. How can that distinctiveness, the community of mind, be maintained if it is not fully appreciated? How can a culture largely unsupported by strong religiosity flourish if its members have only a vague idea of their differentness? Jewish secular humanism and liberality, Jewish tolerance for differentness, and the Jewish emphasis on education are all things that make Jews distinctive—and they are also the qualities needed for a future America. How and why Jews are distinctive needs to be taught so that secular Jews will want to stay a part of a historic and still vital people.

If American assimilative Jews are to pass down their heritage, they must understand how that heritage is unique and what the elements are that have produced it—in short, they need a consciousness of their Jewish culture. While the Orthodox know how and why they are different from non-Jews, assimilative and predominantly secular Jews are, as Nathan Glazer emphasizes, uninformed as to what is distinctively Jewish. This book is but one effort to remedy such lack of knowledge, by identifying some of the specifics, so that the generalities of cultural transmission may have added to them some clear comparative distinctiveness. Jews should know how their culture is different from that of Gentiles, for religious education among Jews is silent about Christianity. (Christian teaching about Judaism, on the other hand, has a history of invidious comparison.) Jewish education needs to address the past and clarify certain important differences between Christianity and Judaism—from a Jewish perspective—as well as defend against the assumptions of much Christian teaching.

Jews need more knowledge of what their heritage is, how it is historically connected to the present, and how their community of thought has been built. Common cultural differences—distinctiveness of thought—need greater clarification and emphasis. The continuity of the Jewish people requires the health of its religious core, the Orthodox, but it also requires a knowledgeable and appreciative ring of Americanized Jews, whose numbers and talents provide protection for all Jews.

I want to speculate on one still-unanswered question. To some questions, such as whether present-day American Jews are disproportionately liberal or progressive in their thinking, more tolerant of difference, and more grounded in secular attitudes, we can find clear answers in the research evidence. But there is a question that such research does not answer: *Why* are Jews so distinctive? Earlier we touched on, but did not answer, why American Jewish accomplishments and prominence in certain fields are disproportionate. Some scholars, mostly non-Jews, have documented such disproportion, but many Jews are reluctant to do so themselves, fearing negative reactions.

When the Europe of 1800 opened the ghettos that had isolated its Jews for centuries, it unleashed, as Raphael Patai noted, a reservoir of intellectual energy that had been largely confined to studying the Talmud. With the Enlightenment, that energy surged into many secular fields, and found no greater opportunity for expression than in America. Thanks to the porousness of contemporary American life, American Jews have reached an exceptionally high level of achievement; they are, in fact, *over*achievers. The researcher Steven Pease found disproportionately high levels of Jewish achievement in terms of Nobel Prizes won and of levels of prominence in business, education, and medicine.[1] Others offer sociological or psychological explanations, seeing Jews distinct from what Freud called the "compact majority." Knowing that they're outsiders has given Jews the courage to be different, to act on their ideas and values, even as a tiny minority. When the late actor Paul Newman, son of a Jewish father and a Gentile mother, was asked why he, a religiously non-observant person, considered himself to be Jewish, he answered, "Because it takes courage."

Not everyone can resist the pressures of the majority; many do not want to be different from their peers. Assimilative Jews, in varying measure, give up a degree of communal protection when they venture out. Some historians say that being different, being viewed as an outsider, spurs greater effort to excel and overcome negative stereotypes by superior accomplishments or generosity. *Business Week* observed that Jews constituted 38 percent of their 2007 list of the fifty most generous American philanthropists.[2] Thus, the effort to excel and to overturn the negative stereotypes, such as that of the money-hungry Jew, is posited as a motivating force.

Such ideas have some modest value, but what appears to be the most critical cause of disproportion is something different; and there is ample, but not conclusive, evidence to support it. Jewish overachievement is primarily linked to the exceptionally intense focus on learning, formal and informal, of Jewish culture, extending even to child-rearing patterns that can be, and are being, duplicated by non-Jews. Both the specific cultural qualities and personal family patterns are distinctive in their emphasis rather than their uniqueness. Many families see the advantages of education today, but for Jews, whether religious or not, an intense focus on education has long been a part of their culture.

Among the elements that have contributed to a high-achieving Jewish culture, none is more valuable than formal education. As in many poor and formerly uneducated Jewish families, parents expected their children to reach the highest levels. My own mother, for example, forced to work a full-time job at age twelve, insisted that her children be highly educated. My family uprooted themselves and moved to a new but hostile community so that my brothers and I could attend a good private school—a social sacrifice made at the altar of education. And in America today, Jewish families have on average two and a half more years of higher education than American non-Jews.[3] The specifics of formal education make this point clear: while over 50 percent of American Jews older than twenty-five have graduated college, only 21 percent of white non-Jews have; and 30 percent of American Jews have completed postgraduate study versus only 9 percent for the corresponding white population.[4] These statistics represent obvious advantages of preparation for professions and businesses that demand more highly educated and more skilled people, and such educational advantages can largely account for Jewish overrepresentation in those fields.

The expectation of formal education is reinforced by the child-rearing patterns of Jewish life. The NORC survey demonstrated the distinctive educational expectations of Jewish parents in the development of their children. The verbal engagement of intimacy between parent and child fostered in Jewish families—teaching and learning from infancy—contradicts the old Protestant standard of decorum that children "should be seen and not heard." Similar patterns obviously exist in Jewish families, but not to the same general extent, and the reported lack of strong discipline in most Jewish families, along with the heavy emphasis on children learning to "think for themselves," evaluating different existing knowledge, I believe, has promoted a child-centric learning environment. It is one that fosters interest in learning, even though it may create more self-centered children.

The focus on learning is not limited to early years or formal education. Jews disproportionately attend adult education classes and lectures, seeking even in old age to increase their knowledge and understanding. Publishers know that their audience for serious hardcover nonfiction is disproportionately Jewish. Jews tend to look to a future that will be better than the past—an outlook that gives reasons for learning and that contrasts with Calvinist determinism, as learning itself is linked to an undetermined future that is open to change.

Since the Jewish fusion of religion with Greek intellectuality, learning has been a religious and cultural demand, first limited to moral or religious concerns, later extended to secular knowledge. In his research into how Jewish culture and intellectuality developed in the Diaspora, anthropologist Raphael Patai points frequently to the fusion of Jewish thinking with knowledge absorbed from the nations and cultures where Jews searched for safety and peace. Their absorption of knowledge from different sources continued a cultural learning process that has found its strongest expression in America, where the opportunity for such expression has been unequaled in Jewish Diaspora history.

High expectations in Jewish families produce a striving for achievement in young adults that leads to excellence, though it can also lead, among the less accomplished, to a sense of failure to reach one's potential. Pride and confidence, however, seem to be instilled through child-rearing patterns, about which we need to know more. The acknowledgment of the value of "good pride," confidence in oneself, by Rabbi Hillel over two thousand years ago—"If I am not for myself, who will be for me"—sounds modern and points to age-old differences with other religious cultures that emphasized self-denial and asceticism.

Other factors may feed into Jewish family attitudes about the future. One is the absence in the Jewish religion and culture of a well-defined sense of the afterlife, as compared with Christian and Muslim beliefs. For Jews, heaven is "the world to come" and has a linear, this-worldly future perspective, which merely prophesizes the arrival of the Messiah to save the Jews and the rest of the world and resurrect the righteous of all peoples. There is little emphasis on heaven and hell. For most present-day Jews, their worldly focus is captured by the poet Wallace Stevens:

> The honey of heaven may or may not come,
> But that of earth both comes and goes at once.[5]

Jews have long believed that the future will be different and better than the past, and that they, as a people, will have a role in shaping it, bringing "light to the Gentile world." It is possible that Jewish optimism about the future promotes the strong investment of Jewish parents in the practical and philosophical education of their children.

For over two thousand years, Jewish life has been disproportionately involved with words and ideas, the building blocks of books, the study of which can be used as weapons of defense, in humor or argument, or as useful and constructive tools for scientific knowledge. Jews believed that study, books, and knowledge would lead to a greater understanding of life, and, in Maimonides' thinking, bring one closer to God. The Torah and Talmud stress the life of the mind because words and ideas, creating a rich interior world, cannot be taken away by physical discrimination. The specialness of this resource, an enriching and life-affirming part of the interior life, is perhaps one reason why there has been a disproportionate number of Jews prominent in fields like psychiatry, which deals with the world of the mind, of the interior. As the non-Jewish psychiatrist Karl Menninger wrote:

> Now, in psychiatry the reduction of relatively intangible things such as feelings and attitudes to verbal expression is highly important. It is necessary to the scientific evaluation of mental processes and it has been shown by the work of Freud to have a therapeutic value for the patient. It is a very old observation that quarreling Irish may throw bricks at one another, and Italians knives, but Jews throw sharp words. This is a destructive

use of the same gift. To convert this talent for verbalization into scientific purposes is in no branch of science more useful than in psychiatry.[6]

Words and their meaning, books with ideas, formal education, and learning in general permeate Jewish culture. The imprint of learning, of skepticism, is carried by a culture that prizes intellect and imparts high expectations of effort and success. Hurling an insult instead of a rock has been said to be the founding of modern civilization.[7] In 64 CE, Rabbi Joshua Ben Gamla issued a decree mandating universal schooling for all Jewish males over six, at a time when over 95 percent of people were illiterate. Since then, Jewish families maintained a commitment to learning and literacy, reading the Talmud and Torah in their search for knowledge.[8] For most American Jews today, the sense of the spiritual, the nonmaterial, has given way to a focus on learning—a metaphor for worship—with an emphasis on the understanding of past connections, the present world, and the future, and a de-emphasis on faith and personal salvation.

The nonmaterial or spiritual aspects of Jewish life have long been linked to connections beyond one's self that give meaning and purpose to life. For most Jews, the spiritual links do not lead upward to an ethereal next world, but inward to parents, to family, to a historical connection to past Jewish life, and ahead to Jewish destiny. Even among secular Jews, it is *transmitted memory* that is distinctively Jewish, rather than dwelling on the mystery of what may come after death. "He has gone to a better place" may be very comforting for some, but it is not an expression used frequently by Jews. Instead, most Jews, religious or not, heed God's admonition to Moses in Deuteronomy:

> I call to witness for you today the heavens and the earth. Life and death I set before you, the blessing and the curse, and you shall choose life so that you may live, you and your seed.[9]

American cultural ideas have possibly diluted the cohesiveness of the American Jewish community, which has absorbed the new ideas of Protestant individualism and materialism, freedom to choose one's own future pathway, and the democratic ethos of equality that was little known in the "old country." Except for the different groups of the Orthodox who try to maintain a geographic and ritualistic community of difference, the great majority of assimilative Jews reside in a varying but distinctly less formal religious state—a community of mind, a way of thinking—that is distinctively Jewish but culturally rather than religiously governed. In short, most assimilative Jews have created a varying, individualized and personalized belief system of their own, unmoved by Orthodoxy's demands for authoritative and traditional Jewish law.

Most American Jews have embraced an American culture that, from its very founding, has worked to contain the excesses of aggressive religiosity. This moderation can be clearly observed in the writings of the Christian founding fathers, in which they denied a special place for their own Christian religion. There is a constant state of tension between religious groups who believe their judgments came from God and a government built on the secular laws of democracy. But the overall religiosity of the American people remains a tempered one that, except for a few brief periods, has moderated its involvement in the public arena.

A scholar of American religion, Alan Wolfe, has noted the transformation of American religion:

> For there are aspects of American religion that have changed dramatically, even in the past decade or two, including a palpable increase in religious toleration that extends to non-Christians; a preference for personalized faith that has influenced all religions, not just Protestant and evangelical ones . . . the acceptance by most Catholics of both American culture and modernity; and a rapid growth in the number of believers who are neither Protestant, Catholic, nor Jewish. Sociologists a few decades ago predicted the decline of religion in modern societies, but in the most modern society of all, religion has neither declined nor advanced; it has been transformed.[10]

Religious extremists do not have a history of tolerance toward other religions, but instead have emphasized the exclusive truth of their
own beliefs. Their preference for revelation over reason tends to put
them at odds with a liberal democracy that organizes itself by secular
rules of consensus. The prevailing ethos in America is for the strongly
religious to withhold their most aggressive demands and generally
work through constitutional rules of an electoral and court system
that is both functional and dilutive of religious intensity.

In this moderate religious environment, most Jews find themselves
comfortable with pragmatic secularists in government, and maintain
for themselves liberal democratic moral values without compelling
religious beliefs. Face to face with a diversity of people, absorbing a
belief in cultural pluralism unique to America, most Jews see that differences have an energy of their own and make the beliefs and traditions of a "people apart" much more difficult to sustain. It is a price
most American Jews have willingly paid. While some Orthodox and
religious traditionalists have trouble seeing many assimilative Jews as
authentic Jews, the lack of a hierarchical structure of authority among
American Jews—an important, specific byproduct of American ideas
of pluralism and individualism—limits the power of any threat to ex-
communicate cultural Jews, there being other Jewish denominations
that will accept them. If Spinoza lived in today's America, he would
not be excommunicated. The wide variety of Jewish religious denominations is not duplicated elsewhere in the world and is emblematic of
the Americanization of the Jews.

While there are books about the contributions of Jews to American culture in humor, art, literature, and science, in this one I have
looked instead at how the fusion of American and Jewish culture has
shaped the thinking and beliefs of American Jews. The growing openness and tolerance of American society, the increased connectedness
of Jews with the Gentile world, and the growing secularity of many
Jews have also fostered intermarriage at the probable cost of some
group cohesion and future solidarity—again, a price most Jews seem
willing to pay.

Challenges from the results of cultural fusion are not new in Jewish history. When Jewish culture absorbed important elements of Greek culture over two thousand years ago, the implanting of intellectualism into Jewish rabbinical life not only changed Jewish life and history, but also upset the religious leaders of that era. Few Jews today realize that the battle celebrated in Chanukah was, in fact, a struggle between differing groups of Jews over the impact of Hellenistic culture. There are serious issues that require creative responses, but pessimists about the Jewish people should look at their past adjustments. As Alan Dershowitz reflected, "This ability to change to keep Judaism relevant, to give the past a vote not a veto has been a key ingredient in our long and mysterious survival against all odds."[11] Culture plants the new and carries along some of the old, making Judaism an evolving and creative force, not the supposed "relic" or "vestige" of many tendentious Christian histories.

The vast heterogeneity of different groups produces the American mosaic of cultures. In this amalgam, American Jews have demonstrated the unique value of their emphasis on learning, on education, on the development of the intellect, on thinking and analysis. In practical terms, the mind has been a great resource in modern America for the millions of impoverished Jewish immigrants of the last hundred years. While other reasons may contribute, only the Jewish focus on learning can explain the rapid ascent of American Jews from an impoverished beginning to the present-day high levels of achievement. Even with the opening of new opportunities for others in higher education—through affirmative action for the victims of racism, or from the meritocratic influx of Asian Americans into colleges and universities—American Jewish students remain today between 20 and 30 percent of the student bodies of the top thirty private colleges and universities, and from 15 to 20 percent of the top thirty public universities.[12] The high level of academic and professional achievement among Asians and Jews has recently stimulated intermarriage between both groups.[13]

Despite earlier periods of anti-Semitism, America demonstrated its ability to evolve closer to its own ideals, as its people became more tolerant of different religious and racial groups. Each successive generation has become more tolerant than the one before. Research has shown that Jews have been leaders in bringing about a greater level of tolerance in America and are both proponents and beneficiaries of such change. Partly from the analysis of moral justice in the Torah, and in even larger measure from their experience of suffering from discrimination and unwillingness to respect "difference," America's Jews have been "educated" to tolerance.

The majority of assimilative Jews are not necessarily nonreligious or without reverence. Still, though they vary in their sense of spirituality, their lives are governed primarily by secular, rational, and scientific values that exist outside of what they consider the responsibility of God. Unlike their Christian and Orthodox Jewish brethren, the great majority of American Jews clearly do not believe in the personal, intervening God of the Bible. I believe they are spiritually a people of books and, at an even deeper level, a people of *transmitted memory*, whether religious or not.

Most Jews feel a specialness about being Jewish, a sense of shared history and destiny with a people long without their own land who have endured with their particular beliefs and culture in just the confines of their minds, and who have survived for almost two thousand years in the Diaspora. Many American Jews (myself included) are still in awe of their ancestors' extraordinary demonstration of belief, courage, and endurance. But what happens now in America as Jewish religious beliefs erode in the face of secularity, as Gentiles become more tolerant, and as intermarriages increase? This is the issue for those concerned about the future of Jews as a cohesive group.

I believe the likelihood is for even greater pluralism among Jews in the future than we have seen already, as a large new body of cultural Jews emerges from intermarriage. Perhaps new Jewish denominations will appear to nurture those who share only the culture of Jews. All assimilative Jews, particularly those new, predominantly secular intermarried couples, will need to know more specifically than they do now about what Jewish culture is. To transmit culture from generation to generation takes specific knowledge about the essence of Jewish life, and requires words, ideas, and books.

Freud claimed there to be an unarticulated essence of cultural Jewish life that exists beyond God and the Jewish religion. My view—with much, but not conclusive, evidence to support it—is one that helps to understand both the special educational and personal family values of Jewish culture and their role in the disproportionate accomplishments of American Jews. Certainly an essence of that culture is its extraordinary emphasis on cultivating the intellect. The belief that learning lights the way has been held by both Orthodox and non-Orthodox Jews alike for over two thousand years. While the subject of study has morphed from religious matters to the scientific, most Jews have clearly understood that knowledge, not just faith, is critical to Jewish life. Knowledge, as Maimonides taught, was a way for the less religious Jew to get closer to God, just as knowledge for the less religious Jew today is a way to understand the world. It is not merely the belief that learning plays a large role in life, but the belief that it plays an intense and crucial one, both inside and outside the family, that is held disproportionately by Jews. Developing and educating the mind is the key to family life itself, to the transmitting of memory and culture, and is the principal reason for disproportionately high achievement by Jews in an open and free America.

Socrates Lagios, a child of Greek immigrants who became superintendent of schools in Brookline, Massachusetts, was asked in an interview why there was such a large influx of Japanese and other Asian-American students to his high-powered school system in the closing decades of the twentieth century. He replied:

> The key factor is the high quality of the school system, and the influx is because of the very predominance of Jewish parents in Brookline. The Japanese and Asian Americans want a top-notch public school system with serious students and families that will feed the budgets of academic demands. They openly admit to seeking out predominantly Jewish public school districts . . . like Brookline, Mass., Scarsdale, New York and elsewhere because they want that educational intensity and support that Jewish people give.

In answering why he thought that Jewish families have such an intense dedication to educating their children, Lagios replied, "I'm not sure, but it seems essential to their lives. Perhaps it's what makes Jews, Jewish."[14]

I perceive a certain irony in the idea that many Jews—particularly the less religious majority—need to further educate themselves in order to better understand the extent and causes of their own distinctiveness. What that cultural distinctiveness is composed of, and how it is connected to the Jewish people historically, is knowledge necessary to pass on to future generations if there is to be continuity. But there is also a lesson, an example, for America itself that is encompassed in the disproportionate accomplishments of America's Jews with their educational and professional distinctiveness. As a cloud of pessimism about America's future stemming from the Great Recession passes over its people, they would do well to ask why America's Jews, and more recently its Asians, have moved forward so fast. America has given its Jews the gift of freedom and opportunity, and it has been received with gratitude. In return, America's Jews have demonstrated the benefits of an intense emphasis on education, which will be needed in a world that is more competitive than ever before. The gift of America's Jews to their country, the true light of their example, becomes clear: in order to produce the scientists, computer experts, and other intellectually capable people needed for the future, we must educate and cultivate the mind.

Prologue to Chapter Eleven

What does the Jewish tomorrow look like? In Europe, home to more than nine million Jews before the Holocaust, there is now only one country, France, with a substantial Jewish population. Numbering slightly under a half-million, French Jews now live in a third era of sometimes violent anti-Semitism, the first occurring during the Dreyfus Affair in the 1890s, and the second being the Vichy-government roundup of Jews for deportation to Nazi death camps in 1942.

Many French Jews now fear for the future, since over the last two decades they have been victims of assassinations, kidnappings, and vicious bullying in schools by French Muslims. Until the terrorism of January 2015, France's acknowledgment of and protective response to this reality was minimal, and Jewish emigration from France is accelerating. What role, then, will America play in a Jewish tomorrow when only Israel and America are home to most of the world's Jews?

Chapter Eleven

Terrorism, Anti-Semitism, and the Jewish Future

This book's analysis of Jews' past attempts to integrate themselves into Western nations reveals failure in every case—except in that of the United States. At the end of the thirteenth century, England expelled all its Jews, a situation that lasted for over three hundred years. Only by the mid-nineteenth century could a Jew be seated in Parliament without first converting to Christianity. The highly integrated Jewish participation in Spain of more than a hundred years ended with the triumph of Catholicism over the Muslim Moors—which brought with it the Inquisition, torture, autos-da-fé (which included burning alive), and the eventual forced emigration of all Jews in 1492.

France, with its mass anti-Jewish rioting in the 1890s during the Dreyfus Affair and its Vichy government's rounding up of French Jews for shipment to the death camps, has a deeply stained record. Germany, home of Kant, Goethe, Schiller, and "Kultur," turned social anti-Semitism into a loss of political rights for Jews under Hitler and then their organized destruction in the death camps. Russia has a long history of anti-Jewish violence and persecution, including pogroms under the czars and, under the Soviets, anti-Jewish show trials and imprisonment in Siberian gulags.

The hostility toward Jews almost everywhere in Europe throughout the centuries is key to the allure of Zionism, which represents the total distrust by Jews in Europe's ability to protect Jewish political rights. Only America (with the obvious exception of Israel) has a consistent record of protecting Jewish *political* rights, despite periods of social anti-Semitism. From the founding, through many recessions, the Great Depression, the Civil War, and two World Wars, the political rights of America's Jewish citizens have not been seriously threatened, as they were in France, Germany, Italy, Austria, Poland, Hungary, Romania, and the Soviet Union.

Although these state-sponsored anti-Semitic attacks were perpetrated for centuries throughout Europe, such governmental attacks on the political rights of Jewish citizens have never occurred in America. Americans' widely held belief in pluralism in government, religion, and culture has restrained tendencies toward authoritarianism and thus also the anti-Semitism that usually follows authoritarianism. A central thesis of this book has been that the American ideas that have shaped Jewish culture—pluralism, democracy, and the protection of *differentness*—are the very same that protect Jews in a threatening world. The strength of America is vested, then, in the idea that it is a country of protected *minorities*, and this very dual nature of good citizenship is the country's unique and underlying strength.

Pluralist American politics has proven what George Washington claimed for his new nation over two hundred years ago: "The Government of the United States . . . gives to bigotry no sanction, to persecution no assistance . . . while every one shall sit under his own vine and fig tree and there shall be none to make him afraid." This emphasis on the protection of difference, in a letter to a congregation of Jews, was a forward-looking advocacy of pluralist democracy, unlike France's protection of pure "Frenchness." The French sense of homogeneity and full cultural assimilation contrasts with America's demand for a less than complete assimilation as something necessary for "Americanness." The understanding of hybrid identity, combining one's past identity with a new American identity of citizenship, has allowed America to absorb great numbers of people of different nationalities, religions, and now also races.

No other major country is even close to America in importing such diverse peoples. Managing such diversity has been, in fact, America's best claim to exceptionalism. This integration of different religious and ethnic groups has been a great success of American pluralism, and with the integration of *races* now well underway, it would be unwise to bet against its eventual success as well. That is because the long history of the country is one of steadily increasing tolerance. Difficult and slow as it has been, inclusion is a crucial feature of American history and belief.

Now, with the third explosion of anti-Jewish violence in France in modern times, the emigration of Jews is a real possibility, and may drastically shrink the last major concentration of Jews in continental Europe. With major anti-Semitic incidents in France rising fivefold from 1999 to 2013, and terrorists' killings of French Jews increasing in the last decade, there should be no wonder why many French Jews are considering emigration—particularly to a welcoming Israel. Israel's prime minister Benjamin Netanyahu implored French Jews to "come home to Israel, your homeland" after four Jews were murdered in a kosher supermarket in January 2015. Though he annoyed many Jews with his appeal, the idea behind it was not at all new, but rather central to the Zionist principle, noted earlier, that Jews in the Diaspora are in "exile" and the only safe and fulfilling life for Jews is in Israel.

That Zionist belief in the "ingathering" of Diaspora Jews has been a major factor in fostering the amazing tenfold growth of the Jewish population in the state of Israel since its founding in 1948. Drawing substantial numbers of Jews from all over Europe, the Middle East, Russia, and elsewhere—everywhere but the United States—that ingathering has been vital to the creation of the skilled population needed to build a modern state. The amazing growth of the Israeli Jewish population is a demonstration of both the "pulling power" of the Zionist idea of an ingathering return, and the "pushing power" of anti-Semitism in the nations of the Diaspora.

France today has the third largest Jewish population in the world (approximately 475,000), after Israel and the United States, but anti-Semitism there is growing, particularly among a radical fringe of Muslims from the former colonies. Already citizens of France by virtue of their colonial origins, these millions of Muslims immigrated to main-land France seeking economic opportunity. But their lack of economic integration and their cultural isolation have produced large numbers of French Muslims who are angry at their lack of economic opportu-nity, angry at French secularist ideas, and angry at a much smaller but well-integrated group of French Jews largely supportive of Israel.

Even before the most recent terrorist attacks, the change in the Jewish environment of France was clear, and that change coincides with the rising number of French Muslims to roughly 9 percent of the French population. Together with lingering anti-Semitism on the po-litical right, Muslim anti-Semitism has resulted in an accelerating rate of Jewish emigration to Israel, which by 2010 had already reached 17 percent of the French Jewish population. More recently, the number of emigrating French Jews more than doubled from 3,300 in 2013 to 6,900 in 2014, and, though hard data is unavailable as of this writing, it is estimated to have reached as many as fifteen thousand in 2015.[1] Shortly after the January 7, 2015, radical Muslim attack on the satirical journal *Charlie Hebdo*, which killed eleven and wounded eleven, and the murder two days later of four Jews at the kosher Hyper Cacher supermarket, French prime minister Manuel Valls declared, "We need to act. France without Jews is no longer France." But on the very same day the French foreign minister, Laurent Fabius, shifted the blame for French inaction to protect its Jews.[2] As the French sociologist Shmuel Trigano observed,

> he [Fabius] affirmed that it is the conflict in the Middle East—read: Israel—that is the cause of anti-Semitism in France. There was no mention of the traditional Muslim disparagement of non-Muslims clearly invoked by the terrorists and reflected in the silence of "moderate" Muslims, who have, with rare excep-tions, refused to combat anti-Semitism. Nor was there a men-tion of the many failures of the French state to deal with these problems. It is to hide all of this that the authorities, at critical moments, again and again point the finger at Israel. The auto-matic exculpation of Islam from any responsibility necessarily

shifts all the blame to Israel and its policy toward the Palestinians. If Islam is not guilty, Israel is.[3]

It took the murders at the offices of *Charlie Hebdo* and the targeted
killing of Jews at Hyper Cacher to force French officials to act on what
was really happening to French Jewry. The killing of French Jews in
Toulouse years earlier, in 2012, was consistently played down.

Earlier, when the Iraq War began in 2003, President Jacques Chirac affirmed a pro-Arab and anti-American policy. According to Professor Trigano of Paris University, "there were huge demonstrations
in the streets against the United States and Israel. Because he [Chirac]
had attributed decisive influence over the Pentagon to Jewish Americans, Chirac feared 'American Judaism' would pressure Washington
to turn against France if the extent of anti-Semitism became public."[4]

In a close and detailed examination of present-day European anti-
Semitism, the journalist Jeffrey Goldberg found dismaying evidence
of renewed and widespread hostility toward Jews in the tiny populations of Scandinavia as well as in France. The old virus was back! The
depth and breadth of anti-Jewish belief and action forced Goldberg to
pose the questions, "Is it time for Jews to leave Europe? . . . Is it still a
place for Jews who want to live uncamouflaged Jewish lives?"[5] There
is no need, at present, for immediate large-scale emigration, because
today's European anti-Semitism is significantly different from that of
the 1930s. There is no state-sponsored hatred and forced expulsion
such as there was in Nazi Germany, and no worldwide unemployment
and isolation. And importantly, there are now real options to go elsewhere. This allows for an un-panicked, considered, longer-term response that may yet lead to a continuing steady emigration of French
Jews to Israel and elsewhere. The younger, less invested go first; but
the ten-to-one Muslim advantage in population will only increase,
bringing further isolation, hostility, and camouflaged living.[6]

After World War II ended and the extent of the Holocaust was fully revealed, it became apparent that only a remnant of Europe's Jews
were left, some with nowhere to go, some with no country that would
accept them, and roughly 700,000 in a Palestine mandate seeking to be

a refuge for displaced Jews while simultaneously becoming a Jewish state.

But in America, uniquely, there was stability for the six million Jews who had lived there in safety, knowing that, had not their parents or grandparents emigrated in the preceding decades, they too might have been among the six million dead. Those Jews had the further good fortune to benefit from the precipitous decline in anti-Jewish attitudes among Gentile Americans (as detailed earlier; see again Figure 1, p. 68), a decline that made possible for Jews (and others) the golden years of integration into American life.

Now, with only small pockets of Jews remaining in continental Europe, only France still has a substantial Jewish population. On one hand, it is the republican France of liberty, democracy, and the first European state to offer full citizenship to its Jews—although with an anti-pluralist warning that still resonates to new immigrants, citizens or not, "everything as a Frenchman, nothing as a Jew." That welcome was devoid of any hint of pluralism, of cultural fusion, or of hyphenated identity. It does not bode well for the absorption, now or in the future, of French Muslims, followers of a faith in which religion and the state are intertwined and secularism denounced.

On the other hand, modern France has sometimes failed to protect its Jews from outbreaks of anti-Semitism—first, as noted earlier, during the Dreyfus Affair in the 1890s, and then again when the Vichy government stripped Jews of all citizenship rights and expelled them from the military, government, and educational institutions at all levels. But if today's French Jews decide their country is unable to afford them the dignity and safety they expect, where should they go? Israel has been their main choice for decades, but should it be their only choice? A case is made here that while some Jews would and should go to Israel for personal fulfillment, many should be encouraged to come to America, which would be good for the Jewish future, good for the safety of Israel, and good for America.

Let us look, then, from the perspectives of French Jews, American Jews, and Israeli Jews, at what might well become the Jewish future should large-scale emigration be required by the anti-Semitism and terrorism that continues to grow. First, let's examine the French Jewish perspective, which is complicated by the fact that France's Jewish population is made up of two divergent segments. One is the remainder of original Jewish families of pre–World War II times, many lost to the Holocaust, who are largely assimilated, secular men and women who had accepted *laïcité*, a law that maintains a strict separation of church and state and incorporates a wide range of secular values: free speech, personal liberty, and a singular non-pluralist and homogenous sense of "French" culture.

The other segment of French Jews—actually a majority—are the Jews who emigrated from the former North African French colonies, such as Algeria, after World War II, holding French citizenship and, more often than not, belonging to Orthodox Jewish life. This latter group of Jews has probably found emigration to Israel to be an easier cultural and geographical transition than have the secular Jews of *laïcité*, given that they would be less concerned about Israel's theocratic elements, that is, the religious influence in Israeli politics.

The first segment of the French Jewish population would likely consider America to be the preferred destination should they decide that emigration is necessary, because America's views on secularity and its cosmopolitan culture is more similar to their own. In addition, America's pluralism allows the retention of "French" culture at a new destination for many years of slow adjustment. Should France succeed in overcoming the Muslim-French tensions that provoke anti-Jewish terror, then large-scale emigration will not occur. But France has a poor history of absorbing large numbers of immigrants from different cultures, particularly from a religious culture, the Islamic, that is used to overriding secular governments.

The pressure toward cultural homogeneity, expressed early in the Republic—"nothing as a Jew"—holds as well for Muslims today, and makes the absorption of the growing Muslim population exceedingly difficult. Despite the French government's determined efforts to subdue terrorism and anti-Semitism in France, the country's long-faltering economy produces high unemployment among young Muslims and increases Muslim isolation. French economic limitations, and

Muslim beliefs that politics and government should be subordinate to religious authority, make the French job of integrating their Muslim population much more difficult. The *Sturm und Drang* of this clash of cultures leaves the Jewish community of France as the group most directly victimized by a sustained period of hostility and terrorism.

The infusion of a significant French Muslim population has already brought important changes to France. According to the Islam specialist Gilles Kepel and the scholar Mark Lilla, while older generations of Muslims practice a somewhat more pacific Islam and see less contradiction of cultures, the younger generation of Muslims—large in number—have been greatly influenced by *fundamentalist* Muslim ideas imported from the Middle East. "Different groups, some strictly Salafist, some associated with the Muslim Brotherhood, compete for control of local associations and actively recruit younger members to the consternation of the more integrated and shrinking establishment." The charismatic preachers that "educate" the younger generation are largely trained in Saudi Arabia or elsewhere outside of France. Their young French-speaking followers are "much more observant and separatist than their parents and have much more extreme views on issues like sexuality (particularly homosexuality), female purity, and Jews and Israel."[7]

The highly valued education system in France, the teacher of the values of *laïcité* to the young, is in a state of trauma. The Obin Report, commissioned in 2004 by the Chirac government, studied over sixty middle-grade and high-school students, and found Muslim intimidation of non-Muslim students to be so prevalent that the report was buried, lest its findings provoke unrest or even violence. And while the report found that the situation was bad for French students in general, for French Jewish students it was even worse, as evidenced in part by the transfers of many Jewish students from public to private schools. As the Obin Report states: "There is a stupefying and cruel reality in France: Jewish children, and Jewish children alone, cannot be educated in all of our schools."[8] Earlier, in 1996, long before the most recent terror attack on a Jewish supermarket, a principal in the French city of Lyons had to move the last two Jewish students elsewhere because he could not protect their security.

The situation for French Jews is dangerous, owing partly to a weak economy and political instability. Efforts to produce even small changes in policy also face a right-wing National Front political movement that is historically anti-Semitic and harshly anti-immigrant—a movement that is eager to seek political advantage from any cultural clash, and happy to see others promoting anti-Jewish acts. Central to any change for France and its Jews is the reversal of a historical trend that has demonstrated that, while France has been long open to fleeing political asylum-seekers, assimilating into French life large numbers of immigrants with different ethnic and religious backgrounds has not been a French experience. Unlike America's long-practiced absorption of large numbers of different ethnic and religious groups (and more recently racial groups), France has not only rejected the pluralism of America, but also made major efforts to keep French life singularly "French," unadulterated by the cultures of newcomers. Keeping the French language and the culture free of fusion with other cultures in order to preserve a singular sense of "Frenchness" contrasts sharply with the American way of allowing, even encouraging, immigrants to retain the unique aspects of their cultures.

While America produces many politically loyal but not fully assimilated (in cultural terms) Italian-Americans, German-Americans, and Jewish Americans, there is no equivalent "Algerian-Frenchman" in France. That a French president (Nicolas Sarkozy) could publicly state the following in 2011 (without major political backlash) gives one a good idea of how France creates a singular national identity without elements of fusion or hybridness: "If you come to France you accept to melt into a simple community, which is the national community, and if you don't want to accept that, you are not welcome in France."[9]

What, then, does the future of the Jewish people look like with the resurgence of anti-Semitism in Europe, growing anti-Jewish hostility in the Muslim world, and increasing fear in America that the same virus may come here?

For Israel, the substantial emigration of French Jews would be a significant plus, affirming the long-held tenet of Zionism that Jews of the Diaspora must return from their "exile" to the "promised land" of the state of Israel. Israel would gain an influx of highly educated, technologically advanced people who would find established institutions that ease language and other problems for immigrants.

For French immigrants to the United States, the strength of America's pluralist, hybrid conception of citizenship makes immigrant entry to the country much easier than it is elsewhere. The cultural requirements for good citizenship in America are lower than the complete assimilation required in France. It allows much more room for the new immigrants to live a kind of dual life as they assimilate, retaining much of their original culture while slowly absorbing into the American one.

A significant influx of French Jews would enhance American Jewry as well, giving fresh blood to its culture as earlier Jewish immigrations have done. With a low birthrate, increasing secularity, and considerable intermarriage, the new immigrants would add new members to an aging Jewish population and add some new dimensions to Jewish culture itself. As skilled and educated people, most of whom already speak English, they should have no trouble finding jobs, and as historical victims of political and social terrorism, their entry into this country should not be difficult politically.

The enlarging and strengthening of the American Jewish community is not only good in itself, but it is also an important positive factor in maintaining the close political and economic ties between America and Israel. Indeed, although Israel claims the right to act independently, Israelis know deep down that America—not just American Jews—is their necessary protector.

When the UN eliminated mandate control of Palestine in 1948 and partitioned the mandate into a predominantly Jewish and a predominantly Palestinian Arab territory, Israel alone declared itself a state. When it came to UN recognition of Israel, England voted against, leaving Harry Truman and America to round up barely enough votes to recognize Israel as a legitimate state. When in 1967 Egypt mobilized its armies, blockaded a key seaport of Israel, and pushed UN peace-keeping troops out of their neutral zone, France's de Gaulle insisted that Israel not strike until they took the first military blow. When they did not accept his advice, France permanently rejected its close military alliance with Israel, becoming its critic instead, and leaving only Germany as a guilt-ridden but supportive friend. And Germany has, in fact, responded by supplying Israel with Polaris-type nuclear-equipped submarines—now sitting at the ready off the coast of Iran.

What this means for the future of Israel and the future of world Jewry in a world of terror is that Israel has no close friends among the major powers except for Germany and America. To the extent that American Jews are strengthened by an influx of French Jews seeking safety and a good life, it helps maintain strong support for America's support for Israel in the future; American Jews should in fact be recommending America as a good alternative to Israel, entreating some French Jews to consider immigrating to the United States rather than passively waiting to respond. America has proven over and over— even in the darkest days of the Great Depression— that it would protect Jewish political rights, whereas other major countries have failed to do so. Bring a substantial group of Jews from France; make plans now, for it is the only large group of Jews left on the continent of Europe. Welcome them to an America which is the most powerful and dependable protector of Jews, and Israel's truest friend.

The unmistakable trend, then, is toward the development of two dominant centers of world Jewry, one in Israel, the Jewish people's biblical homeland, and one in America, the only country in the Diaspora where the political rights of Jews have never been withheld, revoked or curtailed. Together they provide a critical synergy for sustaining and enriching the Jewish future. The continuing cultivation by American Jews of non-Jewish political support for Israel, and the continuing support of both American political parties for Israel, are imperatives. For the American and Israeli relationship to remain close and bipartisan, Israel must examine the reasons, identified earlier, for the defection of younger generations of Jews from the Jewish community, now and in the future. These same younger generations must, in turn, better understand not only the urgency and gravity of Israel's national defense concerns, particularly the potential threat of a nuclear Iran, but also Israelis' distrust of Europe for its history of anti-Semitism, which still finds expression in hostility to Israel.

Israel must take the risk of establishing a Palestinian state, for not only is the ongoing occupation of the West Bank eroding the democratic principles of Israel, but the permanent presence of over a million Arab-Israeli citizens inside Israel and their families on the other side of an unsettled border creates an unstable and untenable situation. The only country with sufficient political power, economic strength, and international clout to mediate a settlement is America. Like it or not, America is crucial to the long-term survival of Israel as a Jewish state, and is also the proven protector of Jews in the last major center of Jewish life in the Diaspora.

American pluralism—in government, in culture, and in citizenship—is thus a gift to the Jewish future, as it directs attention not only to what is common to Jews and Gentiles, but also to what is different. As a nation of diverse peoples and races, America has been slowly gaining respect for "otherness"—the same respect that the Jewish people, the historical "others," have sought for thousands of years.

Postscript

I started this book on a personal note, stating my belief that falling in love with a Gentile woman made me more conscious of "difference," and directed my thinking toward the subject of culture. It was not only the fact of my intermarriage that moved me in that direction, but my marriage specifically to Len—who sensed my connection to the Jewish people even before I realized it myself. As an eighteen-year-old, I felt no link to Judaism as a religion, and yet Len sensed that I felt an unusually strong kinship not only with my Jewish family but with the countless generations of Jews who came before them.

Len had a sense of my connection to a culture that was strong even though I could not articulate it then. Her early and expressed desire to join my family and my people, despite the lineage of the Rice family from the Mayflower and centuries of English prominence before, only assured me of her intentions. Speaking at Brown in 1947, Rabbi James Rudin opposed intermarriage because it would mean "one Jew less." Len added simply, "It won't be true in our family"—and she meant it.

During the early years of our relationship, Len encouraged my growing interest in Jews and their distinctive culture. She saw my skepticism, my probing deeper into things, as part of the Jewish intellectual tradition and my connection to it. In my early twenties, Len gave me a birthday present of the new twenty-four-volume James Strachey translation of Sigmund Freud's complete works. To me, Freud had expressed, long before the idea of cultural pluralism and

221

"Judaism as a civilization," the idea that Jewish life extended beyond the Jewish religion to being a "life-affirming" culture.

Len continued to support the tightening of my relationship to the Jewish people, despite knowing that while I admired Jewish courage and persistence in religious belief, I was not a religious Jew. Knowing the importance of "belonging," she helped to make me what I was meant to be, and made herself, like the biblical Ruth, part of my family and my people.

Appendix

Figure 2 (see p. 72)

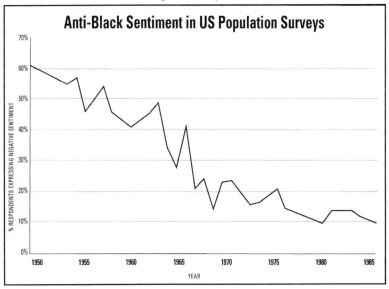

Figure 2 shows trend data detailing anti-Black responses to national survey questions from the period of 1950 to 1988. It is an agglomeration of a basket of three responses: positive responses to whether or not one would mind having a black neighbor, negative responses as to whether one would send their own child to an integrated school, and negative responses as to whether one would vote for a black president. Though the precision of the measured effect would be improved significantly if a single repeated question had been asked throughout, a comparison of the range of possible values at a 95 percent confidence level puts both the direction and rapidity of change beyond a reasonable doubt.

Sources

All NORC General Social Surveys can be found at www.norc.uchicago.edu/GSS+Website/

All National Election Survey data can be found at www.electionstudies.org/

All other survey datasets used can be found at www.ropercenter.uconn.edu/data_access/ipoll/ipoll.html

Notes

Introduction

1. George Washington, Letter to the Jews of Newport, RI, August 18, 1790. As quoted at www.tourosynagogue.org/history-learning/gw-letter (accessed July 5, 2016).
2. Lawrence A. Fuchs, *The American Kaleidoscope: Race, Ethnicity, and the Civic Culture* (Hanover, NH: Wesleyan University Press, 1990), 5.
3. Yosef Hayim Yerushalmi, *Freud's Moses: Judaism Terminable and Interminable* (New Haven and London: Yale University Press, 1991), 14.
4. Ibid.

Chapter One — The Fusion of Cultures

1. Tom W. Smith, "Jewish Distinctiveness in America: A Statistical Portrait," *American Jewish Committee,* 2005. Data is based on studies conducted by the National Opinion Research Center (NORC), 66. See also Steven L. Pease, *The Golden Age of Jewish Achievement: The Compendium of a Culture, a People, and Their Stunning Performance* (Sonoma, CA: Deucalion, 2009), 390.
2. Stephen Greenblatt, *The New Republic* (March 12, 2008): 40.
3. While local and regional studies show somewhat larger numbers of Orthodox, new large-scale random national studies show less optimistic figures for the Orthodox. The estimate for all Orthodox Jews is a combination of the only two national surveys in existence, *The Pew Forum on Religion 2007* and Smith, "Jewish Distinctiveness in America."
4. The Reconstructionist Movement and its founder Mordecai Kaplan are discussed more fully in Chapter 3.
5. For a discussion of declining hostility toward Jews and its effect on Jewish cohesion, see Alan M. Dershowitz, *The Vanishing American Jew* (New York: Simon & Schuster, 1997), chap. 2.
6. Estimates of Jewish intermarriage before 1950 are generally unreliable and less scientifically sound, but the consensus figure is approximately one in twenty Jews marrying a Gentile.
7. This point was made by Nathan Glazer and Daniel P. Moynihan in *Beyond the Melting Pot* (Boston: MIT Press, 1963), and their evidence for the distinctiveness of Jewish values, ideas, and behavior at that time emphasizes its continuity, at least for American Jews, a half century later.

8. Smith, "Jewish Distinctiveness in America."
9. Cynthia Ozick, "Bialik's Hint," *Commentary*, February 1983, 27.
10. Stephen J. Whitfield, *In Search of American Jewish Culture* (Hanover, NH: Brandeis University Press, 1999), 12.
11. For a further discussion of employment restrictions on Jews, see Charles Silberman, *A Certain People: American Jews and Their Lives Today* (New York: Summit Books, 1985), 87–95.
12. Jonathan Kaufman, *Broken Alliance: The Turbulent Times Between Blacks and Jews in America* (New York: Simon and Schuster, 1988), 86–87.
13. Robert Motherwell, interview by the author, Greenwich, CT, June 5, 1990 .

CHAPTER TWO — THE PROTESTANT REFORMATION IN AMERICA AND AMERICAN JEWS

1. Jonathan D. Sarna, *American Judaism: A History* (New Haven: Yale University Press, 2004), 2.
2. Ibid.
3. Ibid., 3.
4. Samuel Huntington, *American Politics: The Promise of Disharmony* (Cambridge, MA: Harvard University Press, 1981), 23.
5. Eric Nelson, *The Hebrew Republic: Jewish Sources and the Transformation of European Political Thought* (Cambridge, MA: Harvard University Press, 2010), 13, 14.
6. Ibid., 135.
7. Leonard Dinnerstein, *Antisemitism in America* (New York: Oxford University Press, 1994), 8.
8. For warning letters back to Europe, see Sarna, *American Judaism,* chap. 2.
9. Ibid., 65.
10. Seymour M. Lipset, "A Unique People in an Exceptional Country," in *American Pluralism and the Jewish Community*, ed. Seymour M. Lipset (New Brunswick, NJ: Transaction Publishers, 1990), 9.
11. Bruce Feiler, *America's Prophet: Moses and the American Story* (New York: Harper Collins, 2009), 102.
12. Washington, Letter to the Jews of Newport.
13. Quoted in Karl E. Meyer, "Who Gets to Be French?", Op-ed in *New York Times*, April 12, 2012.
14. For a full discussion of hybrid or dual national identity, see Lawrence A. Fuchs, *The American Kaleidoscope: Race, Ethnicity, and the Civic Culture* (Hanover, NH: Wesleyan University Press, 1990), 5.
15. Ibid.
16. Jerry Z. Muller, *Capitalism and the Jews* (Princeton, NJ: Princeton University Press, 2010), 29.
17. Ibid., 30.
18. Ibid., 26.
19. See Weber's defense in Muller, *Capitalism and the Jews,* 54–56.

20. See Charles Murray, "Jewish Genius," *Commentary*, April 2007, 33.

21. Sarna, *American Judaism*, 45.

22. Ibid., 36.

23. In addition to Sarna, see Cheryl Lynn Greenberg, *Troubling the Waters: Black-Jewish Relations in the American Century* (Princeton, NJ: Princeton University Press, 2006), and Eric L. Goldstein, *The Price of Whiteness: Jews, Race, and American Identity* (Princeton, NJ: Princeton University Press, 2006).

24. Lipset, "A Unique People," 9.

25. Ibid., 10.

26. Howard M. Sachar, *A History of Jews in the Modern World* (New York: Alfred A. Knopf, 2005), 248.

27. Lipset, "A Unique People," 8. For a fuller explanation of Grant's order and the issue of Grant's anti-Semitism, see Jonathan D. Sarna, *When General Grant Expelled the Jews* (New York: Next Book/Schocken, 2012).

28. Dinnerstein, *Antisemitism in America*, 22.

CHAPTER THREE — THE REACTION: INDUSTRIALISM AND MASS IMMIGRATION
BREED INTOLERANCE

1. Robert Higgs, *The Transformation of the American Economy 1865–1914: An Essay in Interpretation* (New York: Wiley, 1971), 15–20.

2. Richard L. Rubin, *Press, Party, and Presidency* (New York: W.W. Norton, 1981), 78–83.

3. Everett Carl Ladd Jr., *American Political Parties: Social Change and Political Response* (New York: W.W. Norton, 1970), 121–122.

4. Ibid.

5. Ibid., 123.

6. Dinnerstein, *Antisemitism in America*, 50.

7. Ibid.

8. Ibid., 91.

9. Garland E. Allen, "Eugenics Comes to America," in *The Bell Curve Debate*, eds. Russell Jacoby and Naomi Glauberman (New York: Times Books, 1995), 441–475.

10. Ladd Jr., *American Political Parties*, 145.

11. Ibid., 140.

12. Ibid., 141.

13. Leon J. Kamin, "The Pioneers of IQ Testing," in *The Bell Curve Debate*, 492.

14. Carl Bingham, "A Study of Intelligence," in *The Bell Curve Debate*, 572.

15. Ibid., 573.

16. Goldstein, *The Price of Whiteness*, 123.

17. Ibid., 182–183.

18. Werner J. Severin and James W. Tankard Jr., *Communication Theories: Origins, Methods, and Uses in the Mass Media*, 5th ed. (New York: Longerman, 2001), 111.

19. Donald Warren, *Radio Priest: Charles Coughlin, the Father of Hate Radio* (New York: The Free Press, 1996), 98–118.

20. Charles E. Silberman, *A Certain People: American Jews and Their Lives Today* (New York: Summit Books, 1985), 57.

21. Ibid., 55.

22. Ibid., 58.

23. Dinnerstein, *Antisemitism in America,* 131.

24. Howard M. Sachar, *A History of the Jews in the Modern World* (New York: Alfred A. Knopf, 2005), 397.

25. Peter Grose, *Israel in the Mind of America* (New York: Alfred A. Knopf, 1983), 116.

26. For a balanced evaluation of FDR and the Jews, see Richard Breitman and Allan V. Lichtman, *FDR and the Jews* (Cambridge, MA: The Belknap Press of Harvard University Press, 2013).

CHAPTER FOUR — TOWARD THE JEWISH GOLDEN AGE IN AMERICA

1. Ladd Jr., *American Political Parties,* 216.

2. For important aspects of that history see Taylor Branch, *Parting the Waters: America in the King Years 1954–63* (New York: Simon & Schuster, 1988); Richard Kluger, *Simple Justice* (New York: Vintage Books, 1975); and Juan Williams, *Eyes on the Prize* (New York: Penguin Books, 1987).

3. See Rubin, *Press, Party, and Presidency,*154–160, for the significant increase in television news coverage of civil rights activism.

4. Silberman, *A Certain People,* 98.

5. Ibid., 99.

6. David A. Hollinger, *Science, Jews, and Secular Culture: Studies in Mid-Twentieth Century American Intellectual History* (Princeton, NJ: Princeton University Press, 1996), 8.

7. Ibid., 7–8.

8. Silberman, *A Certain People,* 99.

9. Hollinger, *Science, Jews, and Secular Culture,* 25–30.

10. Silberman, *A Certain People,* 109.

11. Richard Kluger, *Simple Justice: The History of Brown v. Board of Education* (New York: Random House, 1977), 80.

12. Ibid., 690.

13. Ibid., 598.

14. See National Opinion Research Center (NORC), "Racial Trends 1943–2009."

15. James Carroll, *Constantine's Sword: The Church and the Jews* (New York: Houghton Mifflin, 2001), 219. For a review of the literature on anti-Jewish statements by the Catholic hierarchy, see Gary Wills, "Catholics and Jews: The Great Change," *New York Review of Books,* March 21, 2013.

16. For an interesting Jewish perspective on the "witness" doctrine see Norman Podhoretz, *Why Are Jews Liberals?* (New York: Doubleday, 2009), 9–16.

17. Quoted in Sarna, 313.

18. Goldstein, *The Price of Whiteness,* 193.

19. Gerald Pomper, "From Confusion to Clarity: Issues and American Voters, 1956–1968," *The American Political Science Review*, 66, no. 2 (June 1972): 420.

CHAPTER FIVE — JEWISH DISTINCTIVENESS AND AMERICAN PLURALISM

1. See Nathan Glazer, "The Structure of Ethnicity," *Public Opinion* (October-November 1984): 1–30 and 32.
2. See National Election-Day surveys, formerly New York Times/CBS News surveys.
3. The surveys of NORC vary in time, but only slightly. The categories for Jews are remarkably stable. Half of all Jews define their political ideology as "liberal" vs. less than 20 percent of non-Jews, and half of all Jews identify their political party as the Democratic Party. Correspondingly, the number of Jews who define themselves as "conservative" and Republican is only about 15 percent. The rest self-identify as independents.
4. See New York Times/CBS 2006 Election Day Congressional Survey.
5. Gerhard Lenski, *The Religious Factor: A Sociological Study of Religion's Impact on Politics, Economics, and Family Life* (Garden City, NY: Doubleday, 1961), 354–356. A non-national survey.
6. See Smith, "Jewish Distinctiveness in America," 20.
7. Ibid., 109–116.
8. Ibid., 22.
9. See National Election Day Survey 2008, formerly New York Times/CBS News surveys.
10. See John C. Green, "American Religious Landscape and Political Attitudes: A Baseline for 2004," Fourth National Survey of Religion and Politics, Bliss Institute, University of Akron, supported by the Pew Forum.
11. Ibid., 20–29.
12. Ibid.
13. Seymour M. Lipset, *American Exceptionalism: A Double-Edged Sword* (New York: W.W. Norton, 1996), 170. The specific percentages were 50 percent to Commitment to Social Equality, 17 percent to Religious Observances and 17 percent to Support for Israel.
14. A comparison of the CBS News/New York Times Survey on Immigration December 2007 and the 2007 Annual Survey of Jewish Opinion November 2007 shows, first, that non-Jewish Americans are 15 percent more convinced that the problem is very serious (57–42 percent). Also, that on the question of deportation, 24 percent of Americans agree vs. only 15 percent of American Jews (comparison with Gallup/USA Survey, March 2007).
15. Stephen Steinberg, *The American Melting Pot: Catholics and Jews in Higher Education* (New York: Carnegie Commission Publication, 1974), 101–103, 120–123.
16. Sherwin B. Nuland, *Maimonides* (New York: Schocken Books, 2005), 12.
17. Ibid., 7.
18. Ibid., 18.
19. Ibid., 64.
20. Irving Kristol, "The Liberal Tradition of American Jews," in Lipset, ed., 115.

21. Green, "American Religious Landscape," 26–29.

22. Norman Podhoretz, *Why Are Jews Liberal?* (New York: Doubleday, 2009), 283.

23. Green, "American Religious Landscape," 22–29.

24. Yuri Slezkine, *The Jewish Century* (Princeton NJ: Princeton University Press, 2004), 64–71.

25. Richard J. Herrnstein and Charles Murray, *The Bell Curve: Intelligence and Class Structure in American Life* (New York: The Free Press, 1994), 286–288.

26. Smith, *Jewish Distinctiveness,* 204–205.

27. Ruth Benedict, "Child Rearing in Certain European Countries," *American Journal of Orthopsychiatry* 19, (Nov. 2, 1949).

28. Smith, *Jewish Distinctiveness,* 143.

29. For an elaborate but unconvincing claim of innate Jewish genius, see Murray, "Jewish Genius."

30. Egon Mayer and Barry A. Kosmin, "American Jewish Identity Survey, 2001," *AJIS Report* (Feb. 2002) Summary.

31. See Sarna, *American Judaism,* 151–159, and Deborah Dash Moore, ed., *Eastern European Jews in Two Worlds: Studies from the Yivo Annual* (Evanston: Northwestern University Press, 1990), 290–299.

CHAPTER SIX — THREATS FROM WITHIN: INTERMARRIAGE AND SECULARITY

1. There has been much confusion over the rate of intermarriage. Although it has, in fact, multiplied ten times over the last five decades, the finding that half of contemporary Jewish marriages are intermarriages should not be used to exaggerate the issue. Even if 50 percent of Jewish singles married a born non-Jew, only one Jew in three, 33 percent, would have intermarried because one "in-marriage" requires two Jews.

2. David Halberstam, *The Powers That Be* (New York: Dell, 1979), 721.

3. Rabbi James Rudin, lecture at Brown University, Providence, Rhode Island, November 12, 1947.

4. Sylvia Barack Fishman, *Double or Nothing?: Jewish Families and Mixed Marriage* (Hanover: Brandeis University Press, 2004), 58 and chap. 7.

5. Ibid., 7 and Appendix, Table 2.

6. See Jack Wertheimer, Charles Liebman, and Steven M. Cohen, "How to Save American Jews," *Commentary* (January 1996): 47–51.

7. Jack Wertheimer, "Surrendering to Intermarriage," *Commentary* (March 2001): 32.

8. See Egon Mayer, "Jewish Education and Intermarriage Among American Jews," prepared for June 14, 1993, meeting of the Network for Research on Jewish Education, Chicago, Table 1.

9. Steven M. Cohen and Arnold M. Eisen, *The Jew Within: Self, Family and Community in America* (Bloomington, Indiana: University Press, 2008), 162.

10. For a major survey (with a sample of 35,000 respondents) by the Pew Forum on Religion and Public Life (U.S. Religious Landscape Survey), 2007, the question of whether Jews

are chosen by God was not asked directly. But because the survey found that only about 25 to 30 percent of Jews define God as personal, transcendent, and intervening, I think it fair to deduce that "chosenness by God" is a distinct minority belief among American Jews.

11. This survey was personally conducted primarily over twelve years, from 1988 to 2000, by personal interviews with both spouses. A total of eighty interviews were conducted. The survey was not done for quantitative analysis but, rather, to obtain a very personal set of insights into intermarriage. As noted, most findings about intermarriage that are used in the text are quantitative studies by other authors.

12. Nathan Glazer, *American Judaism* (Chicago: Univ. of Chicago Press, 1957).

13. Susan Jacoby, *Moment* (May-June 2009): 25.

14. Details are from Pew, *Religious Landscape*, 2007, 5–13 and 18.

15. Ibid., 5–20.

16. Samuel G. Freedman, *Jew vs. Jew: The Struggle for the Soul of American Jewry* (New York: Simon and Schuster, 2000), 243.

17. Quoted in Sander L. Gilman, *Smart Jews: The Construction of the Image of Jewish Superior Intelligence* (Lincoln: University of Nebraska Press, 1996), 120.

18. Ibid.

19. Emanuel Rackman, "Deeds, not Doctrine," *Jewish Week* (December 22, 1989): 30.

20. Jonathan D. Sarna, "The Secret of Jewish Continuity," *Commentary* (October 1994): 58.

CHAPTER SEVEN — ANTI-SEMITISM: IS AMERICA DIFFERENT?

1. Jonathan M. Hess, *Germans, Jews and the Claims of Modernity* (New Haven: Yale University Press, 2002), 7–10.

2. Amos Elon, *The Pity of It All: A History of Jews in Germany 1743–1933* (New York: Henry Holt, 2002), 205 and 206–215.

3. Ibid., 95.

4. Fritz Stern, *Five Germanys I Have Known* (New York: Farrar, Straus and Giroux, 2006), 21.

5. Elon, *The Pity of It All*, 205. See also Peter Gay, *Freud, Jews, and Other Germans* (New York: Oxford University Press, 1979) for a different view.

6. Ibid., 217.

7. Sander Gilman, *Jewish Self-Hatred* (Baltimore: John Hopkins University Press, 1986), 53, 148, 386. See also Gilman, *Smart Jews*, for an analysis of ongoing negative stereotypes and their relationship to claims of superior intelligence.

8. Stern, *Five Germanys*, 33.

9. Werner Sombart, *The Jews and Modern Capitalism* (Glencoe, IL: The Free Press, 1951), 253–278.

10. Adolf Hitler, *Mein Kampf*, archived at www.jewishvirtuallibrary.org/jsource/Holocaust/kampf.html (accessed May 24, 2016).

11. Quoted in Richard Taruskin, "The Musical Mystique," *The New Republic*, October 22 (2007): 41.

12. Howard M. Sachar, *A History of the Jews in the Modern World* (New York: Alfred A. Knopf, 2005), 248.

13. Stern, *Five Germanys*, 22.

14. Raphael Patai, *The Jewish Mind* (London: Jason Aronson, 1977), 339–342.

15. Gilman, *Jewish Self-Hatred*, 139–143.

16. Constitutional Assembly, France, as quoted in Pierre Birnbaum, *The Jews of the Republic: A Political History of State Jews in France from Gambetta to Vichy* (Stanford, CA: Stanford University Press, 1996).

17. Ibid., 207–215 and passim.

18. Ibid., 15, 236.

19. Pierre Birnbaum, *Jewish Destinies: Citizenship, State, and Community in Modern France* (New York: Hill and Wang, 1995), 83.

20. Birnbaum, *The Jews of the Republic*, 376.

21. Ibid., 155.

22. Ibid., 338.

23. Archives of the Central Consistory. Also quoted in Birnbaum, *The Jews of the Republic*, 351.

24. Shira Schoenberg, "The Virtual Jewish World – United Kingdom," at www.jewishvirtuallibrary.org/jsource/vjw/England.html (accessed on May 24, 2016).

25. Robert S. Wistrich, *Anti-Semitism: The Longest Hatred* (New York: Schocken Books, 1991), 107.

26. Anthony Julius, *Trials of the Diaspora: A History of Anti-Semitism in England* (New York: Oxford University Press, 2010), 304–313.

27. Ibid., 149–150, 345.

28. Ibid., 349.

29. For further development of the idea of kinship felt by early American Protestants with the Jews of the Old Testament, see Feiler, *America's Prophet*, chap. 9.

30. Lawrence A. Fuchs, *The American Kaleidoscope: Race, Ethnicity, and the Civic Culture* (Middletown, CT: Wesleyan University Press, 1990), 5.

31. Jonathan Sarna, "Anti-Semitism and American History," *Commentary* (March 1981): 46.

32. Lipset, "A Unique People in an Exceptional Country," 22.

CHAPTER EIGHT — INTERTWINED: RACE AND JEWS IN AMERICAN CULTURE

1. James Carroll, *Constantine's Sword: The Church and the Jews* (New York: Houghton Mifflin, 2001), 318–322.

2. Bruce Feiler, in an interview with *Newsweek* magazine.

3. Feiler, *America's Prophet*, 102.

4. See "Slavery and Justice: Report of the Brown University Steering Committee on Slavery and Justice," 2006, 8–11.

5. Feiler, *America's Prophet*, 173.

6. Greenberg, *Troubling the Waters*, 16.

7. Ibid.

8. King and his fellow civil rights marchers were often jailed in the South, and his supporters in the Southern Christian Leadership Conference, the NAACP, and CORE had lists of donors who could be relied on to post bail for jailed marchers. Many Jews were on those lists.

9. Quoted in Sarna, *American Judaism*, 310.

10. Ibid., 311.

11. James Baldwin, quoted in Gerald Early, "Who Is the Jew: A Question of African-American Identity," *Common Quest* (Spring 1996): 41.

12. Ibid.

13. IJJ (Institute for Justice and Journalism) Affirmative Action Report, November 2006, 1.

14. Quoted in Goldstein, *The Price of Whiteness*, 219.

15. See Jonathan Kaufman, *Broken Alliance: The Turbulent Times Between Blacks and Jews in America* (New York: Simon & Schuster, 1995) for an excellent analysis of the intensity of the divide.

16. Greenberg, *Troubling the Waters*, 236–238.

17. For an interesting analysis of how Jews dealt with their empathy for black people, yet feared being on the wrong side of the racial divide, see "A White Race of Another Kind?" in Goldstein, *The Price of Whiteness*, chap. 6, 138–164.

18. Quoted in Steven M. Cohen, *American Modernity and Jewish Identity* (New York: Tavistock Publications, 1983), 25.

19. A good example of Jewish philanthrophy toward Blacks in the South: Julius Rosenwald, President of Sears & Roebuck, was famous for founding more than 5,000 "Rosenwald Schools" and over 4,000 libraries devoted to the segregated black community, www.searsarchive.com.

20. American Jewish Historical Society, "Jews and the Rule of Law – Ruth Bader Ginsburg," *Heritage* (May 2005): 4.

CHAPTER NINE — THE PROMISED LAND: HERE OR THERE?

1. Theodore Herzl, *The Jewish State* (1896; repr. New York: Dover, 1988), 39.

2. Hasia R. Diner, *A New Promised Land* (New York: Oxford University Press, 2000), 37.

3. Herzl, *The Jewish State*, 85.

4. Melvin I. Urofsky, *American Zionism: From Herzl to the Holocaust* (Lincoln: University of Nebraska Press, 1975), 95.

5. Ibid., 75.

6. Herzl, *The Jewish State*, 70.

7. Ibid., 86.

8. Melvin I. Urofsky, *Louis D. Brandeis: A Life* (New York: Pantheon Books, 2009), 402–406.

9. Ibid., 408.

10. Ibid., 410.

11. Ibid., 520.

12. Ibid., 534.

13. Peter Grose, *Israel in the Mind of America* (New York: Alfred A. Knopf, 1983), 235.

14. Ibid., 270–272.

15. Ibid., 306.

16. Patai, *The Jewish Mind*, 395.

17. For a later manifestation of the same "return" fervor, see VOAnews.com, "238 North American Jews Immigrate to Israel," at www.voanews.com/content/a-13-2009-08-05-voa22-68657442/408253.html

18. Daniel Gordis, *Saving Israel: How the Jewish People Can Win a War That May Never End* (Hoboken NJ: John Wiley and Sons, 2009), 39–45.

19. David Brooks, *The New York Times*, April 17, 2009, A29.

20. A system whereby non-Muslim groups who lived in Muslim lands accepted various limitations of rights but were "protected" by the governing power.

21. The statistics of emigration to Israel come from Israeli archives organized by Professor Sergio Della Pergola, the Shlomo Argov Chair in Israeli-Diaspora Relations, Hebrew University of Jerusalem.

22. Ibid.

23. VOAnews.com, "238 North American Jews Immigrate to Israel."

24. Conor Cruise O'Brien, *The Siege: The Saga of Israel and Zionism* (New York: Simon & Schuster, 1986), 656–662.

25. See Steven M. Cohen and Ari Y. Kelman, with the assistance of Lauren Blitzer, "Beyond Distancing: Young Adult American Jews and Their Alienation from Israel." Hebrew Union College, Jewish Institute of Religion, JCCA Research Center, p. 11.

26. Ibid., p. 13.

27. Interviews conducted by the author confirm Cohen and Kelman's point that most non-Jewish-born spouses had views about Israeli-Palestinian issues similar to those of their Jewish-born spouses, but held those views less intensely.

CHAPTER TEN — FACTS AND SPECULATIONS

1. Steven L. Pease, *The Golden Age of Jewish Achievement: The Compendium of a Culture, a People, and Their Stunning Performance* (Sonoma, CA: Deucalion Publishers, 2009), 392–396. See also Murray, "Jewish Genius," wherein Murray quotes himself and other mostly Gentile researchers in an attempt to make the case for Jews' being genetically endowed with above-average intelligence.

2. Pease, *The Golden Age of Jewish Achievement*, 394.

3. See Smith, "Jewish Distinctiveness in America," 66.

4. Pease, *The Golden Age of Jewish Achievement*, 390.

5. Wallace Stevens, "Le Monocle de Mon Oncle," in *The Collected Poems of Wallace Stevens* (New York: Alfred A. Knopf, 1954), 15.

6. From Menninger's own book, *A Psychiatrist's World* (New York: The Viking Press, 1959), and also from Arnold A. Rogow, ed. *The Jew in the Gentile World*, (New York: The Macmillan Company, 1961), 331.

7. This saying about civilization having begun when people started using words rather than physical force to settle differences is of uncertain origin, but widely attributed to Sigmund Freud.

8. Noted in Murray, "Jewish Genius," 33.

9. Deuteronomy 30:15–20. The translation is by Robert Alter.

10. Alan Wolfe, *The Transformation of American Religion: How We Actually Live Our Faith* (New York: Free Press, 2003), 248.

11. Dershowitz, *The Vanishing American Jew*, 334.

12. Insider Guide to College Life Admissions: Admissions 105 and 106: The Top 60 Schools Jews Choose. Reported in *Reform Judaism* (Fall, 2008): 1 and 2.

13. See Samuel G. Freedman, "On Religion," *New York Times*, June 15, 2012; in reference to a research paper published in 2000 by Colleen Fong and Judy Yung, who found that more than 18 percent of intermarriages among Chinese and Japanese Americans were to American Jews, despite Jews' being only 2 percent of the American population.

14. Socrates Lagios , interview with the author at Brown University, May 28, 1990.

Chapter Eleven — Terrorism, Anti-Semitism, and the Jewish Future

1. Statistics for immigration to Israel from France and elsewhere are from the Jewish Agency for Israel, Tel Aviv, Israel.

2. Shmuel Trigano, "A Journey Through French Anti-Semitism," *Jewish Review of Books* (Spring 2015): 5.

3. Ibid.

4. Ibid., 6.

5. Jeffrey Goldberg, "Is It Time for the Jews to Leave Europe?", *The Atlantic* (April 2015): 68.

6. Ibid.

7. See Mark Lilla, "France on Fire," *New York Review of Books* (March 5, 2015): 16, quoting Gilles Kepel.

8. Ibid., quoting the Obin Report.

9. Quoted in Karl E. Meyer, "Who Gets to Be French?", *New York Times*, April 11, 2012, Op-Ed.

Acknowledgements

This book in its present form is the third and final attempt to write a book concerning these topics: (1) the integration of Jews into America, (2) how America reacted to its Jews, (3) how distinctive from non-Jews they have become despite many generations of assimilation, and (4) why their American pathway is different from others'.

Many people must be credited for helping me persist in my efforts. My oldest friend, from the fifth grade, professor and poet Robert Pack, consistently and enthusiastically pushed me ahead. My first professor in graduate school, Ira Katznelson, who has taught me so much about comparative analysis, provided helpful comments. Thanks, too, to Steve Howard, an assistant on an earlier book I wrote, for valuable insights on the text of this one. I owe much gratitude to Richard Marek, a publisher of note, who brought order and shape to the project. Thanks are also due to my literary agent, Bob Markel, who advised me to add the personal prologues to each chapter; to Matt Chou for his help with statistics; and to all those writers of books and articles that informed this book. Finally, I am especially grateful to my daughter Lynn, who typed the entire manuscript, and to my son Jeffrey, who did the lion's share of the editing.

Index